TOURNAMENTS OF VALUE:
SOCIABILITY AND HIERARCHY IN A YEMENI TOWN

A significant and original contribution to our understanding of the varied experience of Middle Eastern women, *Tournaments of Value* vividly portrays a fascinating world of female socializing and in doing so expands our knowledge of women's social centrality in the Islamic Middle East. Most earlier studies have been written from the vantage point of men, confirming popular Western stereotypes of Muslim women's marginality to public life. Other studies dealing with Islamic systems of 'honour' and 'shame' have concentrated on women's ability to affect their families' status negatively. Meneley supplies us with examples of the opposite: the deep reliance of men on their female kin to establish, maintain, and indeed increase the family's honour in the eyes of the wider community by engaging in the exchange of hospitality. Not only is visiting competitive, but social engagement with others is an essential part of moral personhood. The study examines the associated construction of identity by women, largely through the detailed style and comportment features of their complex social relations.

Meneley's data challenge scholarly assumptions about the cross-cultural validity of a division between household and community and between domestic and public domains. She demonstrates the fluidity of social life and the changing nature of community organization, providing a welcome counterpoint to more rigid formulations of Middle Eastern social structure depicted in other ethnographies. These aspects join Meneley's work to a growing body of anthropological scholarship in which subtle observation, with attention to language, comportment, and gesture, combines with astute contextual analysis to produce a sensitive portrait of a community.

Highly readable and accessible to a wide audience, Meneley incorporates vignettes to illustrate her more analytical points and to enliven the text, allowing the reader to enter fully into the rich world of Zabid. This work touches on many issues of current and enduring importance to both Middle Eastern ethnography and women's studies.

ANNE MENELEY is associate professor in the Department of Anthropology at Trent University.

ANTHROPOLOGICAL HORIZONS

Editor: Michael Lambek, University of Toronto

This series, begun in 1991, focuses on theoretically informed ethnographic works addressing issues of mind and body, knowledge and power, equality and inequality, the individual and the collective. Interdisciplinary in its perspective, the series makes a unique contribution in several other academic disciplines: women's studies, history, philosophy, psychology, political science, and sociology.

For a list of the books published in this series see page 217.

ANNE MENELEY

Tournaments of Value: Sociability and Hierarchy in a Yemeni Town

UNIVERSITY OF TORONTO PRESS
Toronto Buffalo London

© University of Toronto Press Incorporated 1996
Toronto Buffalo London
Printed in Canada

Reprinted 2002, 2003, 2007

ISBN 0-8020-0883-6 (cloth)
ISBN 0-8020-7868-0 (paper)

∞

Printed on acid-free paper

Canadian Cataloguing in Publication Data

Meneley, Anne
　　Tournaments of value : sociability and hierarchy in a
　　Yemeni town

　　(Anthropological horizons)
　　Includes bibliographical references and index.
　　ISBN 0-8020-0883-6 (bound)　　ISBN 0-8020-7868-0 (pbk.)

　　1. Women – Yemen – Zabīd – Social conditions.　2. Social
　　interaction – Yemen – Zabīd.　3. Social status – Yemen –
　　Zabīd.　4. Zabīd (Yemen) – Social life and customs.
　　I. Title.　II. Series.
　　HQ1730.7.Z9Z325 1996　　305.4'095335　　C96-930644-X

University of Toronto Press acknowledges the financial assistance to its publishing program of the Canada Council and the Ontario Arts Council.

This book has been published with the help of a grant from the Humanities and Social Sciences Federation of Canada, using funds provided by the Social Sciences and Humanities Research Council of Canada.

University of Toronto Press acknowledges the financial support for its publishing activities of the Government of Canada through the Book Publishing Industry Development Program (BPIDP).

To my parents, Robert and Rose Meneley

Contents

Preface

The research on which this book is based was carried out in the town of Zabid in the Republic of Yemen in 1989–90. It was made possible by grants from the Social Sciences and Humanities Council of Canada and the American Institute for Yemeni Studies. Permission to conduct research was granted by Dr 'Abd al-Aziz al-Maqalih, director of the Yemen Center for Research and Studies. I am grateful for the aid of Taha al-Qirbi and Dr Abu Baqr al-Qirbi. Ibrahim Sharafuddin, Dr 'Abd al-Malik al-Maqrami of San'a' University, Duncan MacInnes and Donna Ives, and the directors of the American Institute for Yemeni Studies, Jeff Meissner and Scott Ralston, made time spent in the capital enjoyable. Ed Keall of the Royal Ontario Museum gave me advice before I left for Yemen. I thank Drs Steve Cummings and Muhammad Al-Khader for aid and kindness when I was ill.

The wit and friendship of my colleagues in graduate school and beyond – Allyson Purpura, Vilma Santiago, Lindsay DuBois, Noha Sadek, and Susan Kovacs – brightened long days of writing.

My professors at New York University, Tom Beidelman, Fred Myers, and Bambi Schieffelin, offered critical advice with kindness and wit. The expertise of Dale Eickelman and Lila Abu-Lughod in Middle Eastern anthropology has guided and inspired me. I also appreciate the encouragement of Janice Boddy and Michael Lambek of the University of Toronto. The readers for the University of Toronto Press had many excellent suggestions for the revision of my original manuscript. I appreciate the care Virgil Duff, the executive editor at the University of Toronto Press, and my editor, Diane Mew, took of my manuscript during the publishing process.

For their confidence in me and their many years of material and emotional support, I thank my family, especially my parents, Robert and Rose

Meneley. I cannot envision any of it happening without them. Thanks are also due to Nijole and Algimantas Banelis, my parents-in-law, for their interest in this project and their care.

My husband, Vaidila Banelis, took a leave of absence from his architectural firm to accompany me to Yemen. He had the good sense to view the experience as an opportunity rather than an onerous duty, and the grace not to blame me for hardships endured on my behalf. I know he found his own rewards not only in the wonderful Yemeni architecture, but also in his friendships in Zabid. I thank him for his care when I was sick, and his insights into men's lives in Zabid. He took most of the photographs in this book.

We arrived in Zabid, an ancient town on Yemen's coastal plain, in June 1989, just in time for the sweltering summer. We presented our official papers from the Yemen Center for Research and Studies to the governor of Zabid. Our official documents stated that I was the researcher and that my husband, an architect, was my 'escort' [murafiq]. This interpretation of our relationship was the respectable one in Yemen. It is unusual for women to travel without a male guardian, and in this way, the presence of my husband was made understandable.

Within a few days we had found a charming, if tired, house to rent. The once-wealthy owners had fallen on hard times, and the section of their house we were to rent was long past its prime. Its comfort and charm revived a bit after the bats and pigeons had been evicted and our landlords arranged for the windows to be fixed. We also installed a new front door – complete with doorbell – and fixed the wooden partition between the two sections of the house. In this way, we ensured a certain degree of privacy and established ourselves as a 'family' distinct from that of our landlords. I am grateful for the aid of my landlady. Without even feigning the faintest interest in my research, she nonetheless furthered my understanding of Zabidi society a great deal with her explicit lectures on comportment. In time I welcomed her designation of herself as my 'mother in Yemen' who would watch over me while I was far from my mother in Canada. Although I insisted on an independence that was hardly daughterly, we became very close.

We were welcomed in Zabid with a warmth and generosity notable even in Yemen, a country known for hospitality, despite some ambivalence about non-Muslims from the 'decadent' Western world. Our arrival in Zabid coincided with the beginning of the wedding season and before we had finished arranging our house, both my husband and I were swamped with invitations to weddings – my husband to the men's events and I to the women's. In Zabid, weddings are the most important cultural events. Zabidis consider an invitation to a wedding reception the perfect way of introducing a foreigner to the style of Zabidi hospitality of which they are immensely proud. Huge tentlike structures are erected; wooden frames are covered in cotton fabric, and are decorated to convey an air of opulence. The interior walls and ceilings of the tents are covered with brightly coloured carpets. Bunches of bananas and ornaments covered in jasmine flowers are hung from the ceilings. At my first wedding reception, I found couches arranged like bleachers to allow all of the guests – at least a thousand – a view of the raised dais. Here the bride sat in all her finery, surrounded by dozens of wildly excited little girls, who were vying with each other for a chance to dance to the music which was blaring from speakers. The guests were hardly less splendid than the bride, bedecked with gold jewelry and brilliantly coloured gowns. Jasmine flowers set off their hair, and their hands and feet were adorned with henna and *khidhab* (a temporary black tatoo in a lacy design.) I found the sheer scale of such events as astounding and impressive as my Zabidi hosts had hoped I would, and this gathering was only one in a series of week-long parties celebrating this particular wedding, and this wedding itself was only one of the dozens of similar weddings held that summer.

The necessity of recognizing others in the community by accepting invitations to their homes or wedding parties was immediately obvious. I expected women's visiting to be important as it is so often mentioned in ethnographic and travel literature about the Arabian Peninsula. However, I was not prepared for the emotional intensity that accompanied the organization of these visits. Women's social life in Zabid is a hectic one of perpetual motion, and obligations to others are forever being weighed, juggled, fulfilled, or neglected. The process of recognition draws on terms like 'anger' [*za'al*], 'love' [*hubb*], and 'shame' ['*ayb*] and is subject to continual negotiation.

Learning about one's expected social obligations was not mysterious. Zabidi women are not at all reluctant to express what they think of one's behaviour and try to direct it in what they consider appropriate ways. The constant questioning of another's activities is an accepted convention employed in the service of interpreting and often altering the actions of others. In my first few months in Zabid I witnessed countless discussions of who had not shown up at so-and-so's wedding, of a person who had neglected one family for another, of an invitation improperly delivered or neglected entirely, and I was questioned often about my whereabouts. Immediately after I related where I had been the evening before, the interrogating woman frequently would respond with a snort and say, 'Why did you visit *her* instead of *me?*' This intense questioning was not limited to me; indeed, such interrogations are so commonplace as to be practically greetings in themselves. I soon imitated the rest of the women, who answer such queries evasively in hopes of avoiding angry accusations of neglect.

The whirl of the wedding season quieted somewhat with the beginning of the school year in the fall, although daily visits and formal invited parties continued. Keeping up with my social calls was time-consuming, but it was essential to my research. Zabidi women proudly demand respect in the form of proper greetings and visits: without these proprieties, a relationship does not exist, even for the purpose of 'research.' Not only is visiting competitive but, on another level, sociable engagement with others is an essential element of moral personhood. My research would not have advanced without the acceptance granted to me because I behaved like a 'proper' person. Indeed, for the most part people were uninterested in whether I did research or not. My relationships were constituted as friendships rather than as ones of researcher and informant.

It is largely through the training I received in how to fulfil properly obligations to friends, neighbours, and acquaintances that my understanding of Zabidi society is derived. People who come to live in Zabid, I was told, must 'become citified' [*utamaddanu*], a process which is said to be accomplished when strangers begin to participate in social life in the appropriate Zabidi fashion. From a Zabidi perspective, the term connotes sophistication and refinement of manners. The confidence with which they uphold the rightness and superiority of Zabidi social life is immensely 'persuasive' both to Zabidis and to outsiders who move there.

As in many Middle Eastern, Muslim societies, social life in Zabid is governed by strict gender segregation. The Zabidis approved of our conformity to this local norm: my husband avoided the company of women, as did I the company of men. Like Zabidis, we socialized solely with our respective genders. Zabidi women often expressed relief that I was not scantily dressed – as were the European tourists, who periodically paraded through the Zabidi market, the suq – but still my dress was open to criticism. Despite the fact that I was careful to cover my body from ankle and wrist to neck, and to wear a scarf covering my hair, the Zabidi women declared my garb inadequate and began to press me to adopt a chador,[1] a

---

1 I use the conventional spelling of this word of Iranian origin. The Zabidi pronounciation could be transliterated as *shaydar*. In the capital, the same garb is referred to by a word of Turkish origin, *sharshaf*.

long black robe worn over a dress in public places. I resisted at first, feeling uncomfortable with the notion of wearing a chador, but I soon became just as uncomfortable as the only adult woman not wearing one.

By adopting a chador, I solved the other problem Zabidi women had with my clothes, which were modest enough to be worn on the street, but inappropriate for any of the several kinds of festive events. For such occasions, I adopted the gauzy cotton print dress which many Zabidi women wear with a brassiere and a cotton underskirt while attending formal social functions. This dress is considered fancy enough for special occasions but cannot possibly be worn on the street because the cloth is virtually transparent.

I soon became more socially adept under the tireless tutelage of my friends, who were proud of my small accomplishments in the field of Zabidi manners and fashions. They constantly urged me to take the step necessary to becoming a proper social being in Zabid – to convert to Islam. They settled for training me in the proper comportment of a Muslim woman. Many confided before we left that they were sure I would come around soon. Women would tuck strands of my hair into my scarf and lavishly compliment me both for wearing a chador and for avoiding the company of men, as any decent and sane Yemeni Muslim woman would.

Donning a chador had important implications for my research. I gained universal approbation from the women, and several men spoke approvingly to my husband of my appropriate comportment. But once I began behaving as a 'proper' woman, men behaved toward me as 'proper' men should, by avoiding conversations with me beyond brief (and abruptly phrased) inquiries about my husband. As a result, I did not conduct any first-hand research on male views of family, sociability, or religion. All of my time was spent with the women; it was they who taught me and it is primarily their perspective which informs this work.

Although my husband does not claim anthropological expertise, he widened my perspective with his insight into men's social life, which was gained by a participation as constant as my own was with the women. The information I obtained about the men's world was derived in the same way that Zabidi women's knowledge is: through male relatives or husbands, and through other women's commentary on their male kin and affines. I do not present a separate section on men's activities, but the information contributed by my husband or my female friends about male practices is noted throughout the text in footnotes and anecdotes.

My understanding of the nature of Zabidi society came by way of participation in both everyday and remarkable events: I attended special events such as weddings, funerals, and religious celebrations. I participated daily in formal calls in the afternoon and informal calls in the morning. At first I avoided exclusive association with any one family or circle and was invited to many large, formal parties. In this way, I gained a sense of the importance of women's sociability for the social standing of their families in the Zabidi community.

During the second half of my fieldwork I focused as much as possible on informal interviews with women with whom I had developed strong and trusting relationships. My account of Zabidi society owes much to their help and insight. During informal visits in the morning I was able to discuss with them, in relative privacy, various topics: modesty; practices such as female circumcision; the competition for prestige between families; religious practices; and the position of women in families, as wives, mothers, sisters and daughters.

It was difficult in some ways to live in Zabid – coping with the oppressive heat was always a struggle – but it was also very hard to leave. I am particularly indebted to my dearest friend who helped me more than anyone else with her insights into Zabidi society. Her friendship was a source of great comfort to me in the field, and my happiest moments were spent with her. The news of her death after I left the field has caused me much pain. If there is anything of value here, it is because of her. My joy at finishing this work is shadowed by sadness at the knowledge that I cannot again have the pleasure of her company.

The Zabidi women specifically requested that no family names be used in this work, which deals with aspects of life not usually recorded in historical documents. Therefore all the personal and family names are pseudonyms. However, in order to retain ethnographic significance, the relevant facts about the status of the person or family in the Zabidi community are undisguised. Those interested in the notable Zabidi families whose histories (of male members) are recorded in biographical dictionaries and historical documents can therefore gain from this work a general sense of the contemporary lives of female members of these families. There are no photographs of those with whom I worked, as this would be an infringement of their standards of modesty. Instead there are pictures of their male relatives and children, of the men's counterparts of women's social events, and the houses they inhabit.

Rooftop view of Zabid

Zabid's main square [*maydan*], with government building

Street scene with electrical wires

Street scene showing Zabid's high walls and obscure entrances

Wedding *farah*

Door to a Zabidi house

Exterior view of houses

View of courtyard and exterior facade

Interior room

Modern house addition

Qat chew in men's *mabraz*

Children dressed for a 'grown-up' party

Children on an informal visit

Grooms at a wedding

Wedding lunch

Zabidi mosque

Children dressed for the mosque

Men's *khatim*

TOURNAMENTS OF VALUE:
SOCIABILITY AND HIERARCHY IN A YEMENI TOWN

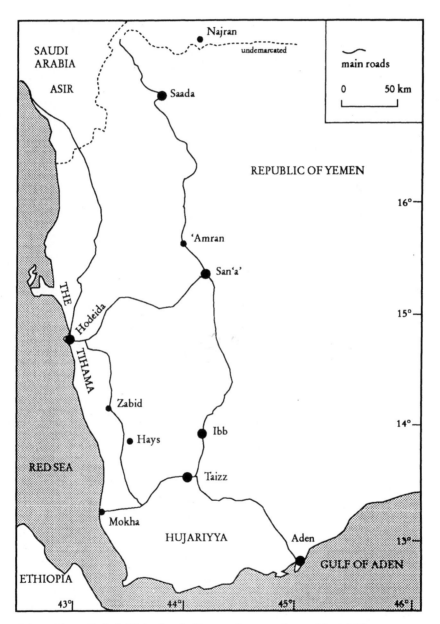

Adapted from Shelagh Weir, *Qat in Yemen: Consumption and Social Change*
(London: British Museum Publications 1985)

Introduction

In the distinctive sphere of our social life, we can never remain at rest.

Marcel Mauss, *The Gift*

Typically speaking, nobody is satisfied with the position which he occupies in regards to his fellow creatures; everybody wishes to attain one which is, in some sense, more favorable.

Georg Simmel, 'Superordination in Lieu of Freedom,'
The Sociology of Georg Simmel

In the fourteenth century Zabid was described by the famous Arab intellectual Ibn Khaldun as one of Yemen's principal coastal 'kingdoms.' By the time I arrived in 1989, however, it was something of a backwater in Yemen, central neither to the national economy or to politics. Zabid is the home of the local elite, the wealthy landowners of estates in the surrounding river valley. It is also a community of deeply religious Muslims, who practise strict gender segregation. This study examines the emotional, political, and religious significance of practices of sociability of Zabid's elite women, with whom I did anthropological fieldwork. These funny, charming, proud, and hospitable women spent a great deal of their time hosting, being guests, preparing themselves for parties, preparing their homes to provide hospitality, evaluating the spectacle of significant social events, and appraising the manners and adornment of the guests, the graciousness of the hosts, and the quality of the hospitality.

Everyday life among Zabidi women involves a complex series of social events, governed by an elaborate etiquette, through which familial social status and community identity are constituted. This vibrant sociability is the motif for this book. This theme encompasses a few of the far-famed characteristics of Middle Eastern societies: the ethic of generosity and hospitality for which the Arabs are famous, and the ideology of 'honour and shame' for which they are infamous. For both men and women, the offering of generous hospitality is a means of creating honourable identities; hospitality is a 'glorious deed' through which honour is constituted (Caton 1990). I want to convey a sense of how these practices are not just entertainment – although they are that – but are also manifestly political and deeply moral. Hospitality does not only signify 'friendliness' but is agonistic as well (Herzfeld 1987, Beidelman 1989). Beyond Mauss's (1970) exposition on exchange's ability to create social solidarity, more recent theorists have focused on the divisive aspects of exchange. Exchange of hospitality in Zabid, like other ethnographically known forms of exchange, has both unifying and divisive aspects.

The social lives of men and women in public are strictly separate. This work deals primarily with the practice of going out [khuruj], paying formal calls and hosting social events, in the women's public sphere. This sphere consists of women from other Zabidi families. Although entirely separate from the male public, the sphere in which women socialize is not 'private,' although the venue is people's homes. Rather, this sphere is a culturally specific public, a fragment of a prenation state kind of face-to-face public, which is continually enacted in everyday women's gatherings.

The domain in which men and women intersect is the three or four generation family [bayt], the members of which share living quarters, a budget, and a common reputation which is actively constructed by its members. Both men and women, in their separate public arenas, are vigilant to uphold their families' good reputations in the eyes of the community by their conformity to local standards of comportment. The capacity of women to affect the status of families negatively through immodest behaviour is well documented anthropologically and in popular stereotypes of Middle Eastern societies. However, the capacity of women to affect familial reputations positively is much less frequently addressed. I suggest that the comportment of women, their modesty, but also their generosity and their appropriate consumption and distribution of material goods, can positively affect their families' reputation. Although the women's public sphere has a notable degree of autonomy from the men's sphere, there is correspondence between the two: obligations to another family must be fulfilled in both male and female arenas, and men and women within families exchange information about public visits and formal relationships.

This presentation of reputations of bayts and the evaluations of them by others in public arenas is inherently political. I have borrowed Appadurai's evocative phrase, 'tournaments of value' (1986:21), to describe this dynamic competition. As the epigram from Mauss cited above suggests, this engagement is endless. The stuff of everyday politics is the competitive hosting and guesting for both women and men in their separate spheres. This fact leads to sociability's ambivalent valuation in Zabidi social life. The style of sociability is in one respect Zabid's finest quality, one that distinguishes it as a superior community; in this respect Zabid illustrates Simmel's observation that the process of sociation itself becomes a 'cherished value' (1950:44). However, the sociable realm is also the site of danger and competition. Differences between women (and their families) are as obvious as any sense of 'communitas' among them; apt here is Bourdieu's observation that the seemingly insignificant details of etiquette and dress are inherently political in their embodiment of the hierarchical order (1977:94–5). The centrality of Yemeni sociable gatherings as a forum for distinctions created through conspicuous consumption is amply documented by Weir (1985), who draws on Veblen's (1979) important study of the display of material goods in defining identity.

In any complex society, gender hierarchies occur with other forms of hierarchy, notably race and class. There has been too little attention in the ethnographic literature on Yemen about how gender hierarchies intersect with the wider forms of inequality, the longstanding status categories, discussed in detail in the next section. This work addresses three forms of hierarchy which structure social life in Zabid: the hierarchical relationship between men and women; that between the elite and 'respectable' people and the non-elite, particularly a servant class of people known as the *akhdam*; and the hierarchical relationships between elite families, which are both more malleable than those in the first two categories and more fiercely contested. The everyday forum of women's socializing is one in which, I suggest, the continual enactment of these relationships takes place.

Competitive behaviour in the Middle East is often described as being about honour. For instance, in one part of highland Yemen, poetic competitions are a central way in which honour is constituted (Caton 1990). In Zabid, the location for competitions over honour is in generosity and hospitality. Status honour is marked by a conformity to a particular style of life within which submission to fashion and strict conformity to standards of deportment, including patterns of consumption, is essential for continued membership in an elite group (Weber 1958:180–95). The style of life of the Zabidi elite includes a mode of consumption which is guided by a moral economy where wealth should be displayed publicly rather than privately hoarded, and in which love [*hubb*] is closely associated with the transfer of material goods. Wealth, derived from agricultural estates and consistently associated with high status although it is not its sole constituent, must be channelled in appropriate ways. The style of consuming wealth through forms of leisure and entertainment are part of the lived hegemony (Williams 1977:110–13) of the relations of domination and subordination in Zabid. The elite, roughly twenty to thirty 'great families,' are not isolated from the rest of the community. In face-to-face societies, 'elites are such because of their superior manifestation of personal qualities shared with non-elites that visibly signify their distinctiveness' (Marcus 1983:12). The elite have the leisure and resources to consume their wealth in sociable practices: they are able to offer gracious hospitality, adorn themselves fashionably, and consume qat, a fresh green leaf containing a mild stimulant which is the ubiquitous accoutrement of socializing in Yemen.[1] None of these practices are exclusively elite, but the elite are able, through their monopolization of productive resources, to conduct these practices in the most admired style, and thus embody most fully the values held by all. Hence, the elite define moral value as that which they themselves are best able to live up to because of their economic domination of Zabid's hinterland and servant class, the *akhdam*. The ordinary Zabidi townspeople emulate as best they can elite standards of consumption while carefully differentiating themselves in their comportment from the *akhdam*.

Within this motif of hierarchy as manifested in sociability are three other themes. One is the connection between hierarchical relationships and women's modesty – the voluntary deference to men, embodied in a style of comportment in which women's bodies are concealed from non-related men. Two, this work investigates the conditions within which emotions are structured; the ability to self-regulate one's emotions and comportment is perceived as an embodiment of social superiority. I further suggest that the style of enactment of emotions like anger is related to the competitive relationships within Zabid's elite where recognition from others is key to one's prestige and position within the community. Third, I explore how religious concepts permeate practices of sociability. For instance, Islam's egalitarian principle prescribes the right of all Muslims to be acknowledged through greetings and visits; 'good' people fulfil these duties. The equality of all Muslims before God is a principle held by Zabidis as intrinsic to their Mus-

---

1 Bundles of qat sprigs are chewed daily, according to a shared etiquette, at both male and female gatherings. The main active component in qat is cathinone; its stimulant effect is similar to that of amphetamine (Weir 1985:46).

lim community, an idea no less tenaciously held for being enacted only rarely. But the egalitarian aspect of Islam is often in tension with the obvious hierarchy of everyday life, where differences between families and individuals are competitively enacted. However, hierarchical as well as egalitarian principles are also evident in Islamic texts which influence Yemeni conceptions of social relations (Messick 1993:159–60).

I first briefly describe Zabid's historical and regional positioning in contemporary Yemen and outline the hierarchical ranking of social categories and their spatial correlates. I then present an extended vignette describing one of the social events I attended in Zabid, which is characterized by the defining features of Zabidi hospitality. The pragmatics of going out [khuruj] in the women's public sphere are addressed in chapters 2, 5, and 6. Chapter 3 examines the organizing principle by means of which specific identities are constructed: the family [bayt]. Chapter 4 investigates the practices of modesty by which gendered identity, piety, and moral personhood are created, while the structuring of emotions in this competitive and hierarchical society is addressed in chapter 7. Chapter 8 considers piety as a foundation of identity and examines a ceremony, the mawlid, in which the tension between equality and hierarchy in Zabid is mediated.

My account of society in Zabid is 'positioned' in a particular manner. The perspective offered here is that of the elite female Zabidis, one which differs from a male perspective. Some of the perceptions held by elite Zabidis would be contested, I suspect, in the self-representations of the non-elite. Another form of positioning involves the relationship between the Zabidi way of life and the lives of other Yemenis with whom Zabidis share a political and historical affiliation as well as cultural affinities. Further, many aspects of Zabidi life are shared by, or are similar to, those of other Arabs and Muslims, particularly those in traditional urban contexts. I have tried to weave in comparisons to and contrasts with other communities while at the same time conveying what is distinctive about Zabid as a community.

Zabid

Zabid is not a centre of either government or commerce in contemporary Yemen. Zabidis are aware of their current marginality, but they retain a pride in their heritage, and they delight in their own customs [adat]. This pride is derived in part from Zabid's history as a place from which, once upon a time, economic, religious, and political influence radiated. The town is, in the eyes of Zabidis at least, not commonplace, but rather a place of distinction, worth, and morality.

However, Zabid is not now isolated (nor was it in the past) from wider political and economic currents shaping Yemen and the Gulf region. It was founded in 820 A.D. by a representative of the Abbasid caliph. The wadi surrounding Zabid was populous and fertile enough to allow intensified agriculture; the Zabidi elite still depend on income from their estates in Wadi Zabid to maintain themselves. Several medieval dynasties ruled from Zabid, supporting their states with tax revenue from the outlying agricultural regions. The town was established as an intellectual capital during the Rasulid and Tahirid dynasties, with elite members of these dynasties sponsoring religious schools and mosques.[2] Zabid was briefly ruled by the Mamluks, and twice by the Ottomans; the second era ended in the early twentieth century after an extensive period of drought, famine, illness, and warfare.

Zabid was noted in the medieval Islamic era as a centre of Sunni scholarship, especially for the Shafiʿi legal school [madhhab]. This legal school is the dominant one in Zabid and the Tihama region, as well as in southern highland Yemen, while the northern highlands are predominantly Zaydi, a Shiʿi sect.[3] In the eighteenth century certain Zabidi scholarly families were part of an informal network of religious scholars all over the Muslim world who were involved in the revivalist Islamic movement of the time (Voll 1987). It is this aspect of their heritage which contemporary Zabidis most often recall, and the loss of which they lament. Zabid's fame as a religious centre is still encoded in the number of mosques extant in the town, over eighty. Religious learning remains an important marker of prestige in Zabid today, although present-day scholars are not as renowned in international circles as were their predecessors.

Following the 1962 revolution, which replaced the Zaydi Imamate with the republican state, there was civil war in Yemen until 1968. Several presidents were assassinated in quick succession, but ʿAli ʿAbdullah Salih, Yemen's current republican president, has remained in power since 1978. For the most part Zabidis seem proud to be part of the 'imagined community' of the Yemeni nation (Anderson 1991). The government-controlled radio and television stations frequently present programs designed to encourage identification with Yemen as a 'nation' [watan] and as part of a Yemeni 'people' [shaʿb]. Zabidis seem receptive to the president's exhortations that Yemen must become strong and modern; they were particularly

---

2 Sadek (1989, 1990) discusses the sponsorship of architecture by Rasulid women.
3 Although the doctrinal differences between the two are minor, this longstanding difference in religious affiliation continues to orient identity in contemporary Yemen.

proud in May 1990 when South Yemen, the socialist regime established in 1967, agreed to reunify with North Yemen, under the leadership of ʿAli ʿAbdullah Salih. In Zabid this was understood as a political coup for the north over the south, but also as a triumph for Islam over the secular ideology of communism, and a move which would strengthen Yemen's position as a nation-state in the international community.[4]

The government schools have been instrumental in engendering affiliation with the nation-state; ideas of nation are implicitly and explicitly addressed in the school curriculum.[5] Given the limited local employment options, and Zabid's much-valued history as an educational centre, the new government schools have become an extremely important focus of activity and source of income. They also provide a basis for a new form of association, as 'colleagues' [zumalaʾ]. Despite regret at the declining significance of religious education, the indispensability of modern education via the government schools for social advancement in Yemen is now recognized. The eight local schools are full to capacity; an afternoon session in the elementary schools was recently implemented to meet demand. (There is now a women's high school and strong local support for the education of women.)[6] University-educated Zabidis are rapidly taking over from the Egyptian and Sudanese high-school teachers, and the lower schools are almost entirely staffed by Zabidis now. School staffing and administration are sources of great interest and politicking for both male and female teachers. The school schedule now shapes diurnal and annual time, which has meant shifts in domestic work schedules and practices of sociability (for example, weddings now usually coincide with the school vacation).[7]

The shared identity as a nation opposed to other similar sorts of units, and as part of a community of Arab nations distinct from other sorts of nations, particularly Western ones, is a primary orientation for contempo-

4 This optimism must have been eroded when civil war broke out in 1994 between the two Yemens which had so proudly unified four years earlier.
5 Messick (1993:99–114) writes insightfully on how Western ideas of education (and implicitly of nation) filtered into North Yemen via the second Ottoman occupation in the nineteenth century. The Ottoman internal reforms were designed to reshape their army, school, and legal systems on Western models, reforms which they also attempted to implement in Yemen. The role of schooling in inculcating new frames of perception is addressed by Mitchell (1988).
6 There is an evening school which teaches older, illiterate women, which also has a small sign language class for deaf children. I discuss the ways in which schooling changes notions of familial obligations and duties as well as marriage and child-rearing in chapter 3.
7 During Ramadan, the school schedule directly conflicts with the local practice of staying up all night, visiting friends, and sleeping as long as possible during the day.

rary Zabidis, as for other Yemenis. The state which was most tangibly a part of ordinary life was Saudi Arabia. During our stay there was a great deal of movement between the two countries. Some Zabidi men work in Saudi Arabia or have in the past: wage labour provided the wealth for consumer goods such as household appliances and accoutrements which are associated with the 'advanced' [*mutaqaddim*] West, but often manufactured in the Far East.[8] Those resident in Saudi Arabia came to visit Zabidi relatives, and many Zabidis went to Saudi Arabia to perform the hajj, shop, or seek health care. The relations between Saudi Arabia and Yemen worsened during the last month of our stay, after the Iraqi invasion of Kuwait in August 1990. The borders between Saudi Arabia and Yemen were closed, leading to much concern in Zabid over relatives who were still in Saudi after the hajj.[9]

Prior to the Republican revolution in 1962, only some of Zabid's wealthier families had electricity, supplied from portable generators (any excess was sold to their neighbours). Now that the national electrical corporation is firmly established, these generators have disappeared, the elegant exteriors of Zabid's houses and its streets are haphazardly garlanded with wires, and all but the very poorest of houses have a regular electricity supply. Water is supplied from a municipal pump and piped to most houses through shallowly buried or exposed pipes. These pipes are often broken by cars attempting to manoeuvre the narrow dirt streets, causing havoc and mud puddles which annoy all but the children. Older women recall the days when houses were lit by kerosene lanterns [*fanus*] and water was peddled from house to house in large vessels drawn by camel or donkey cart. Within living memory, wealthier men used horses for local transportation. Now most families have a motorcycle or two, on which the men zip around Zabid on their daily business, sarongs [*futas*] and flip-flop sandals flapping. Cars, highly prized but impractical for Zabid's narrow streets, are less ubiquitous except among the wealthiest families.

Electricity allows some of the newer 'essentials' of existence: fans, portable tape players, video machines and televisions, all of which have had their particular impact on practices of sociability. Women's visiting schedules are altered so that they can watch the late afternoon Egyptian or Jordanian

8   Migration from Zabid was never as comprehensive as it was from some Yemeni regions, and in any event, the heyday of migration ended in the 1970s. By 1989–90 opportunities for employment had become scarce; several young, uneducated men who had migrated during our stay returned unable to find employment. The economic impact of migration will be discussed further in chapter 3.

9   After we left, many Yemenis who did not have Saudi citizenship were expelled.

soap operas, and men's qat chews often feature video movies instead of conversation. North Yemen was never colonized by a Western power, and very few Zabidis have travelled beyond the Arab world; most impressions of the West are derived from the media. Videos showing Rambo, the World Wrestling Federation, and women and men engaging in immodest activities[10] are easily available in Zabid, and may influence local perceptions that the Western world is characterized by lawlessness and promiscuity. These videos, however, are no less avidly watched for this censure, conveying the sentiment that blame is exclusively the province of the producers rather than consumers. However, blatantly pornographic films are publicly eschewed by most men; those who do watch them are criticized.[11] These movies are held as evidence of the veracity of the criticisms condemning the West as imperialistic and decadent made in Islamist books and audiotapes, which also circulate in Zabid. Radios supply political news from Yemeni, Arab, and Western broadcasting services, and Zabidis are often sharply critical of the domination of the Arab world by the West.

Zabidis may be the wealthy elite of the surrounding area, but that relation, for them, certainly does not hold relative to the country as a whole. They are also aware that the highlanders, culturally distinct from them, hold the Tihamis in some disdain. The locus of the government and political influence which shapes Zabidi lives is San'a'. The governor of Zabid is appointed by the central government; during our stay he was a highlander from a prominent tribal family. A few Zabidis have positions in the central government, which lends them great prestige and influence locally. Permission to open businesses and other bureaucratic affairs must be dealt with in San'a' and the main university campus is there. Most of the wealthy Zabidi families have kin or social connections there, facilitating their access to education or government, giving them an advantage over families who do not have such wide ties.

In 1990 the coastal city of Aden re-emerged as a centre of significance for Zabidis. When the restrictions on travel between North and South Yemen were lifted in the spring of 1990 as a prelude to reunification, Aden became a popular destination for Zabidis, as the health care was rumoured to be vastly superior to that of the north and less expensive than that in Saudi Arabia. Many returned impressed by the orderly arrangement of

10 Almost any contact between unrelated men and women is considered immodest, so most
    Western movies fall into this category.
11 Women's formal gatherings never feature video films. Although sometimes watched in
    small groups of neighbours, anything racy is considered to infringe upon modesty, and
    they seem embarrassed to watch it.

Adeni streets, but baffled by the undeniable social differences between Zabid and Aden; they saw unveiled women and socializing in mixed gender groups, all taken as evidence of the abandonment of Islam. Adeni visitors to Zabid were frequently subjected to lectures on such topics.

Identity and Social Organization

There are longstanding social divisions within the Zabidi community which persist despite government attempts to eradicate them. This hierar-chical ranking of social categories remains a significant principle governing everyday life, as is evident in recent ethnographies of Yemen (Bujra 1971, Caton 1990, Dresch 1989, Messick 1978, Gerholm 1977, Serjeant 1977, Walters 1987). The following social categories, despite some regional varia-tion, are usually described in ethnographies: servants [akhdam], ex-slaves ['abid], those who provide low-status services such as barbering or butch-ering [mazayanah], tribesmen [qaba'il], merchants [tujjar], and descen-dants of the Prophet Muhammad [sadah]. There is no single principle, based on either descent or occupation, by which the Yemeni hierarchical system is constituted (Gerholm 1977:107).[12]

After the 1962 Republican revolution, all status categories were banned in North Yemen, as the state promoted a republican ideology of equality, encouraging people to affiliate with the nation-state. Government televi-sion broadcasts and schoolbooks often invoke the 'people' [sha'b] of Yemen as a whole and the identity which all Yemenis share as members of the nation. This polemic (and the revolution itself) was particularly aimed at eradicating the power of the sadah, who, at least in the upper highlands, comprised the ruling class during the centuries of Imamate government (Weir 1985:23). While this nationalist ideology may have partially trans-formed both traditional ideas about the estates and the position of the estates themselves, the fact that Yemeni society is hierarchically structured has not changed (Weir 1985:23, 168).

The hierarchy of estate ranking in Zabid provides a framework for the broad assignment of identities. Most Zabidis, however, do not belong to any of the above estates. Elite and respectable Zabidis are referred to as al-nas, [literally, 'the people']. From the perspective of the elite, the term nas

---

12 Dresch suggests that the search for a single structure (such as the caste system) within which these groups are ranked in Yemen in general is misleading. He proposes that the term 'estate' be used to denote groups which have various rights and duties in particular places rather than an overarching structure that would 'specify their bounds and relations' throughout Yemen (1989:151 n1).

means the 'socially significant people,' a category from which the *akhdam* and the *mazayanah* are excluded.

Most Zabidis are considered of the *nas*; within this category, the salient identity in everyday life is the family to which an individual belongs. A wealthy, influential family is referred to as a *bayt kabir* [a great house/family]. Collectively, the great families of Zabid are known as *al-kibar* [the eminent/noble]. They are the most prosperous and respected families of Zabid, all large landowners. This category of families has no corporate existence, and they are dispersed throughout Zabid. Although the elite families dominate Zabid politically, socially, economically, and morally,[13] they are not segregated from the rest of the population.

Being a member of the *sadah* does not necessarily guarantee elite status in Zabid. The *kibar* families are both *sadah* and non-*sadah*, but not every *sadah* family is one of the *kibar*. The *sadah* families have intermarried quite extensively with other great families in Zabid. In the past, deference in terms of greeting and address were owed to the *sadah*. The honorific prefix *'sidi'* (pronounced *'sdi'* in Zabid) for descendants of the Prophet is rarely used in Zabid.[14] In post-revolution Zabid, overt deference to the *sadah* is not often offered, nor do the *sadah* demand it merely on the basis of descent. If these families remain wealthy and influential in Zabid they will be respected, and while their descent may add lustre to their reputations, it does not in itself guarantee deferential behaviour.

Between twenty and thirty families are considered *kibar*. Being a *bayt kabir* is more a process than a state, a fact which underlies the competitive nature of society. There is some dispute about which families deserve to be recognized as one of the *kibar*. The Yemeni layer-cake view of estates was never quite so immutable as indigenous descriptions of it suggest. A certain degree of social mobility from one category to the next is possible, as is downward mobility (Messick 1993:159–61). However, for the *mazayanah* and the *akhdam*, the fact of their membership in these two estates largely precludes the possibility of ever becoming elite.[15] But many of the ordinary, respectable people [*nas 'adi*] aspire to *kabir* status.

---

13 The *kibar* in Zabid seem similar to a category of people – 'the families' [*al-usar*] – in Ibb, a highland town described by Messick (1978:84–5).

14 Several *sadah* families were famous in the past for religious scholarship. Some were even thought to have the blessings of God [*baraka*], which they could communicate to sick supplicants through a touch or through bodily substances like spittle. (I heard only joking references to this healing power.)

15 A notable exception is a man of modest birth who was closely associated with the leaders of the 1962 revolution. He is now one of Zabid's most prominent and wealthy citizens.

Zabidis are aware that the social categories, and the terms used to refer to them, are officially banned. As persuasive as Zabidis find the rhetoric of Yemen as a nation, there was no indication that their common place as citizens overcame the distinctions between the *akhdam* and the *nas*.[16] The *nas* ascribe differences in personhood to the *akhdam*; the position of the *akhdam* in Zabid is understood as one of moral opposition to the *nas*.[17] The *akhdam* are said to lack the bases for respectable personhood: modesty, emotional control, and piety. For them, birth constitutes an ascribed identity which is very difficult to alter.

Reasons given for their subordinate position are their reputed non-Arab origin and ordainment by God. Often the *akhdam* were dismissively described as 'from Ethiopia' [*min al-Habasha*], the least illustrious origin as far as Zabidis are concerned.[18] Others said merely that the place of the *akhdam* was 'from God' [*min Allah*] and that nothing could change it. While not segregated from the rest of society, as are the *akhdam* communities of San'a' or Ibb,[19] they are only integrated in specific, and limited, ways into the larger Zabidi community.

The *nas* claim that there are readily apparent phenotypical distinctions by which the *akhdam* are identified; the local perception is that the *akhdam* are 'black,' although I found skin pigment itself is not a reliable indication of social status.[20] However, the *akhdam* do make their livings in ways considered shameful by the Zabidi *nas*, particularly domestic labour in other people's homes. Some have particular associations with certain *bayts*, where they work on a daily basis.[21] Most families hire *akhdam* women temporarily on the occasion of a wedding, or death, or in time of illness. They also support themselves through begging.[22]

The richest families in Zabid owned slaves before the revolution in

16   There was a certain uneasiness about using the term *akhdam*. Sometimes I heard people say, 'I know we shouldn't call them *akhdam* but I don't know what else to call them.'
17   Messick describes a similar understanding of the *akhdam* in Ibb (1978:99–100).
18   People described to me as from Ethiopia described themselves as 'from Zabid,' indicating that they do not accept the disparaging identity ascribed to them. An extensive discussion of the issue of the origin of the *akhdam* is found in Walters (1987:200–30).
19   The *akhdam* in Ibb always resided outside of the town (Messick 1978:99–100).
20   Walters (1987) amply documents this point.
21   Some *akhdam* live in elite households, although this practice is now uncommon.
22   *Akhdam* men frequently beg in qat chews for qat or a few riyals. This regular begging does not occur at women's social events, although female *khadimas* often receive a share of qat from women for whom they work. *Khadimas* also receive five or ten riyals at the end of Ramadan and on the *'ids* [religious festivals] from the wife of the head of wealthy *bayts* in their neighbourhoods. (In 1989, the exchange rate was ten Yemeni riyals to one U.S. dollar.)

1962,[23] although now the ex-slaves [sing. 'abd, pl. 'abid] are rarely mentioned in Zabid. They were of higher status than the akhdam, often freed and given property by their ex-owners.[24] One 'abda was treated with respect and a little fear because she was reputed to be in charge of the zar [spirit possession] ceremony.[25]

The mazayanah (sing. muzayyin) are the barbers, butchers, circumcisors, and formal inviters.[26] They are an endogamous estate, like the akhdam. Unlike the akhdam, the female mazayanah participated regularly in women's visiting; they were usually treated politely. Mazayanah women are often more bawdy in their comportment than the higher-status Zabidis, and while other women may be amused with their naughty commentary, they also view it as a sign of their moral inferiority.

Like the mazayanah in other parts of Yemen (see Dorsky 1986:37–8), those in Zabid are fairly affluent due to good wages for their services at weddings and circumcisions.[27] However, receiving wages for providing services to others, especially those associated with bodily functions, is considered demeaning. Many Zabidis claim that in recent times, the mazayanah have become presumptuous [mutakabbirin] and are unwilling to perform their traditional services at weddings and funerals or are charging exorbitantly for services performed only grudgingly. The mazayanah are often described in unflattering terms by the nas; they are said to be grasping, and people who 'only love money' [yuhibb flus bas], and butchers [jazzar] are often maligned for being deceptive and dishonest.[28]

Zabidi identity is often defined in opposition to that of the rural people,

23 In medieval times, Zabid was a centre of slave-trading.In Race and Color in Islam, Lewis includes a thirteenth-century illustration of the Zabidi slave market (1970:40).

24 One ex-slave I knew farmed land just outside Zabid that his father had inherited from his ex-owner; his family had friendly relations with their ex-owners, whom they occasionally visited. They were received graciously, but their visits were not returned.

25 Only the akhdam and the 'abid participate in the zar. Other Zabidis claim to be frightened of the zar, and say that it is not properly Islamic.

26 In Zabid, the terms ris [m.] and risa [f.] are also used to refer to individuals who perform these jobs. I use the term mazayanah since it is commonly used in the literature.

27 Although male children can be circumcised for no charge in the local clinic, the muzayyin is still considered more skilled, but much more expensive. In addition, he must be invited to a special lunch by the child's father. Female children are only circumcised by the muzayyina.

28 Before an 'id, the jazzar would march a young camel, adorned with jasmine flowers, around Zabid, to advertise that it would be slaughtered the next morning. Serjeant (1991) provides an account of this Zabidi practice. However, sceptics claimed that the butcher substitutes an old, wiry camel for the nice young one, fobbing off bundles of meat to naive customers.

who are referred to as country people [*riffiyin*] or tribespeople [*qaba'il*]. *Qaba'il* identity provides an important foil by which Zabidis define themselves; life in Zabid is seen as infinitely preferable to that in the rural regions.[29] Although from the Zabidi perspective the *qaba'il* are considered unsophisticated, uneducated, and irreligious, they are not considered fundamentally different as persons, in contrast to the *akhdam* and the *mazayanah*, who are deficient [*naqis*] in the qualities of personhood. In many instances, Zabidis even conceded that *qaba'il* are considered more honourable, honest, and forthright than they are themselves. They are respected for these qualities and are treated with circumspection, especially given the fact that they are said to be quick to anger.

There is also a class distinction between the two. Zabid has long been home of the elite of the surrounding river valley, the wadi. Because much of the land in the wadi is owned by elite Zabidis, the relationship with the rural people who work the land is one of owner to tenant. The tribal *shaykhs*, like wealthy Zabidis, are large landholders.[30] The haughty attitude that Zabidi women sometimes display toward rural women extends to the ordinary tribeswomen only. The women of the *shaykh*ly families are considered of equal status to elite Zabidis and are treated with respect. There is frequent intermarriage between the *shaykh*ly families of the surrounding region and Zabidi families.

Social Space

When Fayein visited in the 1950s, Zabid was still walled (1957:72), although now only the four gates remain. Zabid has four quarters: Al-Jiz', Al-'Illi, Al-Jami', and Al-Majanbad. This last quarter houses the government building [*hukuma*] and an ancient citadel[31] and opens onto Zabid's dusty main square [*maydan*], which is usually vacant except for a small shaded teahouse. Zabid's small clinic and the telephone and post office are

---

29 The Zabidi formulation of urban identity can be contrasted to that of the townspeople of the highland town of Manakha, who have an 'ambiguous identity,' according to Gerholm. He suggests that the tribal ideology in the region so permeates the town that the townspeople [*'arab*] are aware of the tribal disdain of the town (1977:141–3). The *'arab* in Manakha try to maintain a tribal identity by emphasizing their distant tribal origin (1977: 141–3, 152–3). In contrast, in Zabid, people of tribal origin have to adopt Zabidi ways to be accepted.

30 See Dresch (1989) for an account of a less hierarchical relationship between *shaykh* and tribespeople in the northern highlands.

31 Ed Keall of the Royal Ontario Museum has an ongoing archaeological expedition in Zabid, investigating this citadel.

also here. The old covered market, the suq, runs through the centre of the town, with permanent clothing and dry-good shops, bakeries and prepared food stalls. The new suq, selling daily staples such as qat, fruits, vegetables, meat and fish, is on Zabid's northern outskirts, beside the new high schools. Zabid is not part of the weekly market system of the lower Tihama.[32] Zabid's quarters, of roughly equal size, have no internal organization or occasions for corporate action; they are relevant primarily as geographical reference.

The social categories structure the social use of space in Zabid. The *qaba'il* live outside the town, while the *akhdam* tend to live on the outer perimeters of town, in all four quarters. The *kibar* are known [*ma'ruf*] by reputation in all four quarters of Zabid and in the surrounding countryside and Tihama towns. The homes of the *kibar* are scattered throughout Zabid's four quarters.[33] Smaller, unnamed neighbourhoods are often small groups of weaker houses (approximately seven to ten *bayt*s) crystallizing around one *bayt kabir*.[34] Geographical propinquity is a requirement, but being considered part of a neighbourhood depends on visiting and mutual aid (the weak houses provide labour and the great houses material aid).

Zabid is still an old-style Middle Eastern town [*madina*] with a population of roughly ten thousand people. While one could not claim, as do some tourist guidebooks, that Zabid has not changed since medieval times,[35] its urban fabric has not been radically altered in the same way as that in Yemen's other towns. The large cities with which Zabidis are most familiar – Yemen's capital, San'a', the provincial capital of the coastal Tihama region where Zabid is located, al-Hudayda, and Aden, Yemen's

32 Bayt al-Faqih, Hays, al-Husayniya, al-Mansuriya, al-Jarrahi, al-Turaybah, and Swag all have one suq day a week. Many men travel to al-Jarrahi daily (ten minutes by car from Zabid) to buy qat.

33 Chelhod states that Al-'Illi is the quarter of the *sadah* and qadis [non-*sayyid* learned families] and Al-Jami' is the quarter of the merchants (1978:87). This generalization appears to be based on the location of the most notable families of each quarter. In fact there are famous merchants, *sadah*, and politically influential *bayt*s in all four quarters. Chelhod describes Al-Jiz' as occupied by 'ancient Abyssinians,' a euphemism for the *akhdam*. Al-Jiz' has several *kibar* families, *sadah* and merchants, as well as several wealthy landowning families of Indian ancestry, settled in Zabid for centuries.

34 These small neighbourhoods seem similar to what are called quarters in Moroccan towns (*cf.* Eickelman 1976:91–9; Geertz, Geertz, and Rosen 1979). Zabid's quarters are more literally a geographical reference to a quarter of the town, whereas Eickelman notes that the Moroccan town of Boujad has between thirty and forty-three quarters.

35 It was in fact considerably larger during the thirteenth and fourteenth century than it is now (Keall 1982:2).

largest port city – have expanded rapidly, and exhibit marked differences in the scale and style of spatial organization. The new sections of al-Hudayda, San‘a’, and Aden have clearly defined houses in sprawling neighbourhoods arranged around long, straight streets while the dwellings on Zabid's narrow, winding streets are so close it is hard to tell where one home leaves off and another begins.

The shift from older forms of spatial organization to new forms of order is described in Messick's *The Calligraphic State*, a study of transformation of Yemeni writing style and textual authority from one based on the embodied knowledge of Islamic texts to a mode of writing dependent on print technology and authorized by new frames of perceiving the world, primarily by abstract, rational principles.[36] He suggests that a similar transformation in the articulation of social space can be discerned in the changed layout of urban space. His example, the southern highland city of Ibb, has an old walled town with a dense, multi-storied urban fabric where houses adjoin each other in narrow, curving alleyways. Ibb's new quarters have wide streets, and a grid-like organization, built from planning maps which project rectilinear as opposed to the indigenous curvilinear street and building form (Messick 1993:246–50). These shifts in building styles and social space, known not only in Ibb, but also in Yemen's other cities, are admired by Zabidi women (and men); the wide streets are considered grand and the square or rectangular buildings touted as fashionably modern and progressive.

Part of the reason for the relative consistency of urban form in Zabid is its marginality in terms of recent economic trends. The mainstay of elite families is still income from their rural estates. They tend to monopolize what little influential or lucrative local employment available. Small businesses such as pharmacies, autopart stores, and gas stations provide additional income.[37] Zabid lies alongside the major Tihama highway, which runs to Saudi Arabia and connects with highways leading to the highlands. But commerce along the highway is much less developed in Zabid than in the neighbouring Tihama towns, as its Local Development Council decided that in the interest of preserving Zabid's heritage, the development of merchant activity along the highway should be restricted. There are only

---

36 This transformation is tied to the Middle East's encounter with the West, the influence of which came to North Yemen via the circuitous route of the second Ottoman occupation and the British colony of Aden in the South.

37 The wealthiest merchant families may have considerable income from business interests outside of Zabid.

a few government posts, administering the local building permits and municipal works, but there is not much building going on in Zabid. Other employment options include the Tihama Development Authority (although international funding to this institution had been cut shortly before we departed), the school board, the local clinic,[38] the electrical company, or the telephone and post office. Cash is increasingly necessary in Yemen's current economy, especially given the local consumption patterns, particularly qat chewing. As a result, local employment, other than the stigmatized occupations discussed in the last section, is in demand and some would doubtless trade the advantages of economic development for those of social stability. However much additional income is desired and 'modern' urban forms admired, Zabidis, particularly women, are less sanguine about the social concomitants of economic transformations which bring about radical shifts in population and space.

In Zabid, as in other traditional Islamic cities, there is no overarching street plan based on an abstract plan by which space is organized. One must learn one's way around the winding streets, a task I found challenging. Even Zabidis will sometimes not know the exact location of a house in another quarter. In this case, one walks to the quarter and asks directions of the children on the street to the house one wants to visit (if bored, they may volunteer to accompany one). The location of a *bayt kabir* will usually be known by all in the quarter. For a less prominent family, one asks for the best-known family in their vicinity, and requesting more specific directions to the smaller house when in the immediate neighbourhood. When giving me an address to write to her, a woman would write 'Deliver to the hand of "X" [the name of the head of her household], Quarter [*rubʿ*] or Neighbourhood [*hara*] of Al-Jiz', Zabid, Province of Al-Hudayda.' Occasionally, a further qualifier would be added, such as 'beside the Mosque of X,' but for the most part, the name of the household and the quarter sufficed. Zabid has not had an influx of newcomers or shifts of wealthier inhabitants to new suburbs. Some rich families have built new homes (huge rectangular structures which sometimes evoke office buildings) closer to Zabid's outskirts, but many have built additions to their old homes, maintaining the continuity of their neighbourhoods.

This change from placing by name to placing by abstract principle is what women miss when living in bigger cities. As a woman explained to me,

---

38 The clinic is rudimentary and all but the most minor illnesses must be treated in other cities.

in Zabid, people are invited to come 'to us' [*ind ihna*] while in San'a' people would have to be invited 'to the address' [*ind al 'unwan*]. This phrase poignantly conveys the sense of familiarity and safety (and freedom, for women) felt in Zabid, where everyone is known, at least by reputation, whereas in San'a', people could not be placed without an address.[39] They are uncomfortable with the social relations that seem to characterize these new neighbourhoods, with strangers whose histories, reputations, and social rankings are unknown, living side by side.

For Zabidi women, this 'known-ness' of townspeople, with its impact on practices of sociability, is key. The relative consistency of urban space in Zabid has ensured a maintenance of common-sense order. The town is small in both population and size, and it is possible to reach any part on foot. More important, the town comprises one moral community wherein a common etiquette and set of expectations – particularly regarding gender segregation – are known and accepted by all, although not all individuals are personally acquainted. As long as women are accompanied by other women after dark, they are free to visit those houses in Zabid that are known to their families. In Yemen's larger cities, Zabidi women accompanying their husbands found themselves isolated in new neighbourhoods where no one knew each other; their husbands would not permit them to associate with strangers and they were dependent on their husbands' whims and schedules to take them to 'known' families. For instance, Zabidi women living in San'a' are dependent on their husbands to take them, by car, to each other's homes every Thursday. Hence, their visiting in San'a' is neither as frequent, nor autonomous, nor spontaneous as it is in Zabid.[40] Ibn Battuta, travelling through Zabid in the fourteenth century, notes the reluctance of medieval Zabidi women to leave their town (1984:108). Zabid is just as beloved by contemporary Zabidi women, particularly for the practice of *khuruj*, which they say makes life beautiful. The following chapters outline the style of sociability which Zabidi women long for during absences from their town.

39 I suspect that life in San'a's older neighbourhoods may more closely approximate the Zabidi experience, but some Zabidi women find the newer districts of San'a' quite alienating.
40 Altorki and Cole note a similar transformation in 'Unayzah, Saudi Arabia: women's visiting becomes much more restricted when families move to new, sprawling neighbourhoods and they become dependent on male family members for transportation (1989:216–217).

1

Going Out in Zabid

Zabid is a hundred and twenty miles from San'a', and is after San'a' the largest and wealthiest town in Yemen. It lies amidst luxuriant gardens with many streams and fruits, such as bananas and the like. It is in the interior, not on the coast, and is one of the capital cities of the country. The town is large and populous, with palm-groves, orchards, and running streams – in fact, the pleasantest and most beautiful town in Yemen. Its inhabitants are charming in their manners, upright, and handsome, and the women especially are exceedingly beautiful ... For all we have said of their beauty they are virtuous and possessed of excellent qualities.

Ibn Battuta, fourteenth-century traveller

Not all present-day visitors to Zabid would echo Ibn Battuta's glowing recommendation of Zabid as the 'pleasantest and most beautiful town in Yemen.' Situated halfway between the mountains and the Red Sea on the hottest and dustiest plain in the Republic of Yemen, its charms can be elusive, particularly in the summer. It is true that Zabid, with its stately houses, palm trees, and minarets appears from a distance more appealing than the surrounding environs, enlivened only by scrub brush and the occasional camel. But from close range, to the visitor unused to the climate it is at first unfathomable why Zabid has been inhabited since the ninth century. During the heat of the day there are few people on the streets. The public places, such as the suq and small teahouses, offer little respite from the heat. From street level the finest qualities of the houses are not apparent; their elaborate bas-relief brick façades are hidden by high walls and their obscure entrances make them impenetrable. The appeal of life in Zabid appears only after one has learned the pattern of daily activities that allows people to exist in relative comfort despite the appalling climate.

Work is relegated to the mornings, while the late afternoon and evening are devoted to socializing. I soon had an opportunity to appreciate not only the beauty of Zabidi women but their charming manners, of which Ibn Battuta spoke so highly. I was quickly absorbed into their daily exchange of gracious hospitality, an intriguing practice with social significance beyond the provision of relaxation and diversion.

Going out [khuruj] was both the joy of my existence in Zabid and the bane of it. I was delighted that Zabidi women seemed as anxious to integrate me into their lives as I was to be integrated, but I was overwhelmed; every day I was faced with a decision as to which of the five or ten invitations received I should accept. Not that I was free to decide according to my own reckoning or preference; rather, I, like any Zabidi woman, was faced with intense pressures from others, who constantly reminded me of my various allegiances.

To give a sense of the flow of everyday interaction, the following is a narrative account of one of the many kinds of social events in Zabid. It is neither the most nor the least extravagant, but it does encompass the central elements of hospitality – greetings, refreshments, adornment – which are commonly found in all women's public interactions. Zabidi etiquette governs every social interaction. Evident in this vignette are the grace and graciousness of Zabid's style of hosting and guesting, the comforts offered and the enjoyment taken, but also the divisive undertones of criticism and competition.

One of the most common formal social events in Zabid celebrates a woman who has given birth to a baby; it is called a 'Fortieth' [arb'ayin]. For the forty days following the birth, the father's family hosts a birth reception [wilada] in their home. All women with connections to the new mother, her family and her husband's family should come to recognize the achievement of the mother and congratulate the good fortune of the father's family. On the last of these forty days, the formal, invited Fortieth party is held.

I was invited to the Fortieth for Nagla, the wife of a schoolteacher whose family was not one of Zabid's wealthiest, yet was reasonably prosperous and generally well thought of in the community. I did not know Nagla that well, but through a schoolteacher friend, Awatif, had become close friends with Nagla's husband's sister, Nadya. And obligations to the baby's father's relatives are as binding as those to its mother. When one is bound to another family, through ties of friendship, kinship, neighbourhood, or even business, one is obliged to recognize the other family's notable events, happy or sad; as Zabidi women say, 'the affairs of your friend become your affairs.' I had attended several reception evenings of their *wilada*, passing relatively quiet nights with the hosts and between five and twenty guests an evening. All those who had visited during the reception period were invited to the festive culmination of the forty-day affair, an evening during which the connections of both the mother's and father's families are made public and concrete by the presence of the female representatives of these families. The final party differed in scale (over one hundred guests attended) and elaborateness of the hospitality offered, the decor of the reception areas, and the adornment of the guests.

A few days earlier, the formal invitations had been issued in person by representatives of the host family. In this respect the Fortieth differs from the other evenings of the *wilada* to which guests are not formally invited but are expected to show up at least once after the word of the birth reaches them through the efficient Zabidi grapevine. Not showing up at a social event to which one has been personally invited is a grave offence, not forgiven without a watertight excuse, and virtually never forgotten. Nadya, the new mother's sister-in-law, accompanied by her cousin (and a crowd of young neighbourhood children looking for a bit of excitement) called around personally at the homes of their guests. When they arrived at my door issuing the formal invitation to the party, they also warned me of how angry they would be with me if I did not come.

Getting the short distance from my house to Nadya's on the evening of the party was fraught with the usual complications. Zabidi women regularly go out in the evening, but they never walk alone on the streets; this is perceived as leaving oneself open to threats to one's reputation or attacks from strange men. Hence, one must arrange female accompanists, a sometimes trying task if several persons are involved. Magda, a friend from a neighbouring *bayt* with whom I often went visiting, called for me at 4:45 p.m., time for the early visiting session. Although she was anxious lest we be late, I reminded her that we had agreed to collect our neighbours, the women of Bayt Mahmud Hazimi.

We entered their unremarkable doorway, walking through a dark and labyrinthine passageway, past the staircase leading to the men's reception room, to the impressive interior courtyard and room where the women received their guests. It was in a chaotic state. Ibrahim, their servant [*khadim*], was trying to finish sweeping and damping down the courtyard after lunch, while the mother and sister of the head of the household frantically tidied the women's reception rooms in case, as often happens in Zabid, guests drop by unannounced. The youngest girls in the family, who were about to start their first year in school, decided they must at that moment – despite all attempts to dissuade them – try on their new school uniforms. They frolicked about half-dressed, disturbing the older daughters who were unrolling their prayer mats in preparation for their afternoon prayers. The youngest boy, aged three, whimpered; he was not yet his usual spirited self after his recent bout of malaria. The brides of the oldest sons were dashing about, fiddling with their hair and makeup and long strings of jasmine flowers, one demanding to know who had made off with her new sandals. For the party that evening, they were wearing – from their matching wedding trousseaus – the sparkly dresses favoured by the young. 'Umara, the wife of Mahmud, came out of the washroom searching for a towel, offering us her forearm to grasp in greeting, instead of her wet hand. She apologized that they were not ready as they had promised to be, saying that her husband had shown up late for lunch. Magda, a close friend and neighbour, teased that they were late every day (which was true); she said, unconvinced they would be able to collect themselves any time soon, that we would meet them at the party. If a woman from a family with whom they had more formal relations had come upon their disarray, 'Umara would have been mortified and likely miffed at the teasing. (I had witnessed these last-minute preparations many times before while waiting for 'Umara; eventually evidence of the chaos would disappear and everything and everyone would be in proper order, ready for the gracious reception of guests.)

We were wearing our chadors over our party finery and carrying small bundles of qat wrapped in pink plastic as we proceeded down the few dusty streets to Nadya's house. Magda told me to cancel whatever I had planned for the following evening, because we had been invited to one of Zabid's most prestigious *bayts*; her half-brother had recently married one of their daughters. We were stopped by an elderly woman, Khayriyya, who supported herself by selling her homemade sorghum bread [*lahuh*] to the neighbours. She greeted us by waving her finger in front of her face, which alone or accompanied by a blunt 'where?' [*fayn*], serves as the ubiquitous interrogative in Zabid, where everyone is interested in the whereabouts and doings of others. One could evasively reply, 'to some people' [*'ind al-nas*], but we knew that Khayriyya would pester us until we cited our destination. She snorted when we told her. She asked why we were always going to Nadya's house, leaving our own neighbours, such as herself, to sit alone in her house. Magda urged her to come along with us and Khayriyya again snorted, saying she had not been invited and dismissed Nadya's family as snobs [*mutakkabirin*]. We extricated ourselves by asking her to give our greetings to her daughter, and assuring her we would visit her soon. I asked Magda what had happened between Khayriyya and Nadya and she said that Khayriyya was angry [za'alana] because they had forgotten to invite her.

Rounding the corner, we were confronted by a crowd of children, playing in an open space abutting the street. They howled with a force that belied their small bodies, 'Where are you going, Anne? [fayn, fayn, fayn ya Aaaannnne], ceasing only when Magda hissed, 'Shut up, just go away' [uskut, yallah bas!]. The children always greeted me, the foreigner, with more exuberant familiarity than they would dare presume with a Yemeni woman, but Magda fussed over my reputation. There were a few old men sitting in a nearby shop – really just a bare room with a few odd boxes of soap powder and matches – and she was afraid they would overhear the children screaming my name; it is considered shameful to mention a grown woman's name in the presence of non-related men. The children lost their limelight as we were enveloped by a crowd of bechadored women headed for the same party, and we walked the rest of the way with them.

We passed through the dark corridor leading to Nadya's house. As we entered the reception room, we shucked our chadors, rolling them up to be tucked underneath ourselves at our places. Magda had long since counselled me on the necessity of keeping track of one's chador, telling me a perhaps apocryphal story about a party where everyone had left their chadors in an indistinguishable pile. Zabidi women would as soon leave the house stark naked as without a chador, so havoc ensued at the end of the party as the dozens of guests tried to retrieve their own chadors from the mass of nearly identical black garments. Magda chuckled as she described one panicked guest leaving in a chador so short her knees showed, another with one so long it trailed behind her, she herself leaving with a face scarf [khunna] she swore could not have been her own because it smelled funny and she always kept hers nicely scented.

Nadya met us at the door, kissing us several times on the right cheek, urging us to come in. Greetings are showered on a guest by a hostess with an exuberance that seems almost aggressive at times, replete as it is with accusations of neglect or of favouring others over the hosts. Nadya asked us why they never, ever see us [laysh ma nashufakum abadan?], although both Magda and I had spent the evening at her house just three days earlier. She said she had heard that we had attended a party at another house the night before and asked if we loved them more than her family. Nadya pressed Magda on the whereabouts of her sisters, her mother, and her brother's wife; Magda hastily assured her that they would all be along later, aside from her mother, who, she said – employing a practical prevarication often necessary in Zabid to avoid enflaming jealousies – was not feeling well. (I knew enough not to mention that I had seen Magda's mother looking perfectly robust that morning as she made plans to visit another friend, saying that Magda and her sister would represent their family at Nadya's party that evening.)

As Nadya turned to greet the next guests ('Tayyiba, where have you been?' echoed behind us), Nadya's mother, Jamaliya, ushered us further into the reception courtyard, and bade us to sit down. Before we did, we circled the courtyard, kissing the hands of the guests already seated. Peers – women of roughly the same age and social status – exchange three reciprocal kisses, followed by kissing one's own hand; younger women bow their heads to be kissed by older women. Sayyida, a dear friend of Magda's whom she did not see frequently because she lived 'far' – in another quarter, a fifteen-minute walk – kissed her three times on one cheek, and sat down beside her. Magda said, in reference to Sayyida's recent return from Saudi Arabia for medical treatment, 'Thank God for your safety (safe return)' [al-hamdulillah 'ala salamatik]. Sayyida gave the response, 'God keep you safe' [Allah yusalamik], reproaching Magda affectionately for not having been at her house when they had arrived home the previous day. Magda protested that only God had known when they were to return; even Sayyida's mother, Magda said, had not known their return date when she had telephoned a few days earlier. When they had dispensed with their recriminations, Sayyida lowered her voice and told Magda the news of the illnesses and treatments; her own skin disorder, her sister-in-law's infertility, and the drugs prescribed and bought on the advice of the doctors.

When Nagla emerged from her confinement on the fortieth day, she looked radiant, adorned once again as a bride: bedecked in a new gown, jasmine flowers, with her hands and feet adorned with henna. Like most new mothers, Nagla had been hardly evident until this last party; for much of the reception period, worn out from a difficult birth, she lay pale and silent in another room away from the guests, her swaddled infant beside her. Now recovered and fully enjoying her celebration – it is the mother who is celebrated rather than the baby – Nagla received special greetings from the guests. Sometimes they quietly teased her about being a new 'bride' ['arusa], implicitly referring to the end of the period of postpartum abstention from sex which this party marks. Nagla playfully slapped these women, saying 'Shame on you' ['ayb 'alayk] or gave a mischievous smile, claiming not to know what on earth they were talking about.

Najat, a crotchety older neighbour, descended upon us after greeting Nagla. Interrupting Sayyida mid-anecdote, she declared that she was angry with Magda for not visiting her when she was sick. She gave a dramatic account of her bout of malaria, saying she had expected a visit from her friends and neighbours, as visits are thought to lighten an illness. She exclaimed that even the foreigner, indicating me, had visited her on what she claimed was practically her deathbed, while the native Zabidis had neglected their well-known duties to the sick. (I had heard this sort of thing before: Zabidis referred to foreigners in the same tone as 'even a child!' or 'even a cretin!' – as people from whom nothing reasonable or considerate could rightly be expected.) I did not diminish the force of Najat's rhetoric by declaring the truth, which was that I had not even known she was sick, but had coincidentally dropped by to see her nephew's wife. In response to Najat's complaints, Magda asserted that she had sent her greetings with her mother, and Najat, still grumbling, hurried to take a place in the rapidly filling interior reception room, claiming that she did not want a further chill. Magda said to me under her breath, 'They [Najat and family] are so quarrelsome' and to Sayyida, she sniffed, 'Sick! She had malaria!' As common as the flu in North America, the seriousness of malaria as an illness was often underrated; women burning with fever often described themselves not as 'sick' [marida] but as merely 'a little tired' [ta'abana shwayya]. Little sympathy is accorded a suspected malingerer in a community where life-threatening illnesses are all too familiar.

The spacious courtyard, roughly twelve by eight metres, looked lovely in the dusk, with a couple of date palms set against the backdrop of the fine patterning of the outer façade of the house. This façade and the enclosing walls, three metres high, which surrounded the courtyard, sported a new coat of whitewash in honour of the festivities. Our hostess, Jamaliya, was often described as a housekeeping 'artist' [fannana], and all the women in her household helped her maintain this reputation. They had achieved the readiness for guests which yet eluded Bayt Mahmud Hazimi, as the reception area looked inviting, clean after the dust of the streets, and cool in the late afternoon as the heat of the day receded. To prevent dustiness, the ground had been swept and dampened down into a smooth, cool surface. The perimeter of the courtyard was lined with two rows of Tihama couches, their high wooden frames strung with twine and upholstered with cushions, cloths, and pillows [farash] newly covered and pressed in honour of the festivities.

A perch on one of these couches – which stand high so the air circulates underneath them, a necessity in the torrid Zabidi climate – is quite comfortable after one has hoisted oneself up. We selected our seat, eschewing the interior room for the hint of breeze and cooler air in the courtyard.

One guest, Imina, asked to wash her feet before she ascended; she had inadvertently stepped into a large mud puddle on the street. It is the height of bad manners to clamber onto a couch with dirty feet.

Jamaliya brought two extra pillows and tucked them behind us, exhorting us to relax. I had finally learned how to sit properly (right knee raised, left leg tucked under); my unconventional seating posture when first in Zabid troubled hostesses, who could not believe I would be comfortable in any position other than theirs. Propriety is satisfied by draping one's long skirts demurely over one's legs.

Placed at intervals were waterpipes [mada'as] for the two types of tobacco, leaf [humi] and a sweet paste of tobacco mixed with ash and molasses [maltut]. Both types had their devotees, who took turns smoking from the pipe closest to them. A few young women brought their own cigarettes, claiming that the shared hose of the waterpipe was a means of passing infections. Older women dismissed this notion by asserting that sickness was from God [min Allah] alone. The health hazard of smoking in general is presented on television and in the high school curriculum. Several young graduates, with the self-righteous tone of non-smokers everywhere, occasionally lectured their elders on the dangers of tobacco. Regardless of one's personal opinion of smoking, however, the provision of tobacco and waterpipes is still recognized as a cornerstone of hospitality.

One feels special and pampered as a guest in a Zabidi home; hostesses are experts at making a guest feel as if her comfort is of pre-eminent concern. We had no sooner sat down than Jamaliya brought us glasses of sweet tea, spiced with cardamom, which we sipped as we chatted and observed the guests coming in. Jamaliya and Nadya – as respected for their generosity as they were known for their immaculate housekeeping – were helped in their hostessing duties by several close neighbours and kinswomen, so no guest would have to wait to have her needs met. These women circulated the couryard, asking the guests if there was anything they wanted [tishti hajja?]. They handed out cool glasses of cola, and put more tobacco in the waterpipe when someone called out that it was empty. High tables are placed in front of the couches, with large thermos jugs of cool, incensed water, to refresh the chewers from the dehydrating effects of qat. Although daily qat chewing is not as universal among Zabidi women as it is among men, many women describe its mildly stimulating quality as indispensable to relaxation although the focus in women's gatherings is more on qat exchange than consumption.

We began rubbing the dust from the qat leaves with our fingers; Magda immediately cleaned a small bunch for me and wordlessly aimed it at my mouth. This kind of qat exchange is commonly performed between women who are affectively, socially, and, of course, spatially close. As is common for affluent hostesses, Jamaliya distributed a generous portion of qat to each of the chewing guests. We protested loudly, claiming that we would never possibly consume that much; Jamaliya merely smiled, and after entreating us to relax, moved on to exchange hand kisses with a new arrival. Later we each tried to press upon her a bunch of cleaned qat as she whizzed about on her hostly duties, but she accepted only a token of what we each offered.

The hierarchical relationships among Zabid's twenty to thirty 'great' families [sing. *bayt kabir*, pl. *al-kibar*] and the rest of the people are palpable in social gatherings. Everyone acknowledged that the *kibar* were the most respected Zabidi families, but this acknowledgment was not without ambivalence. One often heard darkly muttered criticisms of them, implying that their haughtiness with others had more to do with their wealth than any moral superiority. Although Nadya's family were not of the *kibar*, they were quite comfortably off, well respected, and widely and well connected to several *kibar* families in Zabid. At Nagla's party the grand entrance of sixteen or seventeen lavishly dressed women, part of the 'clique' [*shilla*] of women from Zabid's elite families, created a stir. They paraded in, dripping with gold, and asked previously seated guests to move so they might all sit together. The nearby guests obliged, although I heard some grumbled commentary from a couple of older women. Hamuda, one of the *shilla*'s most forceful personalities, called out to me that I had yet to visit her in her home, and virtually ordered Magda to bring me the following Friday. No sooner had they settled in, with no small degree of fuss (one woman demanding another cushion, a second insisting she would die of thirst if not immediately given water, another oblivious to all, checking her makeup in a small mirror), than Hamuda crankily complained they did not have enough waterpipes. All of these requests – rather imperiously delivered, to my mind – were fulfilled immediately, without comment or noticeable resentment, by the hostesses or their helpers. For the hosts to display anything but voluntary compliance, of course, would be a flagrant transgression of the norms of hospitality, making the hosts look worse than even the most peremptory guest. But judging from the extensive behind-the-scene and after-the-fact commentary, slights or evidence of snobbery never went unregistered in Zabid.

The party was soon buzzing with conversation and the ground bestrewn with discarded qat stems. Qat exchanges flew so fast that women barely had time to chew. Those sitting far from each other sent bunches – either a small cleaned bundle wrapped in tissue or several long sprigs – with one of the hostesses. In one exchange, mirrored by dozens of others in this gathering, a messenger delivered the gift of qat to Miriam, naming Magda, her friend, as the donor. Miriam looked up as if completely surprised – although these exchanges are a quintessential part of every gathering – crying to Magda, 'Oh, you must chew!' [*Khazzini anti!*]. Some time later a recipient usually attempts to return the qat to the donor. Those sitting close together may have small arguments, pressing each other to accept these small gifts of qat. Although these struggles are usually good humoured, women may be quite annoyed if they are not allowed to make a return. Jamila, one of the clique of elite women, sent Sayyida a large bundle of qat. When Sayyida tried to make a return to her, Jamila at first refused, waving the qat away, until Sayyida exclaimed loudly (and indignantly) 'Try some of mine!' [*Khazzini min haqqi*]. Sayyida, herself from a great family, did not want to be lumped together with the others to whom Jamila had grandly offered qat. Jamila had earlier given bunches to clients of their family who regularly received charity from them, like the two old servant [*akhdam*] women who stopped in front of Jamila, kissing her hand several times. She made only a token effort to kiss their hands in return, and wordlessly handed them each a portion of qat, which they accepted in like silence, retreating to the furthest couch, a low one by the door.

At the height of the party there were so many guests that we were sitting cheek to jowl and one woman claimed the couches were sagging from the weight of all the guests. This gifted raconteur told an anecdote about one party so well attended that the couches had actually collapsed. Zabidi women are masters of turning unpleasant or frightening experiences into hilarious anecdotes. She entertained us with her vivid description of the chaos which had ensued after the collapse: the spilled drinks, the hot coals from the incense burner, the tangled limbs, and the shrieks.

That evening there were at least one hundred women and girls present, a not uncommon number for a Fortieth party in a prominent family. I had attended three or four similar ones in the preceding few weeks. Wide attendance is a sign of the host family's strong community support and viable social ties, and is a matter of pride. The day after a party, one finds the hostesses lollygagging about, exhausted, but pleased if they can say, rolling their eyes and waving their hands for dramatic effect, 'the house was CRAMMED' [*bayt milan*]. However full the house had been, however, complaints will still be made about who had *not* attended.

I had been in Zabid for several months at this point, and was known to most of the guests at the party, but one woman stopped in front of me, surprised, as my hair and eye colour betrayed me as an outsider, asking Magda, 'Where is she from?' Magda told her that I was from Canada and that she could talk to me herself in Arabic. After making a crack about Canada Dry Cola, a ubiquitous soft drink that seems to constitute Canada's sole fame in Yemen, she asked me the questions I had come to expect: 'Are you married? (Yes) Do you have children? (No) Are you a Muslim? (No) Why don't you convert?' The last question was always difficult, and I disappointed many by not converting on the spot. Magda defended me from the moral questionability which (in local perception) inheres in *not* being a Muslim, by saying that I wore a chador and went out with them every evening and visited the sick. These activities were held up as evidence that although I was not a Muslim, I was behaving as a proper moral person should, in contrast to the outlandish comportment generally expected of Westerners.

The woman noted as well that I had taken up the Yemeni habits of chewing and smoking the waterpipe and asked if I found Zabid beautiful. I said that Zabid was beautiful in many ways except for the awful weather. She agreed, and added the quip which Zabidi women love (after a summer in Zabid, I loved it too), 'If we go to hell [*nar*] after we die, we'll say, "Oh is this all? This is NOTHING, we're from ZABID!"'

Awatif, the young schoolteacher who had introduced me to our host Nadya, squeezed herself in between Magda and me, after berating me soundly for not having visited her. After exchanging similar recriminations with Sayyida – and somewhat less enthusiastic ones with Magda, of whom she was not particularly fond – she turned to me, launching into a whispered tale about a woman sitting across from us. Awatif had once been engaged to her son, but the engagement had been broken once her family heard the rumour that this young man drank alcohol, a stigma in this upright Muslim community, and a charge which carries connotations of bad character regardless of its empirical veracity. Awatif said they had been too hard on the young man, who had been (she believed) temporarily corrupted by some bad friends. She was disappointed as she was eager to get married. This desire – shameful for a Zabidi woman to admit – was suspected by her friends who teased her mercilessly. I was surprised by this conversation; such an intimate (and potentially controversial) topic is usually discussed only with family, and certainly not at large, formal parties. The reason why this is so was inadvertently demonstrated by Magda, who despite her involvement in her conversation with Sayyida, overheard something in ours which caught her interest. 'Who are you talking about?' she pointedly inquired. Awatif gave a vague reply, then looked away and clammed up; I ignored Magda's inquisitive look. Awatif whispered that I should visit her the following morning to hear the rest of the tale, and turned to a less controversial topic: the propensity of students in the elementary school to drive her (their teacher) crazy with their inattention.

A staple element of hospitality in every social event is the provision of various scents. Nadya came around with a large bottle of perfume, thoroughly spritzing Sayyida and me. Sayyida protested humorously at Nadya's generous excess, 'enough, there's no need to wash me!' Awatif fended off the encroaching bottle, insisting she only wanted a tiny bit on her hands. The incense [bukhur] burner, containing an aromatic (and expensive) mixture of gums, woods, and oils, was passed around; we infused our hair and dresses with its fragrant odour. This kind of incense, which is thought to be enticing to men, is proper only for married women. Awatif unleashed an even more fervent protest at the proferring of this incense; she squawked 'No, no' and waved it away with her hands. This type of protest, which I saw in almost every social gathering, seemed almost a tacit staging of a modesty drama: the hostess never expects the proper unmarried girl to accept the incense, but it is inevitably offered, and inevitably declined with exaggerated indignation. Awatif accepted, however, the incense burner bearing aloewood ['ud], an aromatic wood used by both men and women. Nadya also dabbed a strongly scented oily perfume on our hands; once again our chaste Awatif declined.

Adjacent to us sat a congregation of married and unmarried teenaged girls, the banat, giggling and chattering at an impressive clip, away from the older women in front of whom they are expected to be deferential and silent. The waterpipes, lined up at intervals in front of the couches where the older women sit, are not necessary here; in elite and respectable circles, the girls do not smoke or chew qat. They are given tea and cola to drink, and gum and watermelon seeds to munch on; the husks quickly carpet the ground as the qat leaves do in the women's area. No one complained about this implicit segregation; some of the less charitable older women found the indefatigible good spirits of the girls fatuous, while the younger women were not sorry to have their hilarity unchecked.

Awatif and I watched Adila, a beautiful young woman, exquisitely groomed in the latest Zabidi fashion, enter in the wake of her hefty mother-in-law whose girth was matched only by her well-deserved reputation for gossiping and griping. From a tiny Tihama village, Adila was still very much an outsider in Zabid. Her family were rural landowners rather than sharecroppers on Zabidi estates, but all rural people, from the Zabidi perspective, are considered somewhat bumpkinish. Zabidis tend to be ethnocentrically unapologetic for their urban snobbery, convinced of the rightness and elegance of their own etiquette and manners. In addition to this stigma, Adila's husband had a dreadful reputation, as did his female relatives, who were avoided as much as possible. They were notorious for their sharp tongues in Zabid, where gossiping was by no means unknown, but universally feared and condemned. Even their relatives did not like them, and this was suspect in a community where kinship ties are one of the most important means of affiliation.

Adila's husband was alleged to have mistreated his first wife, whom he divorced after she had born him five children. This wife had been very popular in our neighbourhood, and although she now lived in her father's house some distance away, she was invariably greeted like a long-lost sister when she visited her old neighbours. Although Adila's beauty was often admired – and with the Zabidi inclination for invidious distinction compared favourably to that of the first wife – no one seemed to like her. Adila had been in Zabid for nearly two years but had yet to make any good friends, unusual in a place as gregarious as Zabid. She always mentioned the invitations she had received from notable Zabidi families, and never complained of the fact that no one returned her visits, or accepted her as a friend. While they were still invited out, very few people would enter their house at all; her immediate attachment to me, another outsider, suggested a desperate loneliness.

Adila had quickly adopted Zabidi fashion in dress, showing taste [dhawq] in her selection of gowns, but her mastery of Zabidi fashion was in contrast to her gaucherie in the field of Zabidi manners, which remained unmistakably 'other.' She greeted women she hardly knew with several kisses on one cheek which denotes a warm and affectionate closeness. This feigned intimacy made the younger girls collapse into giggles, as did her lavish distribution of candies and gum from her purse. (This is the province of the hostess, and Adila's actions had a peculiar infelicity.) She chattered feverishly in a high-pitched voice about clothes and then provoked another fit of giggles when she began to praise elaborately Awatif's eyebrows. (Zabidis do admire thick eyebrows, and Awatif's were fine, but there was something jarring in Adila's framing of this compliment which was evident even to a novice like myself.) Awatif barely choked back a snort of laughter and abruptly rose, claiming she really ought to see if the hostesses needed any help.

This party, like every one, had two definable sessions, named after the afternoon and evening prayers ['asr and layl]. At sundown [maghrib] many women change venues, to make another call or go home to pray. Magda and I were showing our loyalty to Nadya by staying for the entire duration of the party. Therefore, Magda asked if she could perform her *maghrib* prayers there rather than traipsing back to her own house. Nadya took her into another courtyard with an adjoining room and washing facilities for her pre-prayer ablutions and provided her with a clean cotton headcloth and a prayer mat. After a small exodus at *maghrib*, when many of the girls went home to study for their next day at school, an even greater influx of guests arrived, primarily older women, for the later session of the party.

One of the incoming guests was Zohara, whose quick wit and easy smile made her a pleasure to be around. Before she could say a word, I declared I was angry with her because she had forgotten all about me. She laughed at my imitation of the Zabidi greeting style and teasingly faulted *me* for never visiting *her*, only other people. She introduced me to her two friends, from a well-known family from another quarter of Zabid; they invited me to visit them at their house the following week.

We spent the rest of the evening pleasantly chatting; Zohara, admiring her friend's new frock, special for the evening, leaned over and felt the fabric, asking 'how much?' [*bikam?*]. When the sum was proudly reported, Zohara pronounced 'Oh, that's nothing!' [*bilash!*], which carries the connotation of 'what a good deal' if the quality is good, and if it is not, merely 'cheap' in its derogatory sense. When Zohara's two friends rose to leave around 9:00 p.m., choruses of protests were heard from Zohara and the hostesses. Nadya demanded to know where they were going, and insisted they sit a little longer. Zohara chided them, 'You don't have children or husbands to go to!', referring implicitly to the obligations of married women which have to be balanced with visiting duties. Unmarried women who were beyond marriageable age (usually twenty-five to thirty) were often the social mainstays of their families, visiting widely and providing the organizing force behind social events in their own homes. Zohara's friends made their escape by putting on their chadors while countering the pressure from their hostesses with a description of the length of the walk home ahead of them.

I received a bundle of qat from 'Umara, the wife of Mahmud Hazimi, whom we had called on earlier. Even she and her friends, a group of older women from prestigious households in our neighbourhood, diehard socialites who loved to loiter late passing judgment on neighbourhood affairs, were showing signs of wear at 9:45 p.m. Magda, whose health was not strong, looked completely exhausted, and I was always wiped out by the heat. We were joined by Magda's sister, who had spent the evening chatting with her friends, but was now ready for the refuge of their own house. We gained our release from the warm remonstrations of our hostesses by insisting we were the first ones to arrive – not entirely true, but close enough to pass – only to confront Sowsan, who loudly berated us for leaving early, although it is rare for any guest to stay past 10:00 p.m. Sowsan was a *muzayyina*, a forceful woman, who did not appear to be the slightest bit intimidated by the higher-status women at the party. She made a good living from her services at weddings, which included inviting guests and preparing the bride for the wedding festivities. Higher-status people would sometimes complain bitterly behind her back about her high fees, but no one seemed eager to criticize the fearless Sowsan to her face; she had no qualms about making a scene in public. Nor was she bound as fully by the modesty code. As Magda and I made our way for the door, Sowsan asked me loudly if my husband liked Zabidi incense, a query which is often used to tease young brides about sex and the pregnancy everyone anticipates will be announced shortly after the marriage. I merely smiled, and she called out that they were expecting me to have a Zabidi baby. She then insisted I give her greetings to my husband. Although laughing, several women urged her to stop – sending greetings to an unrelated man is highly improper – and a chorus of 'Shame, shame' [*'ayb, 'ayb*] went up. I was happy enough when Magda sensed my discomfort and hustled me out of the courtyard and into the streets. Even she was laughing, however, and asked me if I was embarrassed [*mustahiya*] by the talk, saying that Sowsan just didn't 'know' shame. She also tried to pump me for the details of my conversation with Awatif, but I prevaricated. Magda knew I was lying, but she did not push further. I had only started to receive information about more intimate and controversial topics as the result of my strict policy of discretion, one which was necessary in a place like Zabid where the fear of having one's private business trotted around town is reason enough not to talk to a stranger. I kept to this policy even with Magda, my dearest friend, who was occasionally irked that I kept things from her, but ultimately reassured, I think, that I would not spread her family's secrets around.

In my field notes for this evening, I had noted how much I had enjoyed the party, how much, for me, it seemed to capture what Zabidis extol in *khuruj*: the sense of a women's community united by a common etiquette, the communal enactment of the values of hospitality and the gracious receipt of it, and the cooperation of guests with hosts in putting on a show of finery. But I had been at parties where I had not been as comfortable with the hosts or the other guests, or had observed controversy between hosts and guests or between guests. And that evening too, there were many possible experiences to be had: Zabid is not the only place in which one person's social pinnacle is another's nadir, after all. A few guests looked bored, some, like Adila, obviously discomfitted, others, like Magda, were vexed by unpleasant encounters. Status differences were marked or contested, and this event, like every social encounter, was charged with both positive and negative aspects and sentiments.

We were quiet on the way home, Magda complaining of exhaustion and me of the heat. Magda and her sister walked me to my door on the way to their house, asking if my husband was home; if he had not been, I would have been invited back to their house so I would not have to sit alone. Given the enthusiasm with which going out is touted, it is surprising to witness the relief that women display on arriving home. On several occasions when I had stopped at Magda's house on my way home, I noticed they tore off their chadors, sighing as they flopped down on the nearest couch, appealing to a sister, mother, aunt, or daughter to bring them a glass of tea, while sharing the news of the party with those who had remained at home. The excitement which characterized the departure is traded for exhaustion and the relief on reaching one's home. This sentiment, I suspect, is related to the fact that every social encounter is more than relaxation; there are always elements of confrontation, of conflict and competition. Each interaction is characterized by a sense of being in the public eye and an intense awareness of the fact that one's comportment – and others' treatment of oneself – are evaluated and could potentially have consequence for familial reputation. Small incidents taking place in these gatherings – snubs, kindnesses, compliments, criticisms, and insults – may or may not have immediately tangible repercussions for a family's status, but are always taken seriously. The sense that one is safest and most secure from the vantage point of one's own *bayt* is evident when women return to their own houses after these formal outings. Although families are not without their strife and internal critism, they are bound by a fierce loyalty which inclines them to protect each other from the critical commentary of others. In this respect, one's own *bayt* is a refuge from the competition and evaluation of public life.

2

Tournaments of Value

Zabid is the only town in Yemen where the women go out in the evenings and the
men stay home to watch the children.

Highland Yemeni man

Generosity said 'I will go to Yemen,' and went to the land of the Arabs; Good
Nature said, 'I will go with you.'

The Sea of Precious Virtues, A Medieval Islamic Mirror for Princes

This chapter addresses how honour is created through the exchange of
hospitality. Hospitality is a well-known value of Arab and Mediterranean
societies; Zabidi society is hardly distinctive in holding generosity as a
central value. Herzfeld (1987) suggests that the specific practices by
which honour may be created, such as hospitality, should be examined in
detail.[1] In Zabid, women are proud to uphold the ideals of generosity
and hospitality shared by both male and female Zabidis. This need to continually recreate one's family's status through social intercourse in public
provides the central dynamic of life in Zabid. In the practice of visiting,
the social structure is enacted and potentially altered in everyday encounters. Inherent in visiting is what Giddens calls the 'duality of structure ...
structure is both the medium and the outcome of the reproduction of
practices' (1979:5).

---

1 The sexual propriety of women is essential to a family's honour, as will be discussed in chapter 4. However, one needs to consider dimensions beyond sexual comportment, such as
generosity, which may be central to the evaluation of honour (Wikan 1984).

Ethnographers of the Middle East have often noted the extensiveness of women's visiting networks. However, the implications of women's social life for the society as a whole are not fully considered. Elizabeth Fernea's *Guests of the Shaykh* (1969) sensitively conveys the texture of everyday life in a gender-segregated society but does not fully analyse the significance of women's activities. And while Altorki describes how Saudi women gather information about new brides, influencing the formation of marriage ties which have considerable political significance (1986:123–47), her analysis ultimately negates the significance of women's social life in most instances.[2] Similarly, Makhlouf contrasts women's afternoon visiting with the 'dullness of the morning' (1979:26), while Wikan suggests that visits merely spice up 'humdrum' lives (1982:125).[3] Makhlouf ascribes to San'ani women's parties a 'manifest function' of entertainment and a 'latent function' as being a 'bonding ritual' (1979:27), but her analysis does not go beyond these most obvious functions of visiting. She does not address the generative potential of women's visiting, or its divisive aspects. Dorsky notes that in 'Amran, women's formal visiting takes place on life-cycle occasions, according to balanced reciprocity (1986:70–1, 158–64, 211 n5), but she does not consider how women's visiting networks, like other ethnographically known forms of exchange, may serve to create relationships between families. Zabidi women, through hosting and visiting, create rather than merely uphold the honour of their families.[4]

Other accounts make clear that visiting and hosting involve the investment of labour, time, and resources into the maintenance of social relationships which are intrinsic to the status of the family. Bourdieu highlights the significance of networks of social ties in constituting prestige (1977:179–80), a fact very much evident in Zabid.[5] These ties do not simply exist: they must be continually renewed. Neither the patrimony of social connections

2   She states, 'This segregation finds its cultural compensation in the elaboration of formal and informal networks of friendship and kin' (1986:99). Women's visiting is merely 'compensation' rather than an activity which has import for the community as a whole.

3   Sweet's (1974) rather elusive suggestion that visiting in a Lebanese town was the 'essence of life' seems closer to the mark.

4   The literature on Turkey (Aswad 1974, 1978; Benedict 1974; Tapper 1983) discusses the *kabul gunu*, a type of visiting among elite women; these accounts describe women as 'expressing' the status of their husbands, but in Zabid women are more than just 'adjuncts of their husbands' (Tapper 1983:76).

5   Abu-Zahra's account of visiting also notes the connection between visiting and prestige in a Tunisian village: 'Social prestige is measured by the number of friends and followers who visit one and pay one their respects on the necessary social occasions' (1974:127).

nor one's family's place in society can ever be taken for granted. C. Eickelman (1984, 1988) explicitly addresses the role women play in the politics of
the Omani community she studied, particularly by trying to effect the
social mobility of their families.

Creating their families' honour and prestige is part of women's work
in Zabid. When I arrived in Zabid it was immediately obvious that visiting involved more than enjoyment, although countless times I was told
that the beauty and pleasure of Zabid lay in the custom of going out; certainly the gracious manners of Zabidi women, their witty conversation,
and cool and comfortable reception rooms made visiting in Zabid more
enjoyable than one would have thought possible given the wretched climate. But beyond the pleasurable aspect of this practice, which unites all
Zabidi women, is the undercurrent of divisive competition. Whether as
hostesses or guests, women are representatives of their families in public
and face the often-critical evaluation of their peers. Women create or
maintain ties between families through visiting, but they also create distinctions. The intensity with which women pursue visits is related to the
constant competition between families in Zabid. The practice of women's
visiting is fraught with the same tensions and contradictions which under-
lie Zabidi society as a whole: the elements at odds are dependence and
independence, equality and hierarchy, solidarity and distinction, and
enjoyment and danger.

Gender and Social Life

Social life is segregated by gender: this is the premise underlying sociability
beyond the family in Zabid, and visiting as a social practice. Women's visiting is strictly separated from men's visiting; no male past puberty is
allowed into a women's visit, unless he is a servant [khadim]. To this
extent, women do make up a separate community (cf. Abu-Lughod 1985).
Although the separation of men's and women's social lives requires continuous effort, the idea that the two must never coincide is an unquestioned
part of the common-sense assumptions of everyday life.

The interior of a man's home is off-limits to all other non-related men.
In his discussion of how an interior space is formed and transformed in a
Lebanese community, Gilsenan writes:

Women will never appear there (the maglis) when any kind of public event is going
on. It is not that a woman's presence pollutes the room. It is rather the nature of the
occasion that determines her presence or absence. As soon as the maglis reverts to

'private' use, then it is part of the 'inside' again and thus belongs to her realm, too. In this space, where inside and outside meet, where nonfamily enters into the one setting in the house into which they may enter without violation or profaning of the basic sacredness of family space, the women remain within the closed and nonvisible space to which no stranger may penetrate. (1982:183)

Only from a male perspective can the interior of others' homes appear closed, non-visible, or private. In Zabid, at certain times of the day, these interior spaces are open to receive the peers of women, whether friends or strangers. Women and children move freely between houses during the mornings and late afternoons and evenings; doors are never locked and female visitors simply appear in the courtyard. Male visitors must either yell for the man outside his door or commandeer a child to announce their presence. In Zabid it is a man who must defer to the female guests in his home. When a man returns home in the evening, he always pauses before entering the interior of his house and calls out 'Fi nas?' [Are there any people here?]. He cannot enter until all the guests have left.

Although women's social life beyond the family takes place exclusively in the company of women, in each other's homes, it is in no sense perceived of as a private sphere opposed to a public sphere which is the domain of men.[6] On the basis of her work in an Omani village, C. Eickelman suggests that the private sphere is the circle of family members, while the public one is where family members encounter non-related others (1984, 1988). This formulation is similar to the divisions in Zabidi society itself; when male and female family members interact with each other in the home, the home then becomes a private sphere relative to both male and female (adult) outsiders. Members of a particular *bayt* share not only the moral space of the house and a budget, but a common reputation as well. All members, male or female, are obliged to uphold the reputation of their *bayt* through their appropriate comportment in public. It is not that the women's social life comprises a private sphere; rather, it is a public sphere that is separate from the public which men face.[7] Unless women are specifically talking about

6 Aswad makes a similar point in her study of visiting between women of elite Arab landowning families in Turkey, reminding us that because visiting takes place within homes, it should not be confused with a domestic activity as opposed to a public one (1978:480). The validity of equating the oppositions of public/private: men/women: political/domestic has also been criticized by Nelson (1974), Rogers (1975), and Joseph (1983).

7 Men's and women's public spheres never coincide for sociable occasions. Non-related men and women do come into contact in the schools and hospitals, but these interactions are strictly defined as work.

men or Zabid in general, when they speak of going out with the *nas*, they are referring only to female people.[8]

Meeker notes that honour [*sharaf*] requires a wider community which recognizes honourable behaviour (1976:250). One meets the community, the *nas*, in the course of going out. *Khuruj* is a competitive practice in that one's family's place in the community – their honour – must continually be recognized by regular visits from those with whom one has connections. These connections that Zabidi families have with other families can be seen, as Bourdieu suggests for the Kabyle of Algeria, as an intrinsic part of a family's patrimony (1977:178). Both female and male family members are responsible, in their separate public spheres, for the maintenance of this valued patrimony, a practice which is the stuff of daily politicking in Zabid. The social connections can be considered part of the family's resource base which, although not necessarily in a direct or incontrovertible way, open up options. In a society where access to resources is, to a great extent, accorded through personal connections, keeping these connections viable is tantamount to keeping open avenues of opportunity.[9]

Varieties of Visits

Any event – joyful, tragic, or mundane – is marked by visiting. In this sense, the practice of women's visiting resembles a Maussian system of 'total prestations,' a society in which the obligation to pay, to receive, and to reciprocate visits is mandatory (Mauss 1970:3, 10–11). The etiquette pertaining to performance of visits is strict; visits are, as Bourdieu notes, formalities which are considered so natural that 'abstention amounts to a refusal or a challenge' (1977:95). There are several occasions when all the women with whom a family has social connections must visit or risk jeopardizing the relationship. Mandatory visits are owed on the occasion of life-cycle events (birth, marriage, and death), religious festivals, and in times of illness.

When a woman gives birth, all her friends, neighbours, and those who have connections to her natal family or her husband's family will visit the new mother at least once.[10] Married women who have given birth bring

8 I confessed to a Zabidi friend that when my husband and I were living in San'a' we had both chewed qat with men. She asked me, puzzled, if I had not known any 'people' in San'a'.

9 See Lancaster (1981) for an illustration of this process in an Arabian tribal society.

10 This practice is widespread in the Gulf region. Saudi women now regularly give birth in hospital; the new mother's family members bring the essentials of hospitality there to host visitors (Yamani 1987).

five or ten riyals to give to the mother of the baby. The new mother will present return gifts of money to them when any of these others give birth. This process was described to me as being an example of how community [*mujtama'*] is created in Zabid.[11] I was told that the first woman to give birth returns twice as much money to her friend as she received from her. However, in actual fact the amount of money given tends to stay stable (equal exchange). Although this escalation does not usually occur, the fact that everyone said it should indicates the competitive aspect of exchange in Zabid; one does not only reciprocate, but ideally gives more than one received, thereby asserting superiority. The procedure is formal: a woman keeps a notebook with a list of the women who attended and gave money, so she can be sure to return it. These exchanges on the occasion of birth evidence the two tendencies in visiting – that which unifies women and that which distinguishes them from each other.[12]

Weddings are invited events which include a number of reciprocal exchanges, not only between the bride's and the groom's family but between both families of the new couple and other families in the community. When there is a death, women who have connections to the family of the deceased must pay at least one condolence visit. The women of the mourning family refrain from public appearances for at least a month, and often longer.[13]

During Ramadan one is supposed to make at least a brief visit to every household in Zabid with which one has a connection, no matter how slight. Serious offence is taken if a Ramadan visit is neglected. Certain great families hold an open house on particular days of the year. One family has a huge reception on the ninth day of Ramadan, others receive guests regularly on other religious holidays. When a woman is sick, or when a member of her family falls ill, she will undoubtedly receive visits from relatives, neighbours, and close friends.

A special invited party, known as a *masaliya*, is common in Zabid. A family invites those in the community with whom they have connections for a party or a celebration with a particular theme, such as the fortieth day

11 I frequently gave money to my friends, but they protested that I would not be around for them to return the money to me when I had a baby. The opportunity to return is essential to the bond. I made a joke that when I had a baby, I would return to Zabid and demand money from all those to whom I had given.

12 This property of exchange – the fact that it distinguishes at the same moment as it unifies – has been discussed by Weiner (1976:213).

13 Visits surrounding marriage and death are particularly significant for prestige, as will be discussed in detail in chapter 6.

after a birth, a party in honour of a bride, or for the recitation of the *mawlid* (a text praising the Prophet Muhammad).[14] Fancier dress is required for invited parties, which are often attended by between seventy-five and a hundred women.

Visiting in other places in the Middle East appears to be more rigid in form than it is in Zabid. Women in Turkish cities pay visits on a strictly reciprocal basis, on the hostess's day in. In 'Unayzah, Saudi Arabia, visits are exchanged by a group of neighbours, each taking a turn hostessing in a rotating fashion (Altorki and Cole 1989:217–18). In Zabid there is a constant flow of women between houses in a fashion more fluid and malleable than that of Turkish or Saudi women, but one which has its own logic and etiquette. Individuals must make choices every day about which of the myriad social events to attend, choices often discussed during informal morning visits. These choices affect their families' relationships with other families in Zabid. Each woman will have slightly different networks of people to visit, depending on her natal and affinal kin, her immediate neighbours, her family's social connections and their status, and her friendships from school or work.[15] Flexibility is an essential element in managing visiting in Zabid; for instance, a woman may put off a long-term event such as a visit to a new mother in favour of a one-time invited event.[16]

The daily visits of Zabidi women are framed by the prayer calls; the main meal of the day is eaten in early afternoon. The first visiting session is known as *'asr*, named after the afternoon call to prayer (between 3:15 and 4:00, depending on the time of year). An hour or so after the *'asr* call a hostess can expect guests to arrive.[17] At the sundown [*maghrib*] call to prayer, women may wash and pray at the house they are visiting. However, women frequently change locale at this time, attending another house for the second recognized visiting period [*layl*]. The *layl* visit begins after sunset, between 6:00 and 6:45 p.m. Women usually return to their respective homes between 9:00 and 10:00 p.m.

14 This ceremony is discussed further in chapter 8.
15 *Zumala'* [colleagues] are becoming an increasingly important category of association now that many Zabidi women attend the local schools or are teachers there.
16 I first tried to book dates to visit people up to a week in advance; no one ever objected but eventually I realized that if I announced a visit, they would be obliged to stay in to receive it, regardless of whether a more enticing obligation turned up.
17 The daily soap opera [*musalsal*] may also frame visits, as those who follow it will not leave their house until it is over. An evening soap opera, around 10:00 or 10:30, is often shown as well. Older women said that in the past, women used to stay out later talking, but now everyone wanted to go home to watch television. However, television or video watching is not common in women's gatherings (unlike men's).

Sociability and Identity

Visiting is an identity-defining practice in more than one way. *Khuruj* is perceived by Zabidi women as an activity which is not only central to social life in Zabid but is in itself social life's finest quality. *Khuruj* is a practice through which identity as a community is formulated: although no one social event includes all of Zabidi women, the idea that going out makes them Zabidis is fully shared. Women say that visiting encourages social intercourse [*ikhtilat*]; they clasp their hands together, intertwining their fingers as if to indicate the social integration that *khuruj* effects.[18]

Visiting is central to a woman's personal identity in several ways. One is not supposed to stay home alone, ever. It is thought to be spiritually dangerous, because Satan [*Shaytan*] is thought to whisper [*yuwaswis*] to those who are left alone, instilling evil in them. In addition, there is a mental and emotional danger in solitude, as being alone is thought to cause anxiety [*diq*]. A considerate and moral person neither stays alone nor allows others to do so. Being unwilling to engage sociably with others is considered a serious moral wrong. 'Every woman sitting in her house with the doors locked' was how Zabidi women dismissed San'ani women, conveying their ambivalence about life in a big city. Although this minor ethnocentric assertion is not true, as some Zabidi women know, it does indicate that the vibrant sociability of Zabidi women is what they consider the most special and positive aspect of life in Zabid.[19]

Zabidi women say that visiting daily is very important for a woman, providing a respite from her children. They consider the presence of children annoying at this time: should children appear, they are hustled away by one of the hostesses or even by the guests.[20] Women declare that it is important to their sanity to have some time away from their children and the responsibilities of housework and husband. I was often told that 'without a little relaxation, a woman becomes a crazy person' [*majnuna*]. Chil-

---

18 As Simmel notes, 'This atmosphere of obligation belongs among those 'microscopic,' but infinitely tough, threads which tie one element of society to another, and thus eventually all of them together in a stable collective life' (1950:395).

19 It is practices of sociability which are used to distinguish Zabid culturally. As noted earlier, the Zabidi women who have experience in San'a' are often isolated in the newer, dispersed neighbourhoods. However, San'ani women in the Old City have well-developed visiting networks, as Makhlouf (1979) notes, which have remained intact in part because of the stable social relations and population in this neighbourhood.

20 A hostess may be occasionally interrupted by squalling children but she will scold them or give them a treat in the hope that her guests will be left in peace.

dren may be around at less formal gatherings, especially babies who are in need of maternal care, but they are not allowed to dominate or become the centre of attention. The visiting hour is a precious time when their identities as adult women are created in the company of their peers.

The cultural construction of visiting intersects with Zabidi conceptions of personhood. To be considered nice or good [*tayyiba*], one has to visit. A positive evaluation of a woman is, 'she is nice because she goes out with the *nas*.' Not surprisingly, given the importance of *khuruj* in uniting Zabid as a 'total society' (Mauss 1970), being willing to engage with others beyond one's own family is defined as a positive moral value. This value is overdetermined: there is also a connection made between politeness and religious morality. A polite woman is also a morally good person; to be a moral and good Muslim is very important to a woman's self-esteem and to the respect she receives from others. It is particularly important to visit the sick and the bereaved, a duty [*wajib*] recommended in a hadith of the Prophet Muhammad. Certain visits were not anticipated with pleasure, but a woman who is good visits out of a sense of duty, in accordance with the norms of moral conduct. Not only do others consider her a good person if she fulfils her visiting obligations, but the fulfilment of them is essential to her own self-image. Personal identity is constructed with the moral obligation to be good in mind. A friend explained this point to me, saying, 'A good person has compassion [*rahma*] for others. She visits people when they are sick, when they are happy, when they are sad, at every hour. She is not hard [*qasiya*].'

Obligations and the *Bayt*

Family members are ever-vigilant in guarding the reputations of their families. As discussed in the next chapter, various complex sentiments and obligations bind family members. Personal status and that of one's family are so closely tied that individuals feel both a responsibility and a pride in behaving appropriately in public in order to 'validate membership' in their families (Riesman 1983:120). This creation of one's own worth and that of one's family through behaving according to the cultural ideal of hospitality will now be addressed.

Families, particularly the *kibar*, have ties to dozens of other Zabidi families, and as a consequence, have many conflicting social obligations. How to manage these relationships to the satisfaction of all is one of the central problems of social life in Zabid, one that is essentially unresolvable. Long-standing relationships between families, whether kin or friends, must be continually recognized through visits, or they literally cease to exist in any viable form.

Visiting and hosting obligations owed to others of the women's public are the collective responsibility of the female family members. These practices are essential for the positive reputations of families. One way in which family members manage to keep all their social ties viable is by dividing their visiting duties among themselves. Because of the shared identity of family members, any (female) adult member can represent her family at a social event. Mothers, sisters, paternal aunts, and daughters may all perform a visit in the name of their *bayt*.[21] However, age and internal hierarchy do matter. Usually a representative of each generation (at least one older member and one younger member), should attend formal invited parties. Older women have the responsibility for making mourning visits, while the younger daughters and brides in all their finery are necessary representatives at festive events. During a wedding, for example, one sister and aunt may go to the home of the bride, while a daughter, mother, and sister will go to the home of the groom, so the family is not seen as being partial to one *bayt* over the other. (A married woman pays calls as a representative of her natal family and her husband's family, a fact which requires considerable juggling of social obligations.) Gifts extended to the bride on these occasions may reflect her mother's exchange relationships as well as those with her young peers, a fact also reported in Altorki's study of Jiddah (1986:114–15).

Family members are expected to be mutually supportive and to present a facade of seamless harmony to their public.[22] In this respect, members of a Zabidi family share a 'face', or collective reputation (Goffman 1976:42), which requires collusion – what Goffman calls teamwork – to maintain (1959:77–105).[23] This is, however, as much a moral obligation as an interested calculation, amply demonstrating how the construction of personhood mediates this sphere of performance. Teamwork is not so much

---

21 As the only woman in my household, I had a very difficult time managing my social obligations. Poor women in nuclear families had very little opportunity to maintain wideranging social connections because unless their husbands agreed to come home in the evenings, they had no one to watch their children.

22 Among Saudi women in Jiddah, visits are occasions when the solidarity of the kin group is displayed (Altorki 1986:102).

23 In using Goffman's framework, I do not want to accept fully the implications of such dramaturgical arguments, which present individual behaviour as calculated solely in terms of the impression made on the audience. As Abu-Lughod suggests, the motivational factor in appropriate comportment is more a matter of self-respect and pride than public opinion (1986:236-7). In most situations, Zabidi women would be ashamed *not* to help their kin.

calculated as it is enacted in the physical comportment of one's body; one's physical presence and postures of helpfulness represent shared identity. Family members are obliged to show solidarity by being present to assist with the hostessing chores. It is considered irresponsible for a member of the family to go out when guests are expected. I once thoughtlessly asked a friend of mine to a party with me, shortly after her brother's wife had given birth, and she said, shocked: 'It would be disgraceful ['ayb] for me to go out when we have people over.' Given the emphasis on presenting a harmonious face to the public, it is not surprising that serious grievances between family members are rarely aired in the presence of guests.[24]

Substantial effort is made to inculcate in children the notion that their comportment is an index of the family itself, an idea which reflects a particular concept of personhood, in which one's personal identity is continually constructed in reference to that of one's kin. Although children younger than five are seldom punished for misbehaviour, they are taught that their comportment affects people's image of their family. I heard young children who misbehaved in front of guests being chided by their mothers, 'What will she [the guest] say about you? She'll tell people that our children are awful.' A friend from a *bayt kabir* invited me to view an end-of-school party for her eight-year-old sister and her fellow students. I agreed reluctantly to attend; after a year in Yemen I was sceptical of the charms of large crowds of Yemeni children, whose behaviour on the street goes far beyond boisterous. I was truly shocked to witness seventy-five children under the age of ten, still and silent, demurely sipping sweet drinks instead of raising their usual hell. I conveyed my surprise to my friend, who laughed at the expression on my face and said 'They become shy when out in public' [*yistahu min al-nas*].[25] This party of clean, immaculately dressed, and perfectly behaved children imitating their elders' etiquette of public behaviour seemed a good example of a training game by which Zabidi values are '*made* body' by an 'implicit pedagogy' (Bourdieu 1977:94). These young girls will not be expected to adhere to adult comportment standards on a regular basis until they are around fourteen years

24 Being able to keep disputes within the family is related to high status, a fact also noted by C. Eickelman (1984) in her study of an Omani community. Elite families in Jiddah are similarly concerned to present an image of solidarity to their public (Altorki 1986:102).

25 Unlike adults, from whom proper comportment is expected in any context, on the streets children are largely anonymous creatures from whom rambunctious behaviour is tolerated resignedly. But even young children are aware that being a guest in someone else's house, particularly a *bayt kabir*, is a public interaction in which they are evaluated as members of a particular family.

old, but their training, and their awareness of appropriate public comportment, begin early.

Families have relationships with other families as units: male and female relatives inform each other about who is attending their respective social functions.[26] Women's visiting has a different structure from men's. They make more frequent visits to each others' houses and often hold large parties.[27] New political and economic alliances between men are mirrored by formal visits between women that solidify and ratify the business relationship. A friend explained to me, 'My father does business with her husband, so she must invite me to visit her, and I must invite her here.' Conversely, women sometimes keep up relations which are temporarily strained by disputes. Our neighbours were mediating a dispute between two families over land. While male members of the family hosted one man involved in the land dispute, at the same time, the female members of the family visited the home of the other family.[28]

Status Equals: Recognition and Competition

Much of the Middle Eastern literature on visiting takes note of how women fervently insist upon equality of visits (cf. Altorki 1986). In the Palestinian village studied by Rosenfeld, men's visiting represents hierarchical reciprocity (low-status man visits a higher one; the great man reciprocates with food, aid, and so on) while women's visiting is strictly non-hierarchical reciprocity. He suggests that because of the common condition of shared subordination to men, women are loath to admit any hierarchy within their own ranks (1974:149). This generalization is not applicable for Zabid: for both men and women, visiting relations between status equals should be strictly reciprocal, while non-reciprocal visiting is common between families of unequal status. However, women's visits in Zabid are negotiated in a discourse which often invokes reciprocity, although the exchange of visits, especially between *bayts* of clearly unequal status, is not reciprocal. Why this discourse draws on the idiom of equality is related, I suspect, to the minimal recognition of propriety which being visited in one's own home

---

26 Men and women do not swap guest lists every evening, but notable guests (or notable absences) will be mentioned in an informal fashion.

27 Men usually attend only one qat chew a day, whereas women may visit two or three houses a day. Men congregate in small groups; women's invited parties are generally much larger. However, men also have public interactions at the suq and at the mosque.

28 Aswad (1974) describes a similar situation in women's visiting where women nurture relationships with wives of their husband's political rivals.

implies. Also, in Zabid, the pervasive notion that good Muslim women ought to be willing to engage sociably with others, rich or poor, high or low, influences the egalitarian bent of the terms in which rights and obligations to be visited and to visit are discussed.

Influential Zabidi men almost always chew qat in their own homes, hosting regular qat chewers daily. Those who wish a favour from the host, or support in a dispute, will attend his qat chew.[29] Other men entertain on a specific day of the week when those who wish to show friendship or discuss business come to chew in the male entertaining space, the family *mabraz*.[30] The poorest men will not have a *mabraz*. Some other men have a *mabraz*, but may not be able to afford the expense of hosting a qat chew on a regular basis, which minimally includes the cost of tobacco, charcoal, incense, and ice.[31] Several of the *kibar* men may also host regular luncheons on Fridays for as many as twenty to thirty guests; others invite guests to lunch on special occasions only. For men, the most important events at which recognition for each other is presented formally are weddings, *'ids* [religious festivals], and *khatims* [celebration of a complete recital of the entire Qu'ran, often held during the last days of Ramadan].

Although the most notable men in Zabid may only occasionally pay visits to each other's homes, their wives will perform frequent formal visits to families of equal status. Women's visiting between equals, however, depends on reciprocity: a woman who stayed in her home every day and expected to hold court would be resented. Other women would refuse to visit her.[32] The emphasis on reciprocity is strongest between those families who consider themselves social equals – especially the *kibar* families, or

---

29 This pattern has been noted in other Middle Eastern societies. In the Tunisian village Abu-Zahra studied, both material power and honourable reputation are at play in visiting: the wealthiest and most influential men attract many visits and pay relatively few (1974). In Jiddah, wealthy men host stable groups of men daily (Altorki 1986:100).

30 The physical structure of *bayts* and their relationship to gender segregation is addressed in the following chapter.

31 One man complained to my husband that as well as the expenses for the chew (he estimated that he spent at least 100 riyals or $10 a day), he also spent 50 riyals ($5) on his own and neighbourhood children who pestered him for riyals for treats. Some of the *kibar* spend considerably more than this, providing soft drinks and bottled water for their guests as well.

32 I heard of only one case in which non-reciprocal visiting was tolerated. One man forbade the women in his family to leave the house when he was absent from Zabid. The friends of these women continued to visit them despite the fact that they could not return the visits. It was explained to me that it was not the fault of these women that their father was so unreasonable; they were all *tayyibat* [nice] and would return the visits when able to do so. Now that the father has died they visit in the accustomed Zabidi style.

those families whose ambition is to become of the *kibar*. By refusing to extend or accept an invitation, one questions the position of the neglected family. Relations between equals are often so competitive that any small sign of neglect is pounced upon. The immediate impact of a slight, such as failure to attend a social gathering, is perceived as a threat; as Mauss observes, 'To refuse to give, or to fail to invite, is – like refusing to accept – the equivalent of a declaration of war; it is a refusal of friendship and intercourse' (1970:11). Such refusals constitute challenges that are taken very seriously; the offended party is usually quick to deny the claims of the other to superiority.

Bayt ʿAbdullah Amir, a rich and influential family, did not invite Bayt Ibrahim Wahhab, another *bayt kabir*, to their wedding. The members of Bayt Ibrahim Wahhab were enraged, especially since they had invited Bayt ʿAbdullah Amir to the wedding of their son four months earlier. On the day of the wedding, when it finally became clear that the invitation was not going to be even belatedly offered, Ibrahim Wahhab's wife, Zohara, stormed around flicking the underside of her chin with her fingers, a common gesture of dismissal, hissing, 'That's finished' [*khallas*]. She said of Bayt ʿAbdullah Amir, 'They shame us' [*yuʿayyibu ʿalayna*]. Bayt ʿAbdullah Amir had invited all the other *kibar* families in Zabid with the exception of Bayt Ibrahim Wahhab, implying that they did not consider them one of the *kibar* in Zabid, one of their equals. I do not know if that was the intent, but it certainly was how the omission was interpreted; Zohara announced to a group of neighbours that, due to this insult, they would never set foot in Bayt ʿAbdullah Amir again. When I left Zabid, the two families were still estranged over the incident.

Attendance at formal events is closely monitored; any indication of lapse in parity between the two families will be reciprocated in kind. Muhammad ʿAbdul Wahid refused to attend the wedding lunch of Bayt Hamud As-Salih on the grounds that Hamud As-Salih had only sent his son to their wedding lunch instead of coming himself. So Muhammad ʿAbdul Wahid sent his son to represent the family at the Hamud as-Salih wedding; to attend himself would be to admit a less than equal relationship.[33]

Women, too, are sticklers for exact parity. I heard many complaints about a woman who had been lax in returning visits although she grandly received them. Her husband is a wealthy man from a prominent Zabidi

---

33 The place of the representative in the internal family hierarchy is particularly important in men's visiting. Women tend to complain if there are not several representatives from each family, although one from each generation is minimally acceptable.

bayt, and although they lived most of the time in Saudi Arabia, they made two extended trips (staying three months) to Zabid while I was there. On her first trip, she received visitors from practically all those with whom her husband's family had connections. Even I was sent for, as the token Christian foreigner who had so quaintly adopted Zabidi customs. During her second trip, however, the Zabidi women were reluctant to visit her again, since she had not returned their calls. One woman said to me, indignantly, 'I'm not going to visit her again when she has *never* come to my home. Why should I visit her when she never visits me?' I was invited again to visit her on the day of a religious festival, and I went, but was teased by several of my friends for 'running after the stranger.' A proud and dignified Zabidi woman would not have deigned to visit her again until she had returned the visit. She did seem to be lording it over the rest of the Zabidis, but after a wide-scale defection of visitors, she finally was forced to return her calls.

Most women go out in groups of two or three; a notable exception is a clique [*shilla*] of young women from the *kibar* families in Zabid. Twenty or thirty of them arrange to attend the same party every day; they pay their calls in a group. Although temporary cliques arise and dissolve in neighbourhoods all the time, this clique was unusual in its longevity and in the fact that it was based on high status rather than residential propinquity. By always appearing together, they present a cohesive face of eliteness to the rest of the Zabidi populace. They confirm their collective equality between their families at the same time as they indicate their superiority over lesser Zabidis. While recipients of visits are honoured (they may say, for example, 'The *shilla* was here last night – you should have seen the house – it was full!'), the *shilla* can be rather intimidating en masse, demanding the best seats and wearing their hostesses out with their sharply issued requests.

In the past, certain *sadah* families considered themselves socially superior to other Zabidis as well as superior in religious knowledge. The members of one *sadah* family, whose patriarch governed Zabid for many years, acted like emperors, according to one consultant. They demanded particular forms of deference such as non reciprocal visits during Ramadan. I was told that even their *khadima* was treated with the greatest respect by other Zabidis, as her association with this illustrious family transcended the stigma of the *akhdam* estate.

In Your Own Home

The sensitivity to non-reciprocated visits is related to the fact that receiving guests has implications for the family's reputation. Being visited in one's own home is a public recognition of the respectability of the host family. The guest, by entering the domain of the host, essentially allows the reputation of her hostess's family to 'englobe' or 'encompass' her own, at least temporarily (Herzfeld 1987). Guests, in this important sense, subordinate themselves to the hostess, although during the visit, as the hostess solicitously fusses over the comfort of her guests, it may appear to be quite the opposite.[34]

I was given one instance of a case in which a person must not be visited in her own home, even if she visits one's home. A woman who has a reputation for being loose with men must be greeted with politeness if she visits one's home, but one must never visit her in her home, lest her bad reputation tarnish yours. I was told a proverb: 'Invite a prostitute [qahba] into your house, but not a robber.' This proverb humorously indicates that bad reputation can be neutralized in one's own home, whereas the danger of a robber cannot. But by visiting a woman of ill repute in her house, one puts one's own reputation at risk.[35] This fact is clearly related to the extreme importance people place on being visited in their own homes: by doing so a guest indicates that the hostess and her family are worthy of respect, and effectively acknowledges that one's reputation will not be harmed by entering their home. Wikan (1982, 1984) describes an incident in Sohar in which a prostitute, polite and generous to her neighbours, was not snubbed by them for her activities; they continued to visit her. She was judged by her peers on the basis of her generosity rather than her improper sexual conduct. The situation in Zabid is different: one Zabidi woman who continued to live in her husband's house after they were divorced (she was commonly believed to be still sleeping with him) did not receive any visitors at all. She said that if she went to others' homes they would be nice to her face but talk about her once she had left.

A man's bad reputation could also adversely affect visiting relationships between two families. Two families, Bayt Muhammad Karim and Bayt Salim Saqqaf, were near neighbours and distant kin, and for these reasons, one would have expected a close relationship between the two. However,

34 It is possible, of course, to look at it the other way around: that by entering someone's house, one is obliging the hostess to provide hospitality. But in Zabid the role of giver is preferred to that of recipient.
35 This seems to hold for men as well as women: several times my husband was told not to go to particular houses because they were associated with men of ill repute – those who watched pornography or drank liquor. Accusations of drinking often seem a stylized condemnation of a person; whether or not the person actually drank was not always verifiable.

Salim Saqqaf had a dreadful reputation: not only did he watch porno-graphic videos and drink liquor – hardly comportment condoned by pious Zabidis – but he was stingy and violent as well. Several times the neigh-bours had to intervene when he was beating his wife, mother, or aunt. The women of Bayt Mohommad Karim would not go near the house. The women of Bayt Salim Saqqaf continued to visit Bayt Muhammad Karim, where they were always received hospitably, but were never visited in return. More than a few times the women of Bayt Salim Saqqaf complained about this fact. Only the oldest woman of Bayt Muhammad Karim would ever enter the house, and then only for the shortest possible time; she would not even sit down. The fact that the women of Bayt Salim Saqqaf continued to visit the reputable family anyway implies that they were anx-ious to maintain at least a fiction of a close relationship. They continued to use the rhetoric of reciprocal visiting, demanding to know why the women of Bayt Muhammad Karim had not visited them, as if they had not stopped going to their house years previously.[36]

The physical structure of the *bayt* is in some key sense the locus of the identity and reputation of the family. Their own reputation neutralizes the ill effects of the bad reputation of a guest visiting their house, but another's bad reputation can equally encompass one if one ventures into their house. If through visiting one confers respect on the family and indicates their social worth, by not visiting one implicitly challenges the family's claim of respectability. These challenges are taken very seriously. A woman, by refusing to visit someone's home, implies that her reputation may be tainted by entering the house of the other. By greeting a woman with bad reputation politely if she enters one's home, one avoids tarnishing one's own good reputation by withholding hospitality. Therefore, the fact that a woman is treated graciously in someone else's home says more about the hostess's honour than about her own. It is being visited in one's own home which truly confers honour.

Unequal Relationships

The intense concern over being visited is also related to the fact that any lapse in the parity of visiting creates an unequal relationship. As Mauss

---

36 When we attended a wedding in the wadi, almost all the women present refused to ride in the car driven by Salim Saqqaf. His aunt later complained vociferously about this fact; everyone present denied that they had meant any insult, but it was clear to everyone that the refusal implied that he was bad [*mush tamam*].

notes, 'To give is to show one's superiority, to show that one is something more and higher, that one is *magister*. To accept without returning or repaying more is to face subordination, to become a client and subservient, to become *minister*' (1970:72). Being able to return hospitality is perceived of in Zabid as a right as much as an obligation.[37] However, some long-standing, often positive, relationships are often characterized by inequality in visiting, particularly those between neighbours [*jiran*].[38]

'Neighbour' is an important social relationship, as it is in so many Middle Eastern Towns. Geographical propinquity to a certain extent cross cuts hierarchical relationships; it is taken for granted that one owes loyalty and attention to neighbours. The concept of *jiran* has an emotionally evocative quality; relationships between neighbourhood women are characterized by comfortableness and familiarity. There is a certain trust between them (and often a jaded awareness of each other's foibles), based on a lifetime of asso-ciation, cooperation, and possibly material support. Neighbours tend to have a great deal of knowledge about each other's families; there are not many secrets between them. They share crises most immediately, and any exciting event happening to one family is, to a certain extent, the property of all. This shared identity between neighbours is evident in the pride women take in the solidarity and helpfulness between groups of neighbours. My neighbours proudly claimed that they were 'like kin' in the closeness of their association. It is considered reasonable to offer duty to one's neighbours as a reason for not keeping another social engagement: everyone agrees that it is *'ayb* [disgraceful] to neglect a social event of your neighbours, no matter what exciting event is going on in the other parts of town.

The focal point of a neighbourhood is a *bayt kabir*; neighbourhoods tend to crystallize around one great family. Close neighbours gather in the *bayt kabir* on religious dates. Despite the fact that inequalities between neighbours are often muted by feelings of solidarity based on proximity and shared experience, differences between families in a neighbourhood are encoded in and reproduced by visiting patterns: lower-status people visit higher-status people more frequently than the reverse. Poor or weak fami-lies cannot afford to provide hospitality on a regular basis, whereas the larger families can. Poor neighbours not only visit a *bayt kabir* more fre-

---

37 Rosenfeld provides several examples of how seriously this right to discharge obligations is taken in a Palestinian village (1974:142–5).

38 Much of the following discussion could equally apply to relationships between wealthy and poorer relatives.

quently but often provide assistance in the considerable tasks involved with hostessing. Two of my *kibar* neighbours held weddings while I was in Zabid. The women of both *bayts* contributed labour to each other's party preparations, but they did not return labour to the lower-status neighbours who helped them as well. Neighbours who want to assert autonomy from their neighbouring *bayt kabir* try to avoid serving in their homes.[39] The relation between weak and great appears to be more that of client/patron, especially if the lower-status neighbours depend on the higher-status family for aid. Poor families may receive charity from the *kibar* or they may be forced to appeal to a *bayt kabir* in times of crisis, such as illness or death of the family's wage earner.[40] Disputes which cannot be solved internally by poor families will be referred to a *bayt kabir*. One poor man appealed to his *kabir* neighbour to chastise his son because he persisted in drinking and beating his mother and would not recognize the authority of his own father.[41]

The tension between equality and hierarchy is evident in visits between neighbours. *Kibar* women do visit lower-status neighbours, not informally, but for life-cycle events, such as birth receptions, funerals, and weddings. (They do not, however, help serve the guests.)[42] Not to visit would only make the *kibar* women appear inconsiderate, or even immoral, and poorer neighbours are perfectly within their rights to demand a visit on these occasions. By periodically visiting neighbours who are either clients or just less affluent, the *kibar* women recognize, at least minimally, their respectability, thereby ensuring future support from these weaker families

39 In one conflict between two neighbours, Iman (from a poor *bayt*) infuriated Zaynab (from a wealthier one) by requesting a service instead of helping. Iman, in this instance and others, attempted to thwart her designation as 'one who serves' by refusing to help. One does not demean oneself by helping a neighbour, as long as the neighbour returns the help at one's own social event. But Iman was aware that, in her case, this was unlikely to happen.

40 These are not the formalized patron/client relations of the Mediterranean region (*cf.* Campbell 1964). Aid and charity are described as helpfulness between neighbours. Poor neighbours have a moral right to appeal to (rather than demand from) their *kibar* neighbours for aid, who in turn are morally obligated, if not legally bound, to help.

41 One *kabir* woman in our neighbourhood was known to be a good mediator and she could be trusted to be discreet; neighbourhood women often turned to her for counsel, consolation, or material aid. One woman from a qadi family was well known for her ability to mediate disputes; women from all over Zabid used to come to her with their problems.

42 Non-*akhdam* women will usually make one token visit at deaths in their client *akhdam* families. A short visit may be made at a wedding as well. *Akhdam* relationships with higher-status neighbours can sometimes be friendly. In such a case, the elite women will not refer to her as a *khadima* but rather call her a neighbour or *miskina* [poor, but harmless].

for their own social events.[43] Herzfeld makes a very significant point: by accepting the hospitality of the client (and allowing themselves to be encompassed temporarily by the client), the patron essentially 'allows the client to maintain self-respect while gaining material advantage' (1987:86).

But every neighbourhood has families who are neither destitute nor wealthy. There are perfectly respectable families, who, while lacking the extensive resources of a *bayt kabir*, are financially independent. These families are still, to a certain degree, encompassed by the identity of the *bayt kabir*, but the relationships between them and the *bayt kabir* more closely approximate egalitarian ones. These families are often the most loyal supporters of a *bayt kabir*, the women of both families united by strong bonds of friendship. The ethos of *jiran* is often invoked to induce helpfulness and solidarity for each others' social affairs.[44] Weaker Zabidi *bayt*s can gain status among their peers for their association with their great neighbours. Small yet respectable families often proudly noted their acquaintance with a *bayt kabir*, speaking of how close their two families were. Neighbours, both very poor and respectable, express this encompassing by throwing themselves into the social events (or crises) of the *bayt kabir* with the same intensity with which they address their own concerns. I often heard weaker neighbours brag about the lavish hospitality at a social function held by their neighbours, a *bayt kabir*. If I neglected a social event held by our *kabir* neighbours, Bayt Ibrahim Wahhab, I was often chided by one of our poorest neighbours, who would say, 'Anne, where were you last night? There were *nas* at Bayt Ibrahim Wahhab. '*Ayb*! [shame!] – we're all neighbours.' If the women of a *bayt kabir* treat their neighbours respectfully (by visiting and providing aid if needed), they will be assured of loyal attenders and helpers as they entertain the other *kibar* in Zabid with whom they have fiercely competitive relations.

The competitiveness that is evident in visits between status equals, when the emphasis is on presenting a grand image of one's family to the guests, is absent in gatherings composed solely of neighbours. Everyone knows roughly where everyone else stands and hence there is little need for (or tolerance of) the affectation or formality which marks visits between status equals. Each interaction is marked by the nuances of one's perceived or desired standing in relation to another family; one may accept disparity

---

43 As Beidelman notes in his discussion of Simmel's ideas on exchange, 'even in the most uneven exchanges the two parties mutually influence one another' (1989:229).

44 The *kibar* may help in their poorer but respectable neighbours' social events by providing room to receive guests. One man from a *bayt kabir* allowed a weaker neighbour to hold the qat chew for their daughter's marriage in his capacious reception room.

between one's family and a *bayt kabir*, be furiously competitive with status equals, and be generously patronizing to those of lower status.

This type of relationship between great and weak *bayts*, where virtue is the basis of domination, appears to be characterized by what Bourdieu calls symbolic domination, a mode of domination that transmutes a family's economic capital into symbolic capital, through systematic 'misrecognition'; thus overt domination becomes 'legitimate authority' (1977:192). The notion that economic resources are transmuted into moral value is apt. However, symbolic capital is a rather elusive notion and the concept of misrecognition underestimates both the degree to which actors understand the system of domination and the extent to which they are able to manipulate it (Eickelman 1979:390). Gerholm's work on Manakha (1977) suggests that in certain situations, lower-status Yemenis may perceive rather clearly how they are being dominated.

Generosity creates an honourable reputation in Zabid; the fact that it is understood as a personal quality is central to the way in which domination is played out. The rich are those who are better able to demonstrate this moral virtue, which everyone values. *Al-kibar* can better afford to offer hospitality (and charity) on a regular basis and their prestige depends on their doing so. Wealth itself does not automatically confer honour; it must be appropriately invested, consumed, and distributed. In a tangible sense, their honourable status is contingent upon the appropriate distribution and consumption of resources.[45]

One Zabidi man had most of the elements of status in Zabid – land, large family and home, and wealth – save generosity and willingness to engage sociably with others. Both the male and female family members were universally condemned by other Zabidis.[46] Although he kept his own family in a lavish style, he was lax in fulfilling obligations to others; his neighbours described him as both haughty and a miser. The women in his family rarely

---

45 Messick notes a similar intertwining of honour, piety, and wealth in Ibb: 'Only the wealthy can attain the valued postures: they alone have the wherewithal to be generous, or derive the pious merit from establishing a *waqf* or providing charity to the poor. Inasmuch as honour, status, and wealth tend to coincide, the important qualities of trustworthiness and good reputation, which underpin much of the economic interchange in the town, are monopolized by the rich. In this set of ideas, the poor lack honour and status, and must be the degraded recipients of charity. The ideal life circumstances, as defined in this community, may only be approached by the wealthy' (1978:423).

46 They were described as bad [*mush tamam*]. The head of the household, a minor government official, had a reputation for corruption. He stayed in his own house to chew in the afternoons, as many wealthy men do, but did not have many men visiting him.

went out, and seldom hosted anyone in their home.[47] The most flagrant transgression of Zabidi norms occurred when he did not host a lunch on the occasion of his eldest daughter's marriage. (This daughter was particularly disliked and described as conceited [maghrura].)[48] I suspect their unwillingness to participate in the practice of recognizing others through offering and accepting hospitality was the key reason this family was not considered of the kibar.

Conclusion

Offering hospitality is one of the primary means by which a family's honourable reputation is created in Zabid. Thus, guests provide the hostess with the opportunity to display generosity. However, guests, if they are or aspire to be the social equals of the hostess, must absolutely refuse to continue to visit the hostess if she will not visit their homes in return. If one always visits and is never visited, one is put in a subordinate position vis-à-vis the visited family. This implies either that there is something potentially damaging about the reputation of the family who is not visited or that the hostess's family is in some sense superior to the family she will not visit in return. The ranking of bayts in Zabid is continually enacted, reproduced, and transformed by this practice of visiting: to maintain its position in Zabidi society, a family must be continually recognized by others in the community. However, the members of a family must keep up with their social obligations if they want to continue to be recognized by their peers, and here lies the tension. Most families in Zabid have many more social obligations than they can possibly fulfil, and therefore inevitably leave some offended. Complete and irrevocable severance of ties between two families is relatively rare, although lapses in visiting continually threaten a relationship. Temporary breaches and heartfelt reproaches are the stuff of everyday life in a society where everyone is continually vigilant for social snubs, real or perceived. The dynamic competition between families in Zabid and the continuous need for recognition cause both the tension in Zabidi society and the excitement.

Although men's and women's publics are entirely separate, in the sphere

47 I was so puzzled by the behaviour of this family, so atypical of Zabid, that I asked someone if they had only recently arrived there. I was told they had been in Zabid as long as anyone, but that they just did not behave properly.
48 She herself told me that she did not like going out because she knew people were always talking about her, speculating on where her father got all the money for her gold (this was, in fact, the case).

of the family the networks of the two intersect. Women have considerable autonomy in the planning and implementation of their social events, but ultimately family budgets which fund hospitality are controlled by men. (This shores up my argument that men implicitly recognize the significance of women's activities, enough to allot them the considerable resources necessary for entertainment and appearing at social events properly attired.) In another Yemeni context, Messick notes how judges depend on their wives and female family members for information about the reputations and activities of members of the community; this sphere of women's knowledge is explicitly recognized in Islamic legal texts (1993:180–1). In Zabid, information about the comportment and resources of other families, and their presences or absences, are exchanged between men and women. Women's networks are particularly significant in reproducing on a regular basis the widest range of familial relationships, which are acknowledged in the male sphere only on special occasions such as weddings. Perhaps most significant for the mutual influence of the two spheres is that having other women visit one's home implicitly recognizes the respectability of the male head of the household and the family as a whole. Men will initiate invitations between women – such as an invitation to a man and his wife to lunch and a qat chew – if the relationship (such as a business one) is to be trusting and close. And the fact that bad relations between men will be announced publicly and irrevocably by a cessation of visiting of the women of the two households says much for the trust and respect men grant each other through women.

From a female perspective, this upholding of the family patrimony is a matter of pride that is taken very seriously. The fact that ultimately the male sphere is more powerful is mitigated by the considerable degree of autonomy and responsibility that women have to run their own affairs, and in this respect Zabid seems distinctive. Men and women are bound in such a way that, within the private sphere of the family, familial interests are held collectively by men and women. The next chapter addresses these ties that crosscut the male and female domains.

3

The *Bayt*: Family and Household

Zabidi women appear at public social functions as representatives of particular families, or *bayts*. The principles by which *bayts* are formed, their transformation over time, the material bases which support them, and the moral bases for their honourable reputations are here discussed. I also discuss how women are situated within families, as sisters and as wives. Marriages are arranged in light of the principles by which *bayts* are formed and the goals individuals are trying to achieve.

Bayts are emergent structures, actively created by people, according to culturally defined principles and goals (*cf.* Eickelman 1976, Bourdieu 1977). Membership is defined by patrilineal descent, and residence is (ideally) patrilocal.[1] Individual identity is inextricably linked to that of the members of one's *bayt*; they share a reputation which must be collectively upheld. A woman's primary affiliation is always her father's family, even after marriage.[2] The term *bayt* has different meanings according to context: it refers both to the household and to the members of the patrilineal descent group after which it is named.[3] *Bayt* as household refers to a domestic group, the physical space of residence, where food is prepared

---

1 Zabidi families share these characteristics not only with other Yemenis, but also with most other Arab Muslim societies. However, in contrast to those who propose that a Muslim family structure can be identified (Behnam 1985), or an Arab one (Barakat 1985), my approach is influenced by Eickelman (1989:151–78), who suggests that kinship forms must be examined in light of their explicit or implicit local meanings.

2 Meeker's (1976) schematic comparison of the way kinship is formulated among Arabs as opposed to Turks, where a woman is cut off from her family of birth at marriage, illuminates on a general level some of the consequences of this principle.

3 H. Geertz in 'The Meaning of Family Ties' (1979) was one of the first ethnographers to reflect on the significance of these different uses of the term *bayt*.

and children are raised. *Bayt* as family refers to the people who live in the moral space of the house, who share a budget as well as a reputation. *Bayt* as household is not coterminus as *bayt* as family, as households include members of other *bayt*s (wives), and possibly a *khadim* or an indigent female affine or neighbour.[4] And the *bayt* as family also includes married sisters residing in other households.

The ideal toward which individuals strive is to have a respected, autonomous, financially independent, and cohesive *bayt*. In Zabid, *bayt*s are usually no more than four generations: the head of the household, his mother, his children, and his sons' children.[5] The *kibar* are those who are able to achieve the ideal most successfully: several generations in a large complex living together and sharing a budget. To outsiders the household will be referred to by the name of the head of the household, for example, Bayt 'Abdullah Amir. As long as they share one budget and eat together, they refer to themselves as one household [*bayt wahid*]. When the sons of a great family marry, a separate house is built for them (usually a room, wash room, toilet and a courtyard) within the family complex. Within the household, this space is referred to by the name of the son or his wife; Bayt Abduh or Bayt Fatima. If a man has two wives, each must have her separate room in the larger complex. Over time, as sons marry and have children who then marry, households as single units simply become too cumbersome to maintain. After the patriarch dies, the sons may begin to eat separately with their wives and children, and they may or may not divide the family inheritance.[6] After the inheritance has been split, the developmental cycle begins again: each *bayt* is financially separate, with a separate reputa-

4 The *kibar* are those who have the space and resources to support these extra members. One *bayt kabir* took in an old female neighbour who had no surviving kin. This was lauded as a charitable act, but the old woman was treated more as a servant than a family member. Even a family taking in an orphaned child unrelated to them genealogically raise it as a charitable act rather than as a member of the family. At one party a woman indicated a small girl, saying within her hearing how good it was of the hostess to have taken in an illegitimate and abandoned child. In this respect, Zabid differs markedly from the Moroccan town of Sefrou, where H. Geertz argues 'the operative, everyday, acted-upon premises do not rely on sharp and simple distinctions among family, friend, and patron' (1979:315). In Zabid, clear distinctions are made between family and others, which are not forgotten no matter how close the relationship.
5 Actual household composition is extremely varied. Almost all households are composed of at least three generations, and they sometimes include unrelated members and affinal kin. Nuclear family households are more common among the very poor.
6 Islamic inheritance laws are practised in Zabid. Sons receive an equal share and daughters receive half the share of sons. One brother may take over all the family land, but he must compensate his siblings.

tion which must be recognized by others in the community. At this stage, brothers orient themselves more toward their own descendants rather than each other.

Economy and the *Bayt*

The material bases by which families are supported affect the nature of *bayt* as household and the contours of *bayt* as family. For the *nas*, land owner-ship provides the ultimate independence and security as well as prestige. However, the *bayt*s which have maintained themselves most successfully over time are those that have sources of income other than land, which allows them to maintain appropriate consumption styles without eroding their landholdings. Income must be derived in ways that are considered respectable, in contrast to the demeaning employment of the *mazayanah* and the *akhdam*. 'Intellectual' work such as teaching, and religious and legal scholarship, is valued over physical labour or petty trade.[7]

The most important economic criterion for greatness is landownership; Zabidi families own estates in the nearby wadi. The landowner does not work his own land but rather hires an overseer to supervise the work of the sharecroppers and day labourers. If the land is pump-irrigated, the share-cropper receives one-quarter of the produce and the owner receives the remainder. The landowner received one-quarter because he owns the land, one quarter because he owns the pump, and one-quarter because he is responsible for repairs and taxes.[8] Wadi-irrigated land is considered a 'gift from God' so the sharecropper receives more of the produce, one-third. The landlord receives the remainder: one-third is his gift from God and the other third is his because he owns the land in the legal sense.[9] The flood water in Wadi Zabid is channelled through a system of canals and tempo-rary deflectors, according to a formal agreement concerning which land

7 Petty trade in the suq is distinguished from being a great merchant [*tajir*], which is respected and lucrative.
8 The information on land tenure was related to my husband by several wealthy landown-ers. Women of landowning families also told me the basics of the land tenure arrange-ments, although they are not involved with the running of the estates.
9 The relationships between owner and tenant in Wadi Zabid are even more stratified than in some of the other Tihamah wadis. In Wadi Mawr, the division of surplus between the sharecropper and the landowner was two-way, after expenses and tithes [*zakah*] (Mundy 1985:29). Land-tenure arrangements in some parts of the highlands award a higher portion to the sharecropper. In Ibb, a fertile region in the lower highlands, the tenant farmer receives three-fourths the produce, but he is responsible for tithes (Messick 1978:149).

receives water and when. The most common legal disputes in Zabid involve rights to water and land; my husband heard of several disputes involving accusations of surreptitious diversion of water from the rightful recipients.

Although the most lucrative Yemeni produce, qat, can be grown only in the temperate highland climate, in Wadi Zabid there has been a switch from sorghum to more lucrative cash crops in the last twenty-five years. By the late 1980s many Zabidi landlords had purchased pumps, as pump technology is necessary to grow crops such as mango, banana, lime, tomato, papaya, and cantelope. This produce, and dates from Red Sea date estates, are trucked into the highland regions, where such crops cannot grow because it is too cool and arid. Those landowners who have been unwilling to invest the capital (or unable to raise it) necessary for pump technology have dwindling incomes from their estates, especially given the drought conditions of recent years.[10]

The great landowner usually deals with farm business from his reception room in the afternoon, during his qat chew, when his overseer comes in to report on the farm. One of the landlord's sons will often be charged with visiting the farm for closer inspection. So strong are the local prejudices against agricultural labour that landowners even refuse to let their sons study agriculture at the university.[11] One great landowner explained to his son that he could not study agriculture because he did not want *his son* 'working in the fields and "turning black."'[12] The body of a great landowner reflects this distance from productive labour: he will be pale, without well-developed muscles, though he may be either thin or fat. Those who work in the fields or perform menial labour in Zabid tend to be darker-skinned and have well-developed physiques.

10 Sorghum and millet occupied 75 per cent of the cropped land in Wadi Zabid in the 1970s (ECWA/FAO Joint Agricultural Division 1978:325). The income from the pump irrigated banana farm of one prominent Zabidi is approximately 25,000 riyals ($2,500) a month; the sharecropper receives 6,000 riyals. The returns for sorghum are roughly half this amount, and although not so much water is required, this crop takes up more land.

11 The relationship between land and honour in this class-stratified society differs from that in the tribal organized highlands, where honourable men work their own land (Dresch 1989:43). Caton argues that both owning land and working it oneself are central aspects of a tribesman's identity (1990:32–3). However, many Tihama *qaba'il* are tenants rather than landowners.

12 This anecdote was conveyed to me by the young man's sister. The whole complex of ideas surrounding 'blackness' or 'whiteness' is complicated by concepts of beauty, morality, and racial origins, as well as manual labour.

Being *kabir* is more a process than a state, and those who have been successful in maintaining their prominence over time must have an eye to their future as well as their illustrious past. A problem for landowners has always been how to meet consumption needs without liquidating one's landholdings. The *kibar* in the past often had additional sources of income besides surplus from their estates. All of the *kibar* owned indigo-dyeing workshops in the pre-revolutionary period; in the early 1950s there were around 150 indigo workshops (Balfour-Paul 1990:44), although only one remained in 1990.

Now, with inflation, additional sources of income are even more necessary, although not widely available locally. The *kibar* often have government posts; the salaries are relatively modest but some corruption is expected, although unreasonable rapaciousness is not respected. As in Ibb, government salaries often become a hedge against selling off land to meet daily requirements (Messick 1978:204). Landownership is often coupled with entrepreneurial activities; the *kibar* are best able to raise the initial capital for investment.[13] Profits may be used to try to increase landholdings. Pharmacies are particularly lucrative businesses in Zabid; one could probably make a decent living selling malaria drugs alone.[14] Those who have made a fortune, as locally understood, in Saudi Arabia are from elite families and are literate.[15] Uneducated men from poor families who went to work there did little more than support their families, returning with a television set and money for a few months of qat chewing.

The school board is the largest employer in Zabid. A university education allows one to teach in one of the local high schools. A high-school teacher's monthly salary (5,000 riyals) is supplementary income for the son of a great man, but for the son of a respectable-if-not-wealthy man it can be an important means of support for the family. The daughters of some *kibar* families were among the first to be educated at the high-school level, and now it is seen as backward [*mutakhallif*] not to educate one's daughters. As one Zabidi told me, 'Once the *kibar* started sending their daughters, it

13 They have the connections to facilitate the acquisition of permits from the central government, and the resources to join the Chamber of Commerce [*ghurfa tujjar*]. With a membership fee of 6,000 riyals ($600) a month, this is a requirement for importation of goods.

14 Expensive medical care in Yemen is often treated as other forms of conspicuous consumption (Myntti 1988:518). In Zabid, people equated the amount of money spent on drugs with the love and value of the sick family member.

15 Some established a service which organizes groups of Yemeni pilgrims on the hajj; others have created joint business ventures with Saudis.

was no longer considered shameful' [*ayb*].[16] Education is increasingly seen as necessary for raising children properly; assisting children with their homework is now a motherly duty. After high school, women can teach in the primary schools.[17]

Having women contribute to the household budget, I was told, was considered shameful; ideally the fathers (and brothers) should provide for the family. The reason it is now acceptable has to do with the fact that education is highly valued, teachers are greatly respected, and the school system in Zabid is an institution representing progress. However, women's salaries should not provide the sole means for the support of the household.[18] Preserving prestige of the family as a whole involves allowing the head of the household to retain control over the finances.[19] I was interested in how much control women had over the money they brought into the household, so I asked one young teacher how she spent her salary. Offended by what she took to be an implication that she was selfishly hoarding her salary, she asked, 'Do you think I only love myself? [*Ahibb nuffsi bas?*], and retorted that she did not keep a riyal for herself, but gave her entire salary to her family. Another woman, from a *bayt kabir*, was angered by my question. She admitted giving her salary to her father, but stressed that her father gave her absolutely everything she needed or wanted. I had unwittingly insulted her family by implying that she was working because her father was inadequately providing for her.

Unmarried women of elite families have little housework to do in the household, and teaching provides them with respect and responsibility; they work, they say, because they find life boring [*mumilla*]. These anecdotes convey a sense of how women are situated in families in Zabid: one, as members who should be concerned with the family as a whole as opposed to themselves as individuals, and two, as the consumers rather

16 Sending daughters to the university in San'a' is still not widely accepted, although in 1990 at least fifteen women from Zabid were registered at the university.

17 The government's teachers' training program [*mu'allimat*] provides support for completion of education (600 riyals per month in intermediate school, and 1,000 in high school). After graduation, they owe at least two years of service [*khidma*] teaching in the local elementary schools or in the afternoon school for illiterate women or girls who are slow learners. They receive 3,400 riyals a month. Another elementary school with a religious orientation [*ma'had ad-din*] provides a salary of 1,600 riyals a month.

18 One woman said of a poor family, 'The father hasn't worked a bit since he returned from Saudi Arabia. He sits in the house while his daughters work. They wouldn't have a thing if those girls weren't teachers.'

19 This is often true for dependent sons' salaries as well.

than the main providers, a point elaborated later. Even learning for women is often perceived as a skill used to help others, their own children, or if unmarried, those of their brothers, rather than for their own intellectual growth.

Zabidis are aware that a university education in technical fields is now a means for securing lucrative, respected employment, and future security. This strategy is common, and effective, for the upwardly mobile. The *kibar* have the political connections to ensure that their sons receive fellowships abroad, and are able to provide them with supplementary income. Although there is no local employment available for engineers, architects, or computer scientists, having a son employed in al-Hudayda or San'a' can be advantageous for a Zabidi family, as he has the opportunity to make connections in the centres of political and economic power in Yemen.

The *kibar* do not constitute a corporate group as such, but these families control most of the land in the surrounding region, and most of the lucrative employment in Zabid. Although there are enough resources in the region to allow some to make a large surplus, both land and the opportunities for local employment are finite. *Bayts* are in continual competition with each other over the material resources which form the foundation for an honourable existence. However, honour resides not only in wealth, but also in the appropriate distribution and consumption of income, in a moral economy which stresses generosity, charity, hospitality, and a high degree of conspicuous consumption.[20] Honour and place in society are realized through the competitive hosting of social events, but consumption has to be balanced with a maintenance of resources. Upward mobility is possible, but so is downward mobility. Those who are forced to sell their landholdings to maintain standards of consumption erode their future security and those of their dependants. There are many examples of quick decline in Zabid: ex-landowners left with fine houses, but no means of supporting dependants.[21] This process translates rather palpably into the erosion of one's reputation; a man who has undercut the security of his family is thought a fool.

Ancestry

The bases for being or becoming a great family involve qualities other than

20 Consumption practices are often central to theories of the elite, such as Weber's discussion of a style of life which includes consumption patterns (1958:180–95) and Veblen's conspicuous consumption as a basis for defining a leisure class (1967).

21 Several young men complained privately to my husband that their fathers had deprived them of their inheritance, by 'chewing their land' (i.e., selling it for qat).

land and property [*al-ard wa al-mal*]; they include illustrious ancestry and a reputation derived from the appropriate comportment of members. The *kibar* are judged in terms of values shared by all Zabidis to be the best [*al-ahsan*] and the most respected [*al-muhtaram*] among them. Those who are not of 'the great' are defined as such by themselves and others by their *lack* of what the *kibar* possess.[22]

The great families often have a historical depth and a respectable origin that the poor or weak families do not have. Several *kibar* families are said have been in Zabid for a very long time [*min zaman*] or are referred to as having deep roots [*asl*]. (The term *asl* also connotes noble descent.) These families have wider circles of extant kin bearing the same patronym, and trace their descent back generations. The term *bayt*, when used in its most general sense, refers to all the descendants of an apical ancestor; the contemporary descendants of the ancestor may be cousins or more distantly related through the male line. 'Bayt X,' for example, will be used to refer to the wider agnatic kin group (and also to the ancestors).[23] One man, of a prominent *sadah* family, described the oldest of the *kibar* as follows, using the term *bayt* in this fashion which refers to historical depth: three *bayts* famous [*mashhur*] for their religious scholarship (two *sadah* and one qadi), two *bayts* famous for their political power (one *sadah*), and three *bayts* famous for their wealth in trade. There are several *bayts* in Zabid now bearing some form of the patronymic of their illustrious ancestors, whose prestige is encoded in their name. Some, although not all, of these *bayts* are wealthy and still of the *kibar*.

Illustrious ancestry encoded in a patronym is not a guarantee of *kibar* status, but is often an element of it. The reputation of accomplished and famous ancestors devolves on current members; on one level, the descendants share the inherited glory of their ancestors.[24] It is thought important that this reputation be upheld by current members through their appropriate comportment. In this fashion, the temporal dimension of prestige enters

---

22 Attitudes toward the *kibar* are not without ambivalence. In almost the same breath, people would say, 'They are the most respected and the best among us,' and then go on to state examples of their moral flaws, concluding that morally they were really no better than anyone else, and in some cases, a good deal worse.

23 The term *bani* [children of] may also be used, i.e., Bani X. Exact kinship links between contemporary descendants may or may not be remembered. 'Practical' kin (*cf.* Eickelman 1989: 151–78) are those with whom relationships are maintained through visiting.

24 This idea of family prestige based on the accomplishments of ancestors is nicely described by Meeker (1976:246): 'The sharaf [honour] of a clan is a totality of significance derived from acts accomplished by its ascendants.'

into contemporary everyday life.[25] The non-*kibar* do not have this sense of family over time and space. Poor *bayt*s have shallow descent groups, encoding only the grandfather's name, for example Bayt 'Abdullah Ahmad. A patronym is not retained; therefore the name of the *bayt* changes with every generation. The name of the *bayt* may also refer to the occupation of the head of the household, for example Bayt Muhammad al-Jazzar [the house of Muhammad the butcher]. In this case, the name of the *bayt* indicates a disreputable occupation instead of an illustrious ancestor. These poorer *bayt*s have smaller circles of kin outside their *bayt*s.

Other *kibar* families trace their origin to other places which are deemed respectable in local eyes, including Turkey and the Hadramawt, as well as several highland regions.[26] One great landowning family, reputed to be one of the richest in Zabid, retains a patronym which refers to the mountain region from which their ancestor came several generations ago. Several landowning families trace their origin to India.[27] The heterogeneity of Zabid's population is not surprising, given Zabid's history of foreign occupations. All these families consider themselves Zabidis and Yemenis now, and their *kabir* status is based on wealth and conformity to local norms.

What distinguishes great *bayt*s from other families is that they have managed to reproduce their prominence over time as well as space. However, contemporary *kabir* status also depends on wealth and the comportment of current members, and not all those with illustrious ancestry meet these standards. These criteria are used to evaluate the status of a *bayt* in its more specific sense, referred to by the name of the current head of the household coupled with the patronym, for example 'Bayt Omar X.' It is this sense of the term *bayt* which is relevant in everyday life. These *bayt*s, even if they share the same patronym, are in dynamic opposition to, and competition with, other similarly constituted *bayt*s. The fortunes of *bayt*s bearing the same patronym often vary widely; some with impeccable pedi-

---

25 In this formulation, I have been influenced by Meeker's (1976) work on Middle Eastern collectivities, and also by Riesman's work on the Muslim Fulani of Burkino Faso, which connects everyday comportment to a historical sense of family. Riesman writes: 'Each Pullo's self includes in some measure the selves of his relatives, both past and present, and his own sense of worth is enhanced by the very admiration which he feels towards those relatives and ancestors' (1983:121). This connection between appropriate comportment and a sense of distinguished family is discussed at length later.

26 Ethiopian, Somali, or Sudanese origin, the imputed origins of the *akhdam*, in contrast, is not considered illustrious.

27 An older informant referred to Mullah Ahmad, a saint [*wali*], as '*Jadd al-Hunud*' [the ancestor of the Indians]. All the families of Indian origin bury their dead in the graveyard [*majanna*] surrounding his tomb, on the western edge of Zabid.

gree may be nearly destitute and dependent to some extent on charity from their wealthier kin.

The Physical House

The word *kabir* also means spacious and extensive, and this sense is reflected in the substantial structure of an eminent family's house. The family complex of a *bayt kabir* contains many smaller *bayt*s in which to house an extended – the ideal – family. The entrances to these complexes are often obscured by long passageways to ensure privacy for the women in the family and their guests. These large complexes are enclosed with high walls; only the second stories rise above them to mark the landscape. The elite families also have spaces where male guests can be entertained without ever contacting the women of the family. In a great house, the men's reception room [*mabraz*] is located adjacent to the house or facing it across a narrow alley. A second-story room [*khilwa*] with a separate entrance may also be used as the men's reception room.[28] Given the importance of providing hospitality to others in one's own home, and given that socializing with non-kin is segregated by gender, separate male and female entertaining spaces are essential for full participation in Zabidi social life. Smaller *bayt*s will not have a *mabraz* or room with a separate entrance, effectively preventing a man from entertaining at home, as women have precedence over the use of the house during visiting hours.

The eminence of the great families is demonstrated in the physical structure of the house. Inside the complex walls in a great house are several long, high rooms [*murabba'*], whose walls are adorned with beautifully carved plaster work [*naqsh*]. These interior rooms are used for sleeping, and during the mornings, and the late afternoon and evening, female guests are received there.[29] The exterior facade of the *murabba'* is decorated with elaborate bas-relief brick work, which is whitewashed with a lime wash

28 There is a separate toilet which male guests can use so they will not need to enter the house proper. Men's *mabraz*s are cleaned and tended by *akhdam*, as they are so clearly men's space that the women in the family will not enter them.

29 Each *murabba'* [*bayt* in its smallest sense] houses one couple and their children. These rooms are lined with Tihama couches. The family sleeps in this room (or in the courtyard during the summer), but during the day, the cushions on the backs of the couches make them into comfortable seats. Clothing is usually stowed in trunks under the beds. Cabinets, sometimes beautifully carved, are built into the wall. A long table in the centre of the room, topped with several waterpipes, completes the simple but functional and comfortable Zabidi furniture.

[*nura*] before Ramadan, or any special event, such as a birth or a wedding. The *murabba*'s face each other across a courtyard [*qabal*] or are placed side by side with adjoining courtyards. In the summer, female guests are entertained on Tihama couches placed in the courtyards.[30] Date palm, lime, fig, or basil trees are often planted in the courtyard for shade and decor.

The most beautiful aspects of the house are located in the interior of the homes, where unrelated men do not enter, and therefore are presented only to the female public. Televisions and video machines are often found in the men's *mabrazs*, but the best television (and the telephone) are kept in the women's part of the house. The cloths covering the mattresses and pillows on the couches are finer in the women's section; they are recovered with new cloth for special occasions. Framed family photographs and other prized items and valuables are kept in the interior rooms as well. These features indicate prestige and reputation, yet they are presented only to the female public. Although the structure of Zabidi houses does not show the same kind of regular structural oppositions evident in Bourdieu's description of the Kabyle house (1979), there are certain affinities between the architecture of great houses, the appropriate display of wealth, and the practices of the body by which gendered identity is established.[31] The walls of the complex which conceal the interior of the house from non-related men are permeable to female non-related guests, where the house's finest qualities can be evaluated. Women's bodies must be concealed from non-related men by veils, but they are revealed in their finest adornment to the female public in the course of formal social events.[32]

It is thought that a family's wealth ought to be displayed in the construction and decoration of a fine house. Criticism was aimed at rich men with poorly appointed houses; for instance, 'He has plenty of money, but his house is a mess.' Poorly maintained houses (and family members) are thought to reflect stinginess.

Although there has not been a massive exodus to the outskirts of the town resulting in a radical reshaping of social space, there have been changes in the style of building houses. Some families have built new cement-block additions to their homes; a few are brightly painted to

30 Illustrations of the decoration of interior and exterior facades in a *kabir* house in Zabid are available in Stone (1985:70–1).
31 Boddy describes the disposition which underlies architecture and treatments of female bodies among the Sudanese, which she calls the 'idiom of enclosure' (1989:74).
32 The fact that men are well informed about the interior decor of houses and the adornment and beauty of women they have never seen is testimony to the effectiveness of transmission of information between male and female family members.

resemble red bricks. New houses tend to be square or rectilinear. The interior walls are flat, without carving, and painted bright colours instead of whitewashed. This new style is thought beautiful and modern, but some new houses have followed a style common in Saudi Arabia – cement-block houses without courtyards. Without air conditioning, these houses are excruciatingly hot in the summer, and people cannot retreat to a courtyard to sleep as is common practice in the summer.[33] Only a few great families have built new houses on the outer edges of Zabid; one family received many fewer visits as their new house was near the highway, on the outer edge of socially acceptable space for women. Although the house was admired and the women popular, it was quite a production to visit them; large groups of women would assemble and go together, offsetting with their numbers the dangers of unfamiliar territory.

In contrast to the complexes of the *kibar*, the houses of poor families have only one room, a small courtyard, and a door which opens directly onto the street. The quality of the interior carving and the furnishings are poor. Sons often have to rent or build small homes elsewhere because there is not enough space to build an additional room. The houses of the *akhdam* vary from small concrete structures little different from other poor Zabidis to thatched huts or tin shacks.

The *bayt* is a moral space as well as a physical one, and both men and women are most secure and comfortable in their natal homes. However, men's experience in the household is different from that of the women. Young boys, teenagers, and men do not perform domestic labour in the household, aside from the daily shopping. Men are waited on in their own homes by their female relatives. Dresch captures this spirit of the *bayt* from the male perspective quite nicely:

The house provides a refuge from the constant disturbance of public life. The workaday phrase 'at home' (*fi l-bayt*) has about it a weight of meaning and is said with a forceful contentment well stressed by the accompanying gesture: the head tips a bit

---

33 Although the style of presentation of wealth in Zabid stresses conspicuous consumption, even elite Zabidis can be quite parsimonious with daily budgets, and paying for utilities is resented. Air conditioning is simply beyond the means of poor families who have built small concrete homes. And regardless of expense, the consistent cold draft of air conditioning is thought dangerous to one's health. Traditional houses are built with thick walls of baked-mud bricks, and remain cool during the day. Only a few houses built in the last decade are decorated with the traditional interior carved plasterwork; these were the houses of men concerned about this trend, which undervalues the aesthetic and practical qualities of the traditional architecture.

to one side, and the hands, palms down, come from chest height to waist height, as if patting in place the bedding, the cushions one sits on, the tea things, and all of life's cares. *Fi l-bayt, murtah!* ('At home and comfortable') *al-hamdu li-llah* ('God be praised'). (1989:57)

For women, however, the household is the site of work as well as relax-ation. For a man, the interior of his household is off-limits to his significant public, non-related men.[34] Women, however, receive their public, non-related women in this interior space, so during the visiting hours it must always be prepared for guests. The interior of the houses are impeccably kept, particularly in the homes of the *kibar*, an impressive feat given the heat and the dust. Women pride themselves on the care of the home, and their reputation depends on it. Zabidi women are very fastidious and are reluctant to accept hospitality in a home they consider unclean; much of women's work in *kibar* households is expended in hospitality-related chores.[35] Housework, especially if there are several adult women in the household, does not take much time, but must be done daily.[36]

The *Bayt*: Obligations and Interdependence

The *bayt* – in the sense of family members that live together and share a common reputation – forms a unit which endows value on its members. Strong bonds of love, loyalty, and obligation between *bayt* members were demonstrated and expressed by all Zabidis. Common to all families is a similar notion of internal hierarchy; all members of the family are subordi-nate to the male head of the household, who ideally controls the budget and provides for the material needs of the members. Men are dominant over women, and the elder members over the younger. These relationships are understood in terms of love [*hubb*], respect [*ihtiram*], and duty [*wajib*]. If a man fulfils his obligations to his dependants, he is said to love them. They in turn express both respect and duty by deferring to his wishes. Families share an identity which is enacted through the fulfilment of mate-rial and moral responsibilities to each other, and a careful protection, through appropriate comportment, of their collective reputation. Hierar-

---

34 On the rare occasion when men do receive visitors in these areas (in times of serious illness, for instance), the regular schedule of women is seriously disrupted.

35 This labour must be juggled with the demands of schoolwork or teaching.

36 Wealthy families often have servants to help with the sweeping of the courtyards. Cook-ing, cleaning, and washing chores are divided up equitably by the women, resulting in either a small number of daily chores, or a rotating schedule of weekly chores.

chical relationships within the family are also muted by a strong sense of shared identity and loyalty rooted in love and mutual concern.[37] As Meeker notes, 'All "unities" in the Near East are based on "love" and refer to "significances"' (1976:406). Insults to one member offend all of them, and one member is, to a certain extent, interchangeable for another.[38] The sense of cooperation and collusion between family members in the image of themselves they present to others in the community is striking.[39] There is said to be no benefit [*maksab*] in conflict between *bayt* members.

Women as Sisters and Wives

Women are situated in families in two ways: as daughters and sisters, and as wives and mothers. Unmarried or divorced women living in their father's *bayt* have unambiguous ties to their natal household and are, for the most part, fiercely loyal to it. Zabid is unusual in Yemen in the high number of women who never marry, particularly among the *kibar*.[40] If a woman is physically or mentally unsound, she is not usually married, but there are plenty of unmarried women who do not fall into this category. Such women may claim publicly that they did not wish to be married, although offers had been made for them. In great families it is not uncommon for a sister of the head of the household to be unmarried, and a couple of his daughters, often the oldest two.

In some families this practice is explicitly related to the inheritance of land; the father and brothers do not want the women's shares going out of the family.[41] A woman's land is supervised by her father (or her brother, on her father's death), and while in most cases she does not control the pro-

---

37 The connection between internal hierarchy and love and mutual obligation is significant for how women experience subjectively subordination to male family members (see Abu-Lughod 1986:81–5). The intertwining of love and power gives family hierarchy its particular force. Joseph notes in her discussion of the brother-sister relationship in Lebanon: 'Patriarchy seated in love may be much harder to unseat than patriarchy in which loving and nurturance are not so explicitly mandated and supported' (1994:58).

38 Some exceptions to this interchangeability were noted in the last chapter.

39 A marked cooperative ethic is present among male and female family members in an Omani community (C. Eickelman 1984).

40 In 'Amran it is unusual for women to be unmarried (Dorsky 1986); and in San'a' an old maid is an anomaly (Makhlouf 1979:32).

41 Women who marry outside the family often choose to inherit a room in the family household, instead of land, as security in case of divorce. Women's right to inheritance is usually recognized in Zabid, although occasionally stories were heard of brothers disinheriting sisters (or their mentally unsound brothers).

ceeds from the land, she has a right to be supported by her father in the same style as her brother's wives. However, there is a potential conflict among a man's female dependants. Many women complained that after a father's death, a brother might be less scrupulous about attending to his sister's needs than those of his wife and children.[42] A wife can mitigate these potential jealousies by being generous to a sister-in-law with whom she lives, and by sharing her husband's gifts.[43] But loyalty to the natal household is so strong that if a woman is ill-treated by her kin, she will often cover this up in public, because she is unwilling to tarnish the reputation of her family.[44]

Another reason for keeping sisters unmarried is that great households need a certain amount of female labour to function properly. Great families have numerous social ties which must be maintained through the exchange of hospitality, and a young wife, saddled with small children, is not able to cope with child-rearing and hostessing. The unmarried sisters often shoulder the responsibility of cooking for the family, and either represent the family in public through visiting or babysit while the wife goes out.[45] After a wife's daughters are old enough to look after the smaller children, the sister and wife often pay calls together. Some young women claim to want a residence apart from their husbands' family for the sake of independence, but the practice of visiting in Zabid is not geared toward a nuclear family structure; it is very difficult for a woman in a nuclear family to care for her children and meet her social obligations to others. In a notable number of cases, a man's sister and his wife have an affectionate, cooperative relationship, and the brother's children are as much a concern to the aunt as to the mother.[46]

In the way that patrilineality is formulated in Arab societies, a woman's identity is primarily derived from her natal family, even after marriage. When a woman is asked, 'What *bayt* are you from?' she always answers first, 'I'm the daughter of X,' and second, 'I'm the wife of Y.' A married

42 Many unmarried women felt that the bond between brother and sister could be undermined by the sexual bond between husband and wife.

43 One woman said she was always careful to give her sister-in-law a taste of what her husband gave her.

44 A woman may not want others feeling sorry for her, and she is aware of her vulnerability; she will have nowhere else to go.

45 Zabid contrasts with 'Amran in this respect, where unmarried women never participate in formal visiting (Dorsky 1986:71).

46 The older children of a sexually active couple often sleep with an unmarried paternal aunt. Particularly if a bride is a teenager, the older kinswomen of the groom will help a great deal in child care.   .

woman's friends frequently address her by a feminized form of her father's patronym. For instance, a woman from Bayt Sulayhi will be known as Sulayhiya to her friends. Her children's status is affected by the status of her natal family. Her natal kin continue to address her by the name they gave her. Women often remain extremely close to their natal kin throughout their lifetime. It was often said that 'a woman always loves her father's house best.'

This sense of collusion in the presentation of the significance of the family – their honourable reputation – to the Zabidi public has particular implications for a woman who marries into the family. At marriage a woman becomes a member of her husband's household. However close her ties to her natal family, after marriage she is obliged to obey her husband and is responsible for her children. Early on in a marriage, the groom's family is anxious to ensure the new bride's deference to their family. This is achieved in part by treating the girl well, and also by continually emphasizing her material and moral subordination to them.[47] The new wife is considered a bride [*arusa*] for a year after her marriage, and ideally has a status more like that of a guest, without having any chores in her new household.[48] Her husband's family is responsible for her financial support, and their status, and her husband's love for her, are shown by the adornment of her body. She becomes a representative of her husband in public and is responsible for paying visits on behalf of his family; and, particularly after her first year of marriage, she shares the responsibility with his female kin for hosting guests in their home.

She should be obedient to her husband (and his mother); being obedient, as long as requests are not unreasonable, is seen as a duty and a virtue. It is said to be shameful for the groom's family if a bride does not defer to their wishes.[49] A bride entering a household is expected to main-

---

47 As in other patrilineal societies, such as the Taiwanese Chinese, the task of eliciting the loyalty of a new woman is key (Wolf 1972).

48 In practice, the bride is given the minimal responsibility of looking after her section of the house. If the girl is still in school, the older female relatives do her and her husband's laundry, which will be her job when she graduates. However, any bride who makes a point of insisting that she, as an *arusa*, should not be obligated to help out with hostessing chores will be mocked behind her back.

49 A few months after the wedding season in Zabid, there were dark mutterings about the insubordination of new brides, but these complaints were only aired to the most trusted friends. One friend, of a *bayt kabir*, told me at great length about the problems they were having with her brother's bride, who spent most of her time at her mother's house. When another woman from another *bayt kabir* asked where their new bride was, my friend said quickly said that her mother was sick and she was visiting her.

tain their standards of comportment. A woman is often given a new first name by her husband's family, as a way, I suspect, of reminding her of her new identity as their bride. Her cooperation is required to present a seamless image of the family to the Zabidi public. She is privy to their secrets, and they essentially have to trust her not to air any internal disputes in public.

Although a woman's identity is irrevocably tied to that of her natal family, to whom she will return in cases of mistreatment by her husband, there are pressures to consider marriage permanent. Women commonly said, 'After marriage, her father's door is locked behind her.' If a woman is not obviously abused by her husband's family, her kin may pressure her to work out the problems. Divorce is not unknown, but it is said to be shameful ['ayb].[50] It is shameful because it is a public scandal, which therefore opens up an opportunity for others to gossip. All parties are potential targets for criticism. The girl may be thought wilful, her family may be thought imprudent for making a bad match, and the groom's family is sure to come under fire from allies of the divorced woman, who blame the husband or his family for the problems. For this reason, it is considered foolish to marry a son or daughter against their will.

Arranging Marriages

In Zabid, as in many Middle Eastern societies, arranging marriages is a family affair: the couple themselves never decide. An unmarried girl having contact with a man is scandalous, and in any event, opportunities for meeting members of the opposite sex are limited.[51] Girls are no longer married before puberty, but they may be married at fourteen or fifteen years old.[52] Men are usually married in their twenties. Potential marriage partners are sought discreetly by the women in families; agreements are kept as secret as

50 There is no obvious stigma attached to a divorced woman, however, as Dorsky notes for 'Amran (1986:152). In Zabid, the children of a divorced couple can choose which parent they want to live with after they develop 'reason' ['aql]; if the child remains with the mother, the husband should pay child support (usually 300 riyals a month). If the mother remarries, the custody of the child reverts to the husband's family.

51 While love cannot be a reason for marriage, it is preferable that the bride and groom be compatible, in the interests of domestic harmony. It is also considered good if the two grow to love each other.

52 Another way schooling has changed perceptions of time is that many now think a girl should graduate from high school before being married. However, many teenagers can continue to attend high school after marriage, even if they have babies, because child care is relatively easy to arrange in the extended family context.

possible until the engagement is announced.[53] When I asked how people arranged marriages, women said, 'Anyone will do.' However, judging from the marriages which were celebrated while I was there, and from those extant, it was not quite so random. The Islamic principle of *kafa'a* stipulates that 'equivalence' should exist between families to be united in marriage. However, in Zabid there are several ways in which equivalence can be reckoned.[54] There are a number of what Bourdieu describes as marriage 'strategies'; as he notes, marriages which look genealogically similar may have 'opposite meanings and functions' (1977:48). Several types of relationships can provide a basis for marriage: paternal kin [*bani 'amm*], maternal kin [*bani khal*], neighbours [*jiran*], and friends [*asdiqa'*].[55]

Although a thorough discussion of the material and moral concerns by which marriages are arranged is beyond the scope of this work, I will offer a few generalizations here. Intermarriage between the Zabidi *kibar* is very common, serving to maintain the distinctiveness of the elite from other Zabidis. Another common practice is for an established *kabir* family to marry a daughter into an upwardly mobile family.[56] Marrying *kabir* daughters to foreign-educated men is also a common practice, as is the tendency for *kabir* families to marry into *shaykh*ly families in the wadi. In all these types of marriage, the *kibar* demonstrate the use of marriage ties to extend relationships outward, including to those families who show signs of becoming influential.

Sociability is essential to the maintenance of practical kinship ties. Affinal ties, like agnatic ties, have to be maintained by constant visiting. In astutely arranged marriages, ties between the two families may become extremely close. They are strong supporters of each other socially, visiting and offering aid at each other's events. If the ties between the two families are viable and warm, a woman often arranges a marriage between her son and a member of her natal kin group.

53 Women are central in arranging marriages in Saudi Arabia which lends them a certain degree of political power (Altorki 1977, 1986).

54 As Meeker notes, 'Marriage means that *at some level* the two intermarrying collectivities are part of one "community" and stand identically with respect to some "significance." This does not necessarily mean that the two groups are of the same sharaf "by descent"' (1976:386).

55 In this respect Zabid differs markedly from tribal societies where agnation is valued above all other potential ties (*cf.* Abu-Lughod 1986).

56 A Zabidi man of modest pedigree who acquired a great deal of local influence in the post-revolutionary period married his son to a girl from a prominent *sadah bayt*. Her sister married into another non-*sadah bayt*, a family of Indian origin said to be one of the largest landowners in Zabid.

Another strategy is for a *bayt kabir* to take a bride from a perfectly respectable, yet non-*kabir*, family, who may be neighbours or poorer kin. The great family encompasses not only the bride but also her family. The relationship between the two groups of affines has aspects of clientship, a relationship which is reflected in unequal visiting patterns. This was especially common in the past, when girls would be married before puberty, and more or less raised by the great family. The unmarried sister of a great man indicated her brother's wife, now the middle-aged mother of fourteen children, and said proudly, 'We raised her [*rabbaynaha*]. She was just a little girl with no breasts when she came to us.' This strategy has the effect, over time, of binding a woman ever more closely to her family of marriage. In some cases, when the class distinctions between the two families had become particularly marked over time, a woman claimed not to even feel comfortable [*murtaha*] in her natal home.

Zabidis often said, 'Everyone says that Arabs marry their paternal kin, but sometimes there are so many problems that it is better to marry far.' They had a relatively jaded view of the advantages of paternal kin marriage, saying that if the marriage did not work out, relationships between the two families might be irreparably damaged.[57] If there are inheritance disputes between the fathers of the married couple (which there frequently are), pressure may be put on the marriage.[58] However, opting for *bani 'amm* marriages seems to be related to the point at which a family is in the developmental cycle. Two Zabidi families practise *bani 'amm* marriage exclusively, as an explicitly stated way of keeping their land together.

Conclusion

The *kibar* are situated in large and economically secure *bayts*, of which they are very proud. Members of the *kibar* often say of their families, 'We are many thanks to the will of God' [*Ihna kathir ma sha'llah*].[59] This chap-

---

57   One failed marriage between the offspring of two *kabir* families bearing the same patronym caused so much havoc that they cut off relations entirely, therefore making public the problems generated between them. Ideally, *bayts* bearing the same patronym are strong supporters of each other socially and can be relied upon for aid in the production of large scale events.

58   Inheritance problems complicated one dramatic divorce (described in chapter 7).

59   The phrase *ma sha'llah* [whatever God wills] is used whenever observing the good fortune of others or commenting on one's own good fortune. It is believed to protect against the evil eye.

ter has focused on the *kibar* because they represent the ideal, the extended family well supported by material resources, which grants them autonomy which the non-*kibar* lack. Poor [*miskin*] or weak [*da'if*] families are largely defined by their lack of what the *kabir* have. They do not have land or financial independence and may be dependent to some extent on the charity of their richer neighbours. Their homes are small; some rent or are allowed to live in small homes owned by their more prestigious neighbours. While having several children is valued by all, it is often said disparagingly of families who have more children than they can reasonably support, 'They have nothing but children.' Among the *miskin*, four generational households (with married sons and their children) are rare. Because of the lack of space in their households, they cannot achieve the degree of gender segregation of the elite, with separate male and female entertaining spaces. Wide-scale entertaining will, in any case, be beyond their means, therefore they cannot fully take part in the competition for prestige among families.

There are plenty of families that fall between the very wealthy and the very poor. Their homes are as impeccably kept as those of the *kibar*, but may not be as large. They have similar consumption aspirations, but are not as able to fund large-scale social events. They have smaller budgets from which to supply the daily needs of the family and long-term reproduction plans like funding marriages of sons. They share, however, the sentiments by which wealthier families are bound, and in these families the loyalties may be put to the test, as some members will be called upon to sacrifice for others.[60]

Honourable reputation and distinction are displayed not only in wealth and the past glory of ancestors but in the comportment of current members. This chapter outlined the economic bases which support families, allowing the appropriate distribution of wealth through culturally valued consumption practices. The structure of families (several generations and many unmarried women), houses (with separate spaces for men and women), and resource base (for consumption beyond the daily needs of social reproduction) allow the labour, space, and finances for large-scale entertaining in a gender-segregated context. The *bayt* is also a moral space, and family members are bound by sentiments and to collude in the image of themselves they present to others.

---

60 For instance, one young woman had to delay her plans to attend university, as her school teacher's salary was deemed by the head of the household necessary to finance her younger brother's wedding. Although bitterly disappointed that she could not start that year, she denied any discontent when in public.

The *bayt* is also the site of the reproduction of religious values and the cultural ideals of generosity and modesty, and reputations; how these qualities are inculcated in children and presented to other members of the community is the topic of the next chapters.

4

Achieving Virtue through Modesty

If you do not have modesty, you can do what you want.

Hadith of the Prophet Muhammad

This hadith of the Prophet alludes to the centrality of modesty [*istihya'*] for regulating the comportment of properly socialized beings in society. This chapter focuses on how, through a series of bodily practices, individuals constitute themselves as moral, pious persons. Modesty 'lies at the heart of ideas of the individual in society,' as Abu-Lughod notes for an analogous concept – *hasham* – among the Awlad 'Ali Bedouin (1986:105). Modesty is the basis for moral personhood and gendered identity, and is also an emblem of, and justification for, social hierarchy. If, as Butler suggests, gender identity is a performance, realized through time by a 'stylized repetition of acts' (1990:140), in Zabid, feminine identity is achieved through a range of modest behaviours. In a sense, *istihya'* can be understood as an umbrella-like concept to which other emotions are structured in reference.[1] *Istihya'* is also closely related to conceptions of piety, deference, status, sexuality, and family. It is used to describe a personal state of embarrassment [*mustahiya*] brought about either by inappropriate behaviour (usually inadvertent) or by the presence of someone higher in the social hierarchy. It also refers to a style of appropriate comportment, which

---

1 Its relation to other emotions is discussed in chapter 7. The nouns for modesty, *istihya'* or *haya'*, are not frequently used in Zabid. Ubiquitous, however, is the imperative *Istahi!*, the use of the verbal forms like *tistahi* (pl. *yistahu*) to refer to an individual's proper comportment, and the adjectival form *mustahiya*, referring to an internal state.

involves a range of behaviours, including gender segregation, female circumcision, veiling, the submission of physical appetites to the will, and self-expression.[2]

The style of comportment in Zabid is similar in many respects to that displayed by women in many other Middle Eastern societies. These superficial similarites have been ascribed by anthropologists to an ideology of 'honour and shame' (Peristiany 1974). Herzfeld (1980, 1987), on the basis of his work in the Mediterranean region, suggests that this gloss obscures more than it clarifies. Wikan (1984), in a similar vein, argues that honour and shame are not binary concepts, and that to ascribe honour to men, and shame to women may misrepresent people's understandings of themselves and others. Finally, Abu-Lughod (1986) argues that among Awlad 'Ali Bedouin, modesty *is* the honour of the less powerful. This formulation is persuasive as well with regard to the subjective perceptions of the modesty practices of Zabidi women.

Underlying the practice of modesty is a concern to control and channel sexuality appropriately, into the context of legal marriage. Several Middle Eastern ethnographies (for example, Delaney 1991, Dresch 1989, Abu-Lughod 1986, Meeker 1976) note how female sexual comportment affects male honour. Dresch, for instance, in his discussion of how female sexual impropriety can break the honour of male kin in highland Yemen, states: 'Sisters and daughters must therefore be "controlled" or "defended"' (1989:44). However, women in Zabid are so fiercely concerned with the honour of their families that modest comportment cannot be understood as merely being enforced by male members (although it is occasionally spoken of this way); rather it must be seen as a family affair.[3] From the perspective of Zabidi women, through self-restraint women earn self-esteem, and at the same time they protect the reputations of their families. Women create or uphold the status of their families by their proper comportment, which involves a studious and continuous denial of sexual desire

---

2 This dual aspect of modesty, referring both to an internal state and to appropriate comportment, is very similar to that described by Abu-Lughod for the Awlad 'Ali Bedouin (1986:107-8). C. Eickelman (1984) glosses a similar concept, *khajal*, as 'propriety.' Her account describes this concept as central to all social interactions in an Omani community.

3 Meeker (1976) discusses meanings of honour in terms of who is required to respond to the violation of a woman. In Arab societies, it is the male kin of the woman, while in Turkish societies, it is the husband. In Zabid, the proper comportment of wives is important for the reputation of the marital household. However, in the one case that I heard of in which marital infidelity was alleged, the man divorced his wife, dissociating himself from her rather than punishing her.

or interest in men, enacted through practices such as female circumcision and veiling.

Another way in which analysts have attempted to come to terms with the similarities in the position of women in Middle Eastern cultures, particularly with reference to practices of gender segregation and veiling, is through an examination of Islamic principles. Many researchers have questioned whether practices such as veiling, separation of male and female domains, and general attitudes toward sexuality can be interpreted as merely reflecting Islamic principles laid out in sacred texts. (For example, Joseph [1986] criticizes several books which propose that Islamic texts determine the position of women.) As Kandiyoti notes, both Western and Muslim scholars tend to discuss the implications of the central tenets of Islam for Muslim women in an ahistorical fashion (1991a:1).[4] Variations in the practices between Muslim societies (or even within them) clearly indicate that Islamic texts alone do not provide an adequate explanation of local practice. This is not to argue that sacred texts are irrelevant to social life, but rather that they have to be understood in the context of how they are drawn upon in everyday life.

As Asad argues in a more general sense, Islamic traditions are drawn upon in the shaping of 'moral selves' (1986:7). In Zabid, the ideology of 'honour and shame,' in which appropriate comportment, particularly the sexual comportment of female family members, affects the reputation of the family as a whole, is in some respects embedded in local understandings of Islam, in that modest comportment is thought to demonstrate piety.[5]

As locally understood, both modesty and piety are also closely linked to Zabid's competitive, hierarchical society. Modest comportment is related to the place of one's own family in relation to other families and to the subordination of the *akhdam* to the *nas*. The fusion of propriety and

---

4 Kandiyoti criticizes approaches which 'treat Islam as a unitary ideology from which practices related to women can be automatically assessed in any given Islamic society' (1987:317).

5 The most thorough attempt to account for both ideologies of honour and shame and religion is provided by Delaney (1987, 1991). She argues that ideas of honour and shame are embedded in monotheistic religions. She suggests that in Islam, men are understood to be the primary instigators of life; women are not seen as providing essential identities or attributes to the child – they merely nurture it. The male concern with honour is rooted in this understanding of conception, as the legitimacy of his seed is at issue. In Zabid, however, women are thought to contribute moral attributes and capacities to the child, as well as identity-giving attributes like skin colour and beauty. More important, the mother's social status plays a great part in determining the status of the child.

piety lends persuasive force to the hierarchical relationships in the community.

Female Circumcision

The close connection between modesty and control of sexuality is evident in the practice of female circumcision. Female circumcision in Zabid does not have the cultural centrality that it does in the Sudan, where the operation is not only much more radical, but is connected to beliefs about fertility, procreation, and cosmology, including spirit possession (Boddy 1989).[6] In Zabid, the operation is specifically concerned with controlling sexual desire, and is not ritually elaborated. There is no public celebration for the circumcision of female or male children; both are circumcised when they are between one and three weeks old.[7]

When I pressed people about why this practice was done, I received a variety of uneasy answers relating to local ideas of femaleness and femininity. Some women said that female circumcision is performed merely because it is recommended for Shafi'i Muslims.[8] One older woman said that a woman was made *tahir* [pure] by the operation, and that if she did not have it she would be considered deficient [*naqis*]. Underlying this practice is, nonetheless, a certain understanding of the nature of female sexual desire. While watching a video of Adeni dancing with my husband,[9] a Zabidi man described the women dancing as hot [*hami*]. He said that the women in Zabid were cool [*barid*], because their clitorises had been circumcised.[10] Another man relayed to my husband a story told to him by a highland *shaykh* about why women in the highlands do most of the agricultural labour. One day a man came home exhausted from his work in the

6 When I described pharaonic circumcision to them, Zabidi women pronounced, in disgust, this radical operation as *haram* [forbidden].

7 Boys may be circumcised in the local clinic or by the *muzayyin*, but girls are always circumcised by the *muzayyina*.

8 The jurist al-Shafi'i states that circumcision is obligatory for women as well as men in his *fiqh* [Islamic jurisprudence] (Eickelman 1987b:402). See Serjeant for a discussion of circumcision in Aden and Tarim (1962:205–6). Most Zabidis are Shafi'i. All Muslims believe that circumcision is obligatory for males. The Zaydi sect, to which most northern highlanders belong, does not practise female circumcision.

9 Aden is considered a racy town by Zabidis. Adeni dancing is thought to be particularly provocative because it shows men and women dancing together. Many Zabidis think that it is forbidden even to watch it.

10 Ideas of hot and cold are important to local understandings of emotion and illness (discussed in chapter 7).

fields and found himself unable to perform sexually. So he sent his wife out into the fields to work, because women's passions [nafs] were so much greater than men's; thus his sexual prowess remained unhampered while her desire was tempered by labour. The man said that since Zabidi women did not perform physical labour, it was necessary to circumcise them to cool their passions.[11] One woman made a joking reference, in the context of a discussion about why highland Yemenis do not circumcise their girls, about how circumcision was for the harara [ardour, passion], and that they had enough harara [heat] in the Tihama. The implication in Zabid is that the heat of female passion has to be cooled.

Contact with women from Yemen's capital, San'a', led some Zabidi women to question the practice of female circumcision. One woman lived in the Old City in San'a' where her husband was a teacher. She told us that the San'ani women had been greatly amused by the idea of female circumcision because it seemed ludicrous to them and teased her to show them.[12] She subsequently gave birth to a daughter, and did not want to circumcise her, but her husband insisted. Another Zabidi woman, returning after a long absence with her new baby girl, announced to a gathering of neighbours that she was not going to have her daughter circumcised. She also cited mockery of San'ani women, and mentioned a magazine article that claimed that circumcision was responsible for vaginal infections. She held firm despite one woman's claim that the baby's clitoris would grow large or long, like a man's penis. Since San'ani women are perceived as more concerned with modesty (for instance, they are more heavily veiled), the fact that modesty is possible without circumcision led these Zabidi women to question whether it is really necessary.[13]

I was told that only a small bit of the clitoris [bizr] was removed.[14] However, the removal of even that from an infant can be presumed to have

---

11 The idea that women have more passion [nafs] than men is a common theme in many Muslim societies. Boddy (1989) discusses the opposition between 'aql and nafs in the Sudanese context, as does Rosen (1984) for Morocco.

12 This request was mocking, as it is highly improper to show one's genitals to anyone except one's husband, and even her three-year-old refused to have her genitals inspected. The woman was pregnant at the time, and insisted on giving birth in the hospital, because she was afraid that a San'ani midwife would make fun of her.

13 The assumed depravity of the Western world meant that the disapproval of a non-Muslim Westerner such as myself of this practice was irrelevant, as Westerners were assumed to be entirely without modesty anyway. It was the disapproval and mockery of San'ani women, who were within the same moral universe as the Zabidis which led them to question their practices.

14 Alternatively salt is rubbed into the clitoris. I did not see either operation performed.

considerable significance, although the exact impact of this operation on female desire and pleasure is hard to determine.[15] My attempts to elicit how the operation affected female sexual pleasure were not all that successful; women either did not seem to know what I was getting at, or else they were too embarrassed to continue the conversation. However, the significant point is the *intent* which underlies this practice. Although it is not a source of continual preoccupation as are other modesty practices, its relation to the enclosure and curtailment of women's sexuality is implicit in informants' statements and practices. In Zabid, circumcision is performed on a baby girl as a result of the decision of her parents and therefore is an example of 'the corporate control of sexuality' (Kandiyoti 1987). Whereas the other practices which focus on the denial of sexual desire depend on the young girl's development of self-control through training and example, an accomplishment of which she can be proud, this operation is carried out on her infant body.

Discussions of female circumcision are relatively rare.[16] Inquiries eventually met the fate of most conversations deemed inappropriate: the other participants lapsed into silence or refused to pursue the topic. So much of women's training to be modest is explicitly focused toward a denial of sexual interest that the topic of the impact of circumcision on female desire is seen as an infringement of modesty.[17] From a female perspective, procreation rather than female desire or pleasure is the appropriate reason for sexual activity.[18] And sexual activity is appropriate only in the context of legal marriage.

Inculcating Modesty

Female circumcision is thought to accomplish only a predisposition toward a capacity to control passion – a capacity which must be developed through training. Modesty training is central to the development of a sense of gen-

---

15 The issue of what constitutes sexual desire or pleasure is complicated; neither one can be reduced to physiological sensation or processes of signification, as Knauft (1994:420–1) indicates.

16 One woman told me privately that some Zabidis had stopped circumcising their daughters; however, they did not advertise this fact, perhaps being afraid that the uncharitable in the community might cast aspersions on their respectability.

17 'Amrani women seem to be more willing to discuss female sexual desire (Dorsky 1986:134–9).

18 Male sexual desire and pleasure is more explicitly legitimized. While we were discussing the arrangement of marriages, a woman told me a Zabidi proverb: 'His penis is erect, marry him quickly.'

dered self, based on the control of physical and emotional bearing. As in many other Middle Eastern societies, the concept of *istihya'* is related to the notion of reason [*'aql*], or the ability to behave appropriately in public contexts (*cf.* Eickelman 1976:130–41, and Abu-Lughod 1986:90–1). *'Aql* is also the capacity to submit one's body to one's will. Training in the modest comportment of one's body begins in earnest after a child begins to develop *'aql*, usually around the age of five or six. Older children and all female adults in the household begin to instruct the female child in the rudiments of modesty, especially the covering of her hair and avoidance of men. Little girls are encouraged to wear head scarves from a young age. If a girl begs to wear her mother's face veil, she is affectionately indulged.[19] One young woman chastised her eight-year-old niece for running around with her hair wildly messy, with her scarf half off her head, by saying, 'Do you want people to say you are a *majnuna* [crazy woman]? Why is your hair like that?' Little boys who show a preference for the company of women are teased into leaving the gathering. One woman was annoyed by the desire of her four-year-old brother to help her with the cooking. She finally yelled for him to go sit with the men. Similarly, little girls, after the age of five, while they do not yet veil, are discouraged from playing with boys or attending men's gatherings, although they may be sent to deliver messages.[20]

Being modest and capable of acting with self-restraint is a quality which everyone values. Abu-Lughod's (1986) argument that voluntary modest comportment is how women are able to gain honour in a situation of inferiority could equally apply for Zabidi women, because modest comportment is perceived as a personal virtue. It is a matter of some pride for women to have daughters who have a proper sense of how to behave. The fact that comportment affects a family's reputation is evident not only in

19 Mauss writes of the process of education in imposition of body techniques: 'What takes place is a prestigious imitation. The child, the adult, imitates actions which have succeeded and which he has seen successfully performed by people in whom he has confidence and who have authority over him. The action is imposed from without, from above, even if it is an exclusively biological action, involving his body. The individual borrows the series of movements which constitute it from the action executed in front of him or with him by others' (1979:101–2).

20 During the course of our stay, a few little girls who had visited our home frequently, gradually began to *tistahi* [verb, to act modestly] in front of my husband. Similarly, a young boy of about eleven decided that he was a young man [*shabab*] and would no longer speak to me. Avoidance of the opposite sex is related to adult male status as much as adult female status. If a woman does not *tistahi* in front of an unrelated man, it questions his status. The only adult men in front of whom women do not veil are the *akhdam*.

the members' pride in modest children, but also in their close monitoring of each other's behaviour.[21]

As noted in the previous chapter, the implicit assumption of gender segregation guides the architecture in Zabid. Although gender segregation is inculcated as a disposition which is unquestioned, the maintenance of the moral boundary between non-related men and women requires continual work. The cooperation and trust of all members of the community, male and female, are required.[22] Men should avert their eyes from women, respect the boundaries of women's gatherings in their homes, and assiduously avoid all but essential conversations with non-related women. Women who practise proper modest comportment can expect, as their right, to be undisturbed by men. At one wedding, a few men had to enter the tent to fix some light fixtures; as they had not adequately announced their arrival, the guests threw their chadors over their heads, many crying, indignantly, 'Haram 'alaykum' [curses upon you!]. The houses in Zabid are surrounded by high walls so neighbours cannot see into each other's courtyards. If any maintenance work has to be done on the roofs of houses, the workman lets out a long, loud yell, which warns women in the neighboring yards to take cover.[23]

Veiling

Veiling is a complex practice which in Zabid serves to conceal the bodies of women from all non-related men except close affines.[24] The principle guiding veiling practices in Zabid is for women to veil from those men who are

21 Kandiyoti (1987) has written insightfully about the 'corporate control of sexuality' in Turkey. She notes: 'Parents, siblings, near and distant relatives, and even neighbors closely monitor the movements of the postpubescent girl, firmly imprinting the notion that her sexuality is not hers to give or withhold' (1987:325).

22 C. Eickelman also notes the existence of trust within the Omani community in which she worked to describe the expectation that standards of comportment will be met by all those in the community (1984:131-2).

23 During the first week of our stay, my husband inadvertently caused an outcry of righteous indignation by not calling out before climbing on the roof. He conveyed his apologies to our aged landlady, who passed them along to our neighbours. This transgression was excused at this point because 'he did not know.' Any later in our stay, it would have been a good deal less forgivable.

24 Veiling is a widespread practice; close attention to how women veil, from whom they veil, and perceptions of what veiling is supposed to accomplish is necessary to understand this practice in its local context. Cf. Abu-Lughod (1986), Papanek and Minault (1982), Wikan (1982), Makhlouf (1979), Anderson (1982), and Olson (1985).

not members of their *bayt*.[25] Women do not veil in their natal households, from their older male kinsmen; rather they veil themselves from all men outside their *bayt*, except for their father's brothers and their mother's brothers.[26] Married women do not veil in front of their male affines with whom they live. The integrity of the *bayt* is maintained in this fashion. Through these veiling and avoidance practices, membership in a *bayt* is marked. Male membership in (or close relationship to) the *bayt* is indicated by his access to the interior space of the house (providing no female guests are present), and female membership is marked by going unveiled within the house at any time of the day.

Any time a woman leaves her house, she dons a black chador, a garment composed of an ankle-length skirt, topped with a headpiece that extends to below her waist. Her face is covered by a sheer piece of black muslin [*khunna*].[27] A girl appears on the street wearing only a head scarf and a dress until her breasts develop, at which point she dons an ankle-length coat [*balto*] and a black scarf that covers her head but leaves her face exposed.[28] These garments are worn outside of one's own home, on the street, to the school, or to the hospital. (Women do not go to the suq or the mosque.)[29] Chadors now comprise a woman's 'means of entrance' into respectable society, as Steedman notes of decent clothes for nineteenth-century women (1986:89). Women, especially the younger ones, were reluctant to admit that this particular form of dress was not always worn by Zabidi women, so firmly established is its hegemony in terms of con-

25 This is in contrast to veiling among the Awlad 'Ali bedouin described by Abu-Lughod: 'The operating principle here is that women veil for those who have authority over them or greater responsibility for the system' (1986:163).

26 Sometimes they do not veil for their *awlad 'amm* [father's brother's sons] or *awlad khal* [mother's brother's sons] although as one woman told me, 'According to the Qur'an we should, but often we don't.' However, if a woman is to be married to one of her cousins, she will veil from him. This is yet another reason why women may dislike *ibn 'amm* marriages; her cousin may be as familiar as her brother.

27 In her discussion of San'ani dress, Mundy (1983), states that this style of street wear, of Turkish origin (known in San'a' as the *sharshaf*) became widespread after the revolution in 1962. The fashion spread to Zabid in the 1980s and is now established as the appropriate street garment for adult women, aside from the *akhdam*. Unlike the San'ani women, however, not all Zabidi women wear a *lithma* (a scarf wrapped in such a way as to leave only the eyes exposed), although this style is becoming fashionable, particularly among young Zabidi schoolteachers.

28 An adult woman may also wear a *balto* if she covers her face with a *khunna*. Sometimes a Saudi-style *cabayah* is also worn. All acceptable street garments are black and enveloping, disguising not only the woman's figure but also her clothing worn underneath.

29 Elsewhere in Yemen, mosques do have separate women's sections.

temporary fashion and propriety. However, one older woman of a wealthy family showed me an older style of veil, which was an oblong piece of woven cotton, dyed a deep blue-black.[30] In the mornings women wear long skirts and blouses with a small head scarf as they do their chores. When visiting in the afternoons, women always remove their chadors and often leave their heads uncovered.[31]

Women do not veil in their marital households. The new bride marrying into the family must learn not to *tistahi* from her husband, his brothers, and his father. After years of strict training in the avoidance of men, she is confronted with a set of men she should neither veil from nor avoid. In this fashion, a new bride is initiated into her family of marriage and her new affiliation is emphasized. I saw one bride run from the room when her husband's brother entered; his sisters chastised her. Another new bride was having a hard time even facing her husband: his sisters and a few neighbours gave her a coaxing lecture on how she must not avoid him. They incensed and perfumed her and assured her that she would learn to relax [*turtah*] in his presence. The women of the husband's family were socializing her in her new duty to be sexually receptive to her husband and produce children for his family.

Although a bride never loses her identity based on her natal family, she does participate to a certain extent in the shared identity of her husband's family: her new affiliation with them is enacted by her lack of veiling within her marital household. To the extent that there is any variation in the general pattern of avoidance of all non-related men, a wife is particularly concerned (and obliged) to avoid men of the same status of her husband, particularly his closest associates.[32]

---

30 Younger women associate this cloth with death because they are now used to cover old women's bodies on the way to the graveyard. An alternative style of street wear in the recent past consisted of large coloured scarves wrapped around the hair and upper bodies when they left the house, a style no longer acceptable.

31 During the day, older women wear a simple skirt [*futa*], with an elastic waist, and a very brief shirt with short sleeves and two buttons, leaving much of the chest area and the midriff exposed. When going out in the evening, they wear a chador as well. Postmenopausal women tend to be less concerned with veiling; if a non-related man enters her house unexpectedly during the day, she may not run for cover as would the younger members of her household.

32 One bride continued to attend a high school where her husband taught. She wore a *lithma*, which covers her face so only her eyes are visible, because he did not want his male colleagues to see his wife's face.

The fact that women do not veil in front of their male kinsmen or affines does not mean that they do not show deference to them: defiance of fathers, older brothers, or husbands is not usually approved by women. I saw several mothers-in-law make a great show of having new brides ask permission of their husbands every time they wanted to go out, although usually women regulate their visits themselves.[33] In this fashion, women create manhood and men's status, using the authority of their male kinsmen to subordinate the new bride to the interests of her family of marriage. These reminders continually stress the wife's new identity as her husband's representative in public gatherings.

Public Evaluations and Modest Comportment

In the public forum of women's visiting, women present not only the wealth of their families in their expensive adornment but also their good breeding [adab].[34] In public interactions, unmarried girls of elite and respectable families refrain from certain treatments of the body which are understood to be related to sexuality. For instance, unmarried young women will not accept perfume or one kind of incense[35] which is thought to be enticing to men. Hostesses always offer both perfume and incense to all guests; girls often push the incense burner away from them in a standardized gesture of indignation, saying, 'I do not use incense!' [ma abakhkhar!]. In this way, a girl stresses publicly her lack of interest in attracting men. Unmarried girls do not use makeup (aside from kuhl, a black eyeliner). They also do not (if they are from respectable families) chew qat, which is thought to be sexually stimulating. Smoking is not associated with sexuality per se, but it is thought to be inappropriate for unmarried girls to display any physical appetites.[36] All women who are likely to have any contact with men (such as teachers or students) should refrain from getting

---

33 In one instance, the mother-in-law actually retracted her son's permission for his wife to attend a party that the mother-in-law considered inappropriate.

34 The religious connotations of adab are discussed in chapter 8.

35 This is a kind of special incense which is concocted from a number of expensive aromatic ingredients; several families have their own particular variations to the basic recipe. A bride brings a stock of it to her husband's home when she marries.

36 As noted in the last chapter, many women in Zabid remain unmarried. After the age of twenty-five or so, when it becomes clear they will never be married, they may start to smoke or chew qat freely in public without any threat to their reputation. However, I have seen akhdam girls, no more than twelve or thirteen, smoking and chewing qat.

henna or *khidhab* on their hands and feet, lest they be thought to be trying to attract men.

Zabidi women are not particularly prudish about sexuality for the purposes of procreation, in contrast to the extreme reserve they display with reference to the subject of female desire. Many jokes are made, especially to new brides, about incensing and perfuming her so she will become pregnant [*tajib nunu*].[37] The husband's role is merely alluded to – through jokes about the perfume and incense which are thought to attract him – rather than discussed in any concrete fashion. Many married women, exhausted by constant pregnancies, queried me about birth control in hope of finding an alternative to the pill (which is said to cause madness) or condoms (which many men did not like to use). When these conversations took place in front of young unmarried women, they frequently raised protests, saying that they did not want to hear that sort of talk. They may urge a married woman to '*Tistahi qalil!*' [Have a little decency!][38]

When looking for wives for their sons or brothers, women evaluate a girl's propriety and her comportment in the presence of older women as well as men. Women are concerned not only with a potential daughter-in-law's chastity, but also with her appropriate deference to older women. They do not want a girl who will be cheeky or defiant. Acts of deference between women of different status, like deference to one's elder male kin, represent that dimension of modesty which extends beyond sexual comportment per se and guides appropriately respectful demeanour in the company of those more powerful than oneself.

Modest behaviour is required for interactions between older and younger women. In the context of visiting or receiving guests, unmarried women should indicate their respect for older women by not laughing or initiating conversation. Modesty is associated not only with control of sexual desire, but also with control of emotions and of one's body. Modest girls are 'composed' [*razina*] as opposed to 'silly' [*sakhifa*] or 'chattering' [*lawka*]. There is also the opposition between 'bitter' [*murra*] and 'sweet' [*hali*]; girls who are behaving in an obnoxious fashion may be instructed to

---

37 While it is not considered shameful to beautify oneself for one's husband (indeed, a certain amount of attention to one's appearance is expected and encouraged), one young bride was criticized for being a flirt [*ghazala*] because she seemed to be overly concerned with monopolizing her husband's attention, at least according to the older women in his family and the neighbours.

38 In private conversations with me, unmarried women indicated a clear idea of the rudiments of sex and childbirth. However, in public, proper young women may profess their ignorance and lack of interest.

'compose yourself and sweeten!' [*irzini tahali!*]. Graceful carriage, erect posture, and stillness of limbs are valued.[39] The contrast between teenaged girls in the presence of older women and among their peers is striking: in the company of older women they are quiet and still, whereas in the company of their peers they are often high-spirited and giggly. At large formal parties the girls sit in one section and the older women in another. Modest behaviour is apparent between women of the same age but of different status: often a poor woman will become very quiet and embarrassed [*mustahiya*] in the presence of a woman from a *bayt kabir*. Several women of respectable, if not wealthy, families told me that they did not feel comfortable [*mush murtaha*] in the presence of the *kibar* women and preferred not to attend the same parties as them.[40]

The imperative *Istahi qalil!* [have a little decency!] is heard in a myriad of contexts. It commands (and implores) others to comport themselves appropriately. *Ihtaram nuffsik* [Respect yourself!] is also used to encourage appropriate comportment. It implies that respecting oneself is closely tied to offering the appropriate respect to others. A woman's 'goodness' and her self-respect are contingent on her modest behaviour, which in turn reflects upon the goodness, worth, and honour of her family.[41] In Zabid, the concept of *istihya'* and conformity to the range of behaviours associated with it are not only connected to goodness but are also related to the perceived sense of superiority relative to those who do not 'act properly.' The most common way of expressing the moral superiority of Zabidi society over Western society was to say that people (particularly women) did not *yistahu*.[42] Other categories of inferior beings who do not *yistahu* are children, who have yet to be trained in proper comportment, the insane, and the *akhdam*.

The *Akhdam*

The inferior position of the *akhdam* in Zabidi society is understood to be

39 One woman told me that babies are swaddled for the first month or two of their lives so they will not develop gangly or floppy limbs.

40 Any breach of etiquette is said to result in embarrassment.

41 Abu-Lughod notes, 'This is the great strength of the ideology of honour and modesty as a means for perpetuating a system of power relations: by framing ideals as values, in moral terms, it guarantees that individuals will desire to do what perpetuates the system, thus obviating the need for overt violence or force' (1986:238).

42 In the first few months of my stay, I heard comments of this sort daily; tourists in Zabid were said to scare children, who think they are insane because of their scanty dress.

inextricably linked to their lack of modesty. Behaving appropriately involves an acknowledgment of where one stands in relation to others in the social hierarchy. The fact that *akhdam* women do not display deferential modesty in front of the more powerful contributes to their subordination in Zabidi society. *Akhdam* women do not wear the chador; they go to the suq; and in general, they do not avoid men as assiduously as do other Zabidi women. At one *kabir* home, a young *khadima* took a container of water into the men's reception room. The two youngest girls in the family, aged four and five years old, audibly laughed at her for going 'among the men.' Even at this young age, the children of the *kabir* are aware that respectable women never enter a men's gathering.

I witnessed a further example of this crucial difference between *akhdam* and non-*akhdam* women. I was invited for lunch at the home of a friend who had just returned from a trip to Aden. The taxi driver who had driven them from Aden to Zabid was to return that day to Aden with another family from al-Hudayda. The rendezvous point was my friend's Zabidi home. Her family invited the taxi driver and the family from al-Hudayda to lunch, although they were not previously acquainted with them. The two teenaged guests were quite high-spirited; they laughed and chattered after lunch as they changed into fresh dresses and applied makeup. When Fahad, the head of the household, appeared at the door to wish them a safe journey, the young girls did not run to hide their faces, but chatted freely with him, saying that he had a beautiful house, and they would just love to stay there forever. Fahad stiffly said, '*Ahlan wa sahlan*,' a formulaic phrase of welcome, and quickly departed. The women gathered their things, and exuberantly kissed Fahad's wife, grandmother, and aunt on their cheeks.[43] The teenaged girls of Fahad's household refused to be kissed, stiffly extending their hands and withdrawing them quickly. After the guests had left, Fahad's teenaged daughter made the gesture which indicates a crazy person (shaking one hand at the side of her head).

I was startled by this interaction. I had been in Zabid for over a year and had become accustomed to the idea that casual, almost flirtatious contact between a man, especially the head of a household, and a woman, especially a teenager without her chador or even a covering for her hair, was unthinkable. I asked the hostesses after the guests had left why the guests had acted that way. They replied, 'They are *akhdam*,' which I had not realized. They were less shocked than I at the comportment of their guests for this reason; in retrospect, I realized that Fahad would not have entered the room at all

43 Greeting practices and hierarchy are discussed in the next chapter.

if they had not been *akhdam*. Elaborating further, they said, 'They are different from us. They do not behave modestly. They don't know what is shameful or respectful.' The fact that *istihya'* is understood as a personal quality, which respectable and responsible individuals display as a result of reason and self-control, makes the inferior position of the *akhdam* seem deserved, owing to their 'improper' moral conduct.

One *khadima*, trying to improve her position, started to wear a chador. When she came to pay a visit on the occasion of a death, a *kabir* woman teased her about it. She joked shyly that she was going to adopt the face veil as well. This small incident exemplifies two key points. One, the *akhdam* are not as morally distant from other Zabidis as the Zabidi *nas* may claim. The young *khadima* clearly shared the same understanding about the connection between status, comportment, and morality as do those higher up in the social hierarchy. Two, the *kabir* woman implied that the *khadima* was adopting a style of comportment inconsistent with her place in society. While the position of the *akhdam* is justified by their lack of appropriate comportment, they also lack 'appropriate biographies' (Harre 1984:274), particularly noble descent, a situation which is considered irremediable by the *nas*.[44]

As a comparative case, Riesman's (1983, 1992) discussion of the Muslim Fulani and their ex-slaves, the Rimaaybe, wherein hierarchy is justified and enacted through differing styles of comportment, is insightful. He suggests that Fulbe emphasis on restraint is related to belonging to lineages – hence, possessing both a history and family, both living and dead – which endows them with a sense that they must behave with self-restraint not only for the sake of their own identities, but for the sake of the wider collectivity (by which a personal identity is constituted). The Rimaaybe, in contrast, behave with less self-restraint because, as ex-slaves, they have no lineages and their current descent groups are shallow. A Rimaaybe who behaves like a Fulbe is considered uppity and a Fulbe who behaves like a Rimaaybe is considered to debase not only himself or herself, but also his or her family and lineage.

The *akhdam*, even more stigmatized than the Zabidi ex-slaves, are considered without honour, without prestige, so any attempt made by one of them to behave honourably is seen merely as amusing or pointless by the

44 In his discussion of identity projects, Harre notes that identity is not only a function of attaining attributes but also one of establishing 'that one has the attributes as a right' (1984:274). A chador is an attribute of status, but without an appropriate biography it is meaningless.

nas. *Akhdam* do not have *bayt*s in the same sense as upper class Zabidis – *bayt*s which extend back into time to an ancestor of noble descent, and which are economically autonomous. Other Zabidis, men and women, have a sense of their families as the significant unit of value from which their own value as individuals derives. They understand that a family's place in society depends not only on the collective wealth of the family but also on the proper comportment of its members in public. The *akhdam*, lacking these larger collectivities to which proper comportment is owed, have less incentive to behave according to the standards of the wider community, which, in any case, is unreceptive to their attempts.

The centrality of female practices for male identities is apparent in the comportment of *nas* women in front of *akhdam* men, from whom they do not veil. A *khadim* in a women's gathering will be ignored, while the rare appearance of a non-related high-status man will cause a flurry as women scramble to cover their bodies. The structural position of the *khadim* is inherent in the act of not veiling; he is constituted as inconsequential – someone who has no power to tarnish anyone's reputation – someone unworthy of voluntary deference.

Modesty and Piety

As is evident in the above discussion, practices of modesty cannot be explained solely in terms of Islamic prescriptions. However, in Zabid, these practices of modesty are continually negotiated with reference to local understandings of piety. As heirs to a tradition of Islamic learning which stretches back centuries, it is not surprising that Zabidis discuss proper comportment in terms of piety. As Abu-Zahra notes, the word *haya'*, from which *istihya'* is derived, 'refers primarily to the instinct that deters a person from committing what is forbidden by Islam. It is therefore considered part of the faith and is emphasized in the traditions of the prophet' (1970:1080). Piety, along with wealth and generosity, is the value by which honour is constituted; it is perhaps the most central value for social identity in Zabid. As modesty is thought to indicate piety, modest women ensure the reputation of their family as devout Muslims. The hegemony of the *nas* over the *akhdam* is further reinforced through the fusion of piety and propriety: the lack of modesty of the *akhdam* throws into question whether they are truly Muslims.

Zabidi women, who are no less concerned with piety than are men, discuss *istihya'* in Islamic terms. The primary reason Zabidi women give for their practice of modest comportment is 'our religion' [*din haqqana*]. Zabidis would essentially agree with Delaney's description of comportment in a Turkish village: 'The way one comports one's body is a sign to others that one recognizes and submits to God's order; it is the way one demonstrates one is a Muslim' (1991:25). The relatively recent adoption of the chador is given force by the fact that it has come to represent piety as well as respectability.

Conclusion

It is clear that the nature of the practices which are thought to constitute appropriately pious comportment – styles of veiling, circumcision, and gender segregation – change over time. Nonetheless, Zabidi women understand modesty as proper pious comportment. In Zabid, the persuasive force of modest practices is that they both ensure family honour and also constitute a woman as a pious subject of God. Circumcision is thought to provide a predisposition for the ability to control passion. This predisposition, an example of the corporate control that families' exert over the sexuality of female members, is reinforced through training. The eventual achievement and continual performance of modest feminine identity is a matter of pride, through which a woman constitutes herself as a moral person. The modest comportment of individual members ensures that their families will be considered families of worth in the eyes of the community. The connection between *istihya'* and piety, given the association of piety and prestige, serves to reinforce and justify the relationships of hierarchy within the community, between *bayts*, and between the *nas* and the *akhdam*. From the perspective of the Zabidi *nas*, the *akhdam* are an ever-present 'other' against whom their conceptions of moral personhood are defined.

To indicate through one's comportment that one knows one's place in Zabid, as in many other societies, is to prove not only one's virtue, but also one's intelligence and even sanity. The basis for hierarchical relationships is thought to reside in qualities of personhood and to be exhibited through comportment. Women actively (and consciously) strive to become virtuous persons as locally defined; these female bodily practices are essential to the good reputations of their families. The containment of elite women's sexuality is a basis for social superiority over others. The achievement of the ideals of feminine virtue is something of which women are proud; it also involves them in the curtailment of their own sexuality and that of their female family members, including such radical practices as female circumcision. The complicated ways in which moral virtue is intertwined with class distinctions, 'enlists women in their own subordination,' as Boddy's discussion of the politics of aesthetics suggests (1993:1). These actions and practices of women are central to the social reproduction of the hierarchical relationships in Zabidi life. The capacity of women, even elite women, to shape their own destinies, however, is still constrained by the society which they help to reproduce.

5

Distinction and Display in the Visiting Scene

On these more formal occasions when we want to put our best foot forward, an understanding of traditional etiquette is practical as well as reassuring.

The Amy Vanderbilt Complete Book of Etiquette

And the people of the palace flocked in crowds; nay the common run of the people came together for this event in an immense assemblage. And they invited about eighty ladies, all modest, virtuous women, and they also invited the wives of the Emirs, of the military commanders, of the judges, or the farmers-general of revenue, and of the notables of the city, and there was not a single woman of the whole who stayed away.

Al-Khazraji, *History of the Rasulid Dynasty*

Zabid does not have a written etiquette manual like Amy Vanderbilt's, but the etiquette for conduct in public social events is formalized. Among Zabidi women, there is general agreement about what sort of conduct is 'right.' Shortly after the unification of North and South Yemen, one Zabidi family spent a few weeks in Aden to seek medical care. Upon their return, all of their neighbours gathered in their home to welcome them back. The travellers regaled us with tales of Adeni life, telling us that the Adeni streets were straight and regular, but the people's social life seemed to have no order [*ma nazzam*]. What shocked them most was that from a Zabidi perspective, Adeni women had absolutely no concept of how to behave appropriately in public. They would chew qat anywhere, even on the street, with anyone, including men. They did not wash and change their clothes before they went out in the afternoon. They did not necessarily know or associate with their neighbours and certainly did not seem to make the rounds of social calls to which Zabidi women are accustomed. My neighbours had never been out of Zabid before, and for the first time their assumptions about their own patterns of sociability, and about how one ought to behave when out in public, were thrown into relief.

This chapter explores this Zabidi style of sociability and its strict and explicit rules, which govern appropriate comportment in public interactions between women. The etiquette of hospitality, the exchanges which take place within visits, and the grooming and adornment practices appropriate for public interactions are described.

Hostesses and Guests

A guest's physical presence in the hostess's home serves to create the worth and identity of the hostess and her family. A hostess is honoured by the presence of her guests but must make her guests feel welcome, desired, and comfortable, to ensure that they will continue to visit her. The hostess's insistent hospitality, implicitly at least, recognizes her dependence on her guests. The hostess clearly honours her guest by graciously extending her hospitality, and, to a great extent, a guest can expect this as her right. This etiquette of interaction mediates tensions between equality and hierarchy, and identity and distinction, facilitating the process of the reproduction (or alteration) of relationships.

A primary principle of visiting is that guests in one's own home must always be given precedence over obligations to others in the community; if guests arrive, it would be churlish to admit to previous plans to go out. Zabidi women are very skilled in making one feel as if they, the hostesses, had been doing nothing but hoping for one's visit. *Kibar* families, whose connections are wide-ranging, can expect guests at any time. Ideally, homes are kept in a state of readiness to receive guests: clean and stocked with the essentials of hospitality. It is very unusual to find a house with the door locked; in most cases, at least one teenaged girl or adult woman is present to receive guests and supervise the youngest children.[1]

Just as the reception room should be neat and clean, so should the guests. Washing and donning fresh clothing is a prerequisite for attending

---

1 In 'Amran, according to Dorsky, women leave their babies locked in rooms and go out to visit (1986:81). I never heard of such a practice in Zabid. In poor families with only one adult woman, men return home around 7:00 p.m. to watch the children while their wives go out.

any afternoon gathering. It is considered crass to go out without washing or changing from work clothes into the fancier clothes appropriate for visiting.[2] Further, personal cleanliness is not only an important element of comportment of properly socialized adults; it is an aspect of moral behaviour toward others. Zabidi women rub alum [*shabb*] a deodorizing substance, under their arms before they go out because, they say, 'How can one relax if one is disturbed by a bad smell?' Zabidis are very sensitive to odours and certainly do not want a reputation for smelling bad. Cleanliness is connected to religious morality, as the hadith of the Prophet Muhammad frequently mention that the considerate person is the clean person (Kanafani 1983:93).[3] Filthy guests not only leave themselves open to criticism, but insult the hostess as well. Both men and women are very fastidious about their clothing when they appear in public. Garments are always freshly ironed and spotless, at least among the higher-status families.[4]

One of the most apparent aspects of the etiquette of hospitality is the aggressive welcoming that the hostess gives her guests. A hostess urges her guests to come in, and when they make a move to leave, she entreats them to stay longer. The hostess also tries to extract her guest's recent social engagements to discern if her family has been neglected for another. When the guest is finally able to extricate herself, the hostess orders her to return again soon.[5] As Bourdieu (1977:180) notes, giving or 'squandering' time is a gift, one which is certainly necessary to social life in Zabid. This importance of giving time to the hostess is evident in her

---

2 Occasionally a woman returning from a late errand would drop in to see her neighbours but she would adamantly refuse to take off her chador, on the grounds that she would be embarrassed [*mustahiya*] because she had not washed or changed. Clean, but not fancy clothes, are worn on informal visits in the morning.

3 Zabid is similar in this respect to the United Arab Emirates as described by Kanafani: 'Smelly or ugly guests in dirty surroundings would inspire repulsion and aloofness and prevent the enjoyment of conversation and hospitality' (1983:2).

4 Women are proud to have pristinely turned-out family members, although keeping them that way in Zabid's heat and dust requires considerable labour.

5 The visitor is bade to come in [*Idkhuli!*], and then asked 'Why haven't we seen you for so long?' This question is ubiquitous; it may be asked even of people one has seen a few days earlier. A guest is instructed to sit 'up' [*Itla'i!*] on the high Tihama couches, is urged to settle herself comfortably, and is offered additional pillows. When the guest makes a move to leave, the hostess will demand, 'Where to?' [*Fayn?*]. She will argue that the guest has only just arrived, even if she has been present for two hours. The hostess will insist that the guest stay for just a while longer [*Ijlisi qalil!*] or urge her to put off a visit to another home. As the hostess sees the guest to the door, she will exhort her to come again soon ['*Ajili, 'ajili!*].

reproofs to a guest for having been absent, in her reluctance to let the guest leave, and in her insistence on a return visit. Being willing to spend the time to visit someone's house, to relax and enjoy oneself by accepting hospitality, is necessary for the maintenance of the relationship. A hostess will feel slighted if the guest sits only for a token period, hurriedly drinks a cup of tea, and departs in a rush.

The hostess is responsible for the comfort of her guests; she provides tea, incensed water, the waterpipe [mada'a] for those who smoke tobacco, and often a 'Canada,' a Canada Dry cola. The hostess urges her guests to relax [fasha'i!].[6] Women who chew qat bring small bundles of it with them, but the hostess, if she is of a bayt kabir, will usually present her guests with an additional ample portion of qat. Toasted watermelon seeds and chewing gum are provided for those who do not chew qat. Cooked food is never served at this time, as it is said to be impossible to relax with food odours around.[7] Qat chewing and eating are, of course, mutually exclusive. Scents are an integral part of hospitality: they are thought to enhance relaxation. Guests are offered two types of incense, for the hair and clothes, and liberally doused with two types of perfume, a scented oil and a spray.[8]

It is understood that the hostess and her hospitality will be evaluated by her public, her guests. The often-expressed fear of people's talk is not unfounded. Indeed, one of the ways status is constituted is by talk. Guests create the status of the hostess through praising her, not to her face, but to others. Positive evaluations include reports that the party was 'heavenly' [jinan] or that 'the house was packed' [bayt milan].[9] However,

---

6 This word is most often used as an imperative and also as an interrogative – Fasha'ti? (Did you relax, enjoy yourself?) Fasha'i was described to me as a distinctively Zabidi word; my consultant impishly told me that the reason is that the only place one could truly relax is Zabid. It is interchangeable with istarihi or irtahi. I suspect the origin of the word is from the root fasha, which means 'to make the rounds or circulate'; it is always used in the context of going out. In one respect at least, relaxation is going out.

7 Zabidi women claim to be sickened by the habits of the Yemeni women who live in Saudi Arabia (where qat is forbidden), because they leave trays of food around as they visit. Meals in Zabid are dispatched quickly and without much conversation. Hands are washed thoroughly afterward, and perfumed, as lingering food smells are thought unpleasant when exchanging hand kisses.

8 Along with khuruj, Zabid is said to be made beautiful by its luxurious scents [rihas]. Almost every elite family seems to have a special recipe for mixed perfume oils and incenses.

9 Caton describes how at weddings in tribal areas of Yemen, the guest makes a formalized 'return' to the host by praising him with poetry (1990:28).

if the house is dirty, a guest feels justified in describing, in graphic terms, the horrors which confronted her. It is clear, however, that the motivation to offer hospitality does not stem merely from fear of negative public evaluation, although that is certainly an explicitly recognized element. Women take pride and satisfaction in offering hospitality generously and ensuring the comfort of their guests. A gracious older woman explained to me that although she had never in her life smoked the *mada'a*, she would treat the hoses of the pipe with cardamom and perfume to make them pleasant for the guests who did. Kanafani, discussing hospitality in the Emirates, states: 'To honor a guest is a duty (wajib) of the hostess: if a woman honors her guest she honors herself and if she does not, she demeans herself' (1983:101). There is a similar understanding of hospitality in Zabid. Wikan also notes that in Sohar, Oman, honour is created through being gracious to others, 'The person's own honour, in the sense of value both in own and others' eyes, in fact requires that she or he honours others' (1984:641).

The solicitous insistence of the hostess is in contrast with the stylized, decorous refusal of the guest to show any need or desire for the hospitality of the host. When women accept tea, they often do not drink all of it; they say this is because of honour [*namus*].[10] Women are reluctant to appear as if they are in desperate need of the refreshment offered, or as if they are greedy and vulgar. When a woman is given a cola or a glass of water, she will drink only half, passing the rest to the guest seated beside her. I was told that a display of *namus* is only necessary if one is out in public; with family or close friends, one drinks as much as one desires. Guests often protest mightily when the hostess gives them qat or perfume; they try to accept only a token amount. This calculated reluctance expresses the fact that the guest is delicate, restrained, and in control of her physical appetites.

On the other hand, it is not impolite for guests to request something or even to order the hostess to perform a service.[11] I never saw a hostess express resentment at these initiatives from a guest; rather, putting a finger under one eye and then the other, she would commonly say, '*Min*

---

10 *Namus* is honour or code. I never heard Zabidi women use *namus* to refer to the sexual honour of women which has to be protected by the men (as discussed by Meeker 1976 and Dresch 1989). In Zabid it refers to self-respect derived from appropriate comportment in the sense of conforming to etiquette.

11 The most petulant requests usually came from the nicotine-addicted, urging the hostess to add fresh tobacco. Non-smokers were rather disdainful of this obviously expressed physical dependence.

'uyuni' (literally, 'From my eyes,' a phrase which expresses sincerity). It is not considered necessary to say thank you [shukran] for hospitality. (I was thought odd for always thanking people when they handed me something. The hostess frequently murmured in response to my thank you 'no thanks are necessary for a duty' [La shukr 'ala wajib].) The guests never immediately recompense their hostess; a hostess today will be a guest tomorrow who can expect the same hospitality in return.[12]

The guest and the hostess are mutually dependent on each other: the guest is allowing herself to be temporarily encompassed by the host family, and the hostess is concerned to ensure that the guest will continue to honour her with her presence. The etiquette of visiting reflects not only the centrality of visits to constitution of honourable status in Zabid but also its centrality to moral personhood. By honouring others through conforming to this etiquette, one creates oneself as a moral person. Transgressions harm oneself more than others.[13]

Greetings

In Zabid, as elsewhere in Yemen and the Middle East, proper salutation is closely governed by etiquette. Greeting signifies at least a minimal recognition of the social personhood of the other, which most individuals can expect as their right; it provides a base line for interaction (Caton 1986:296). While greeting is far too ordinary to be performed with sombre reverence, it does have a quality of moral compulsion about it.[14] Before taking a seat at a social gathering, a woman must greet those present. Greeting often subtly encodes closeness and not-so-subtly encodes hierarchical

---

12 This style of receiving hospitality from a hostess reminded me of how Zabidi women receive presents. When I brought a friend a present from the capital, she said, in a rather aggressive tone, 'Why did you bother yourself?' The gift was quickly tucked away, without thanks or even inspection. Later she described her delight, not to me, but to another woman within my hearing. Betteridge describes a similar mode of gift receipt in Iran (1985).

13 Veblen wittily remarks that adherence to etiquette is a feature of the 'worthy human soul' (1979:48). This connection of etiquette and personhood is also made by Elias (1978), and by Beidelman (1986:60) who notes that etiquette 'lies at the heart of how people imagine themselves as cultured beings.' Beeman (1986) discusses Iranian etiquette in terms of ideas of the person and the nature of the social order.

14 'When greeting a person one is in a very real sense engaging in a religious act, calling on God to bestow his favor on the addressee' (Caton 1986:294).

relations, but refusal to greet a woman at all is rather startling and much criticized. One girl refused to greet a friend with whom she had had a quarrel. Another woman angrily intervened, saying that 'Greeting is *wajib*' [duty].[15] If the room is very crowded, rather than greeting every guest personally, a woman may pause at the door, crying out, 'Peace be upon you, all of you' [*Salam 'alaykum, kullukum*]. She accompanies this greeting with a sweep of her arm, encompassing all the guests, and kisses her hand. The others, involved in conversations or settling in, murmur the response 'Peace be upon you' ['*Alaykum as-salam*].[16]

While each person must be greeted, gradations of greeting indicate how the person stands in relation to oneself: in an equal but formal relationship, equal and close, superior or subordinate. In a small gathering, a woman circles the room, exchanging greetings with each guest personally. Equals exchange reciprocal hand-kisses; then they both kiss their own hands, or draw a hand to their chests, as if gathering a bit of the essence of the other and drawing it close.[17] Women mark closeness by greeting with special attention. Friendship or kin ties are indicated by warmly kissing each other on both cheeks, or by kissing each other several times on the right cheek. Older women kiss each other's shoulder several times, formally but affectionately, especially if their families have a longstanding relationship.

Hierarchy is also encoded in greeting. A high-status guest, or a guest who returns to Zabid after a long absence, is honoured and welcomed by heaped greetings (*cf.* Caton 1986:295). The guest is repeatedly kissed, and subject to a torrent of queries concerning her health and that of her family. These types of greetings are part of the hospitality owed to all guests, but a particular fuss is made over special guests, who are led to the best seats. Respect due to older women is also indexed in greeting practices. A young woman places her head in the hand of an older woman, who draws the girl's head toward her to kiss it. Young girls, after the age of eight or so, are often urged to greet guests formally. I once saw a girl of about ten years greet her grandmother as if she were a social equal by kissing her grand-

---

15 In Jiddah, 'ignoring an outstretched hand is the highest insult and completely suspends relations, placing the insulting party in the wrong, even if the case were reversed prior to the incident' (Altorki 1986:105).

16 This seems similar to the collective greeting '*Salam tahiyah*' given in highland tribal areas, described by Caton (1986).

17 A similar style is evident when greeting babies. A woman pinches the baby's cheek and draws her hand to her lips and lightly kisses her fingertips.

mother's hand instead of bowing her head to be kissed. Her grandmother was incensed and complained long and loud about her granddaughter's lack of *adab* [manners]. This insult was made more galling by the fact that her daughter-in-law, with whom she had had tense relations for years, did not punish the girl for her cheekiness or urge her to show the proper deference to her grandmother.[18]

As Bourdieu notes, 'The concessions of *politeness* always contain *political* concessions' (1977:95), and in Zabid, relationships of dominance and subordination are clearly marked in greetings.[19] In recent years, greeting has become more egalitarian. The descendants of the Prophet [*sadah*] are not singled out for particularly deferential greetings as they were in the past. One old woman said, 'Now the *akhdam* just greet us and we greet them,' implying that in the past, this requisite of social personhood was not extended to the *akhdam*. Now *akhdam* women tend to kiss the hands of those higher in status, sometimes three or four times, without the higher status women kissing the *khadima*'s hand in return. I never saw anyone actually refuse to give her hand.[20]

As Konig notes, etiquette is the intermediary between 'ethics and aesthetics'; it provides a certain aesthetic varnish to social interaction (1973:131). This became clear to me when I and my Zabidi friends faced a different sort of varnish when we attended a wedding in the wadi. When we returned to Zabid, I commented on the rural greeting style: a woman offered her hand and quickly pulled it away. The Zabidis collapsed with laughter and treated me to a rather ethnocentric discussion of the unrefined manners of the rural people.[21]

Some form of greeting is a prerequisite of social interaction between women, but the opposite is true between non-related men and women. Modest and proper Zabidis ought not to engage in casual interactions with non-related members of the opposite sex. Men who came to inquire after

18 Metcalf has written insightfully on *adab* as both an external and internal quality in South Asian Islam. '*Adab* means discipline and training. It denotes as well the good breeding and refinement that results from training, so that a person who behaves badly is 'without *adab*' (*be adab*). *Adab* is the respect or deference one properly formed and trained shows to those who deserve it' (1984:3).
19 The ambivalence, or resistance, inherent in unequal greetings is noted by Messick (1993:164–6).
20 In men's gatherings, the *khadim* circles the room once, and all the men hold out their hands and he lightly slaps their hands in greeting; the second time the man circles the room, he receives qat or a few riyals from each guest.
21 Aesthetic judgments are not neutral, as Boddy (1993) notes.

my husband would not offer any verbal or gestural greeting to me, but simply ask 'Where is he?' [*Fayn-uh*?], often avoiding my eyes. Women looking for me would aim similarly unadorned interrogatives at my husband.[22] The omission of greetings marks the interaction as strictly utilitarian rather than sociable: therefore it is not an immodest act.

Qat Exchange

Recent research has emphasized that in the process of exchange, personhood is created (Myers 1993, Beidelman 1989). In the exchange of visits, the value or honour of persons, and by extension, their families, is created. The exchanges of greetings during visits are themselves creative of the value of persons. Qat exchange within visits mirrors the exchange of visits themselves. Every woman's visit is marked by exchanges of qat between the participants, contributing in a small way to the social construction of differently ranked persons.[23] There are two kinds of unilateral and equal exchanges of qat between hostess and guest: the first signifies honour and the second, dependency. A special guest, invited for lunch or for a wedding, is given a generous amount of qat. This kind of hospitality honours a guest; although she may protest a bit, she accepts the qat because she will reciprocate to her hostess in the future when her family holds a special event. The second common form of unilateral qat exchange is from hostess to client; at the beginning of a party, the hostess hands, without ceremony, a portion of qat to the client. The client accepts wordlessly. In this context, the non-reciprocal exchange reproduces inequality of persons.[24]

All social events are punctuated by a series of small exchanges of qat between guests which are agonistic as well as integrative. Women sitting

22 Yelling questions and answers through a closed door is preferable to face-to-face exchanges in these contexts.

23 A woman generally chews a quarter or a third the quantity that her husband or father chews. Qat constitutes the biggest daily expenditure for all families in Zabid: anywhere between 50 and 1,000 riyals is spent on qat. This is a considerable sum and strains the resources of even the wealthiest families. Qat is used to make invidious distinctions between men (Weir 1985:159–61). Not chewing qat suggests that one is miserly and antisocial, or that one cannot afford it. It is very difficult not to chew once one has started; as Veblen notes, it is 'difficult to recede from a scale of expenditure once adopted' (1979:102).

24 Employers of the *akhdam* often provided food and qat to them daily, as well as small sums of money.

too far from each other to converse recognize each other by sending small bundles of qat, wrapped in a tissue.[25] Especially in gatherings of older *kibar* women, these exchanges are fast and furious; sometimes women are so busy exchanging that they hardly have time to chew. In this way, qat exchanges, on one level, indicate respect and recognition of one's peers. However, women always try not to accept any qat in return, or only a small portion of that offered, although it is very difficult to refuse entirely without offending the giver.[26] Like the exchange of visits themselves, in exchanging qat women indicate both affection and equality and compete with each other, continually manoeuvring so as not to leave gifts of qat unreciprocated. These exchanges also mark those who are not included as distant, unknown, or irrelevant.

The Meaning of Adornment

Dress in Yemen is a means of establishing and marking personhood. Prior to the 1962 revolution, there were styles of dress which distinctively marked each social category (Mundy 1983, Weir 1985, Bujra 1971). These styles of dress no longer unambiguously identify estate membership, but the idea that one's dress says something about one's social position and one's personhood has not changed. Imposing dress was one of the ways in which important scholars aroused respect and awe in their subordinates (Messick 1993:163–4). In Zabid, respect is thought to accrue to those finely adorned.

The particular style of comportment through which moral womanhood is constituted in Zabid includes the appropriate outfitting and adorning of women's bodies, displayed to the female public. Just as distinctions between women are created by greetings and qat exchange, so are they also by various kinds of adornment. Fashion and conspicuous consumption during visits play a central role in the competition between Zabidi families

---

25 A woman cleans each qat leaf by rubbing it between her fingers to rid it of dust. The recipient cries 'Oh, you chew!' [*Khazzani!*], while the giver instructs her to 'Relax!' The recipient accepts the qat, saying, 'You relax!' [*Shuli rahatik!*].

26 Even on ordinary occasions, *kibar* hostesses often distribute bunches of qat to their guests; poorer families cannot afford to do this. The recipient sets up a great protest, but the hostess insists. Later, the recipient will clean a small bunch of qat for the hostess, who only accepts a token bit. Her role as hostess implies that she is the provider, not the recipient of bounty. A woman who normally accepts qat from her friends resists receiving it in return when she is a hostess.

as much as invitations and visits. The visiting circuit provides a stage on which fashion is displayed (Konig 1973:57). When women go out to meet their public, they are very much aware that this is where they and their families will be evaluated. This competitive dimension of *khuruj* is evident in the conspicuous display of luxury goods such as party dresses, flowers, cosmetics, and jewelry.

During *'id al-kabir*, the religious festival after the hajj, the national radio station broadcast an interview with a Zabidi man, who poked fun at the competitiveness of Zabidi women and their preoccupation with fashion, particularly new dresses. Wondering how women would react to this rather unflattering male commentary, I asked my friends what they thought of these comments. They took this criticism with good humour; they laughed and said that it was true. One must have not one but two new dresses for the *'id*.[27] My friend explained to me that it was not that people would say explicitly, 'That's the same dress you wore yesterday,' but that one would know it oneself and thus be embarrassed [*mustahiya*]. The *'id* is by no means the only event for which a new dress is more or less mandatory. Any invited party requires a 'good' dress, whether new or only worn on a few special occasions.

There is a very small range of acceptable dress, and women are extremely sensitive to wearing the wrong clothes. This sensitivity to being out of place means that those who do not have the right clothes or adornment would, in most cases, rather forgo the party. The constant, blunt comments on adornment and the hegemony of brand names which are established as 'genuine' [*asli*] ensure that there are only very small innovations in the range of fashionable clothes.[28]

Simmel notes: 'Fashion ... is a product of class distinction and operates like a number of other forms, honor especially, the double function which consists in revolving within a given circle and at the same time emphasizing it as separate from others' (1957:544). The style of dress most fashionable while I was in Zabid was a fine, patterned, transparent

27 It should be noted that although this man criticized Zabidi women for their concern with new clothes, Zabidi men are preoccupied with fashionable and expensive clothing as well. When my husband showed up for the *'id* in a new sarong [*futa*] which to him was indistinguishable from those worn by Zabidi men, his friend pointed out that his own sarong was much more expensive (he had paid 500 riyals). He said, 'It doesn't matter for you – you are a foreigner. You could wear a bag [*kis*] if you wanted. For us it is important.'
28 This sensitivity to quality and brand names is evident in Ibb as well (Messick 1978: 317–18).

cotton dress [*dur*],[29] worn with a brassiere[30] and a lacy cotton under-skirt. Dresses with the brand name Kanebo, (a Japanese label) were considered the genuine ones and were the most highly prized.[31] Whether a dress is genuine is quickly established by the trained eye or the touch of a sophisticated Zabidi woman. Women notice new acquisitions: they finger the cloth of a gown and immediately query how much it cost [*Bikam?*] if they do not already know.[32] The poor cannot afford genuine gowns even for special occasions; their dresses are of polyester cloth, which are cheaper (70 riyals) and are disdained by the elite.[33] Although the style is identical, the fabric and the price serve to distinguish those who can afford to wear the genuine dresses from those who cannot.

Distinctions between women who can afford *asli* dresses are played out mainly in the realm of personal choice (a tasteful selection of colour and pattern) and quantity of gowns. Women are unwilling to attend formal parties in a dress that has already been seen. The members of the *shilla*, since they see each other every day, must have a considerable stock of new gowns. In an informal, private conversation with a friend, I was told of the tactics for managing fashion requirements on a restricted budget. Non-elite women have fewer *asli* dresses; some said they did not need them because they did not go out much. They also carefully plan to wear a good dress at a party with new guests, washing it and stowing it away for the next use, until the dress finally, through wear and familiarity, becomes an everyday one.[34]

Adornment for an invited party includes more than a special dress; jasmine flowers are also expected. Several times I was told by friends that they would not attend a party because they did not have any *full*

---

29 This style of dress is said to have been imported from the Gulf States or Saudi Arabia in the late 1970s.

30 These items are seen more as an essential element of fashionable attire rather than as underwear. They are only worn to parties.

31 It retained its popularity during my stay; the price rose from 220 riyals in June 1989 to 320 riyals in August 1990.

32 Prices for dresses are informally fixed in Zabid.

33 Cotton *dur*'s are much cooler. However, price rather than comfort is more central to how an object's value is established. There are several brands of cotton *dur*'s which are less prestigious because they are cheaper. *Asli* does not necessarily refer to natural fibres versus synthetic ones; there are also expensive polyester dresses adorned with bead work that are enjoying a certain vogue among younger women which are considered *asli* as well. *Asli* is often opposed to fake [*falso*], from, I presume, the English word 'false.'

34 Unless San'ani women are dramatically different from Zabidi women, Makhlouf (1979: 26–7) underestimates the significance of differences in dress fabrics.

[Arabian jasmine flowers] and it would be 'ayb [disgraceful] to go without it.[35] Jasmine flowers are expensive, especially in the winter, when women may pay 50 to 100 riyals for an evening's flowers. Many women described paying this much money for flowers as forbidden [haram][36]; in the winter, women often wear a small amount in their hair instead of long (expensive) strings around their necks. Another form of adornment for festive occasions is khidhab, a black pattern drawn on hands and feet. This pattern is conspicuous consumption par excellence: it is expensive,[37] time-consuming to apply, and signifies distance from labour: no work like washing or cooking can be done without ruining the pattern. Henna is an important beautification ritual (it is applied to the palms of the hands and the soles of the feet); it is much less expensive than khidhab and thought to have medicinal qualities as well as decorative ones.[38]

Gold is an essential element of feminine attire. All women (except the very poorest) have some gold; it is virtually a requirement of proper dress for public events. A woman would no more attend a party without gold jewelry than she would appear at such an event unwashed or in work clothes. Marriage is the most important occasion when a woman receives gold, but even unmarried women have considerable amounts of gold, particularly if their family is wealthy. One of the first presents a little girl receives is a pair of gold earrings; in wealthier families, little girls sport small gold bracelets on special occasions.

The significant audience for women's fashion is always other women. Although men never attend women's gatherings, their presence is felt in the adornment practices of Zabidi women. Women's position in families is essentially that of consumer; the material support of the family

---

35 Jasmine flowers are strung on threads and there are several styles, to adorn both hair and neck. They are wound on small sticks for men to put in the pocket of their shirts.

36 When I asked what the difference was between haram and 'ayb, women explained to me that haram means forbidden in the Qur'an, while 'ayb means disgraceful in an ordinary sense. However, haram was commonly used as an evaluative term in all manner of ordinary contexts; in this context women were trying to impose some kind of ceiling on this form of consumption.

37 One application of khidhab costs between 10 and 500 riyals, depending on the expertise and reputation of the applier.

38 Henna is thought to cool the body, and is often applied to infants with fevers. Kapchan (1992:153–6) notes that in Morocco, henna is thought to convey baraka [God's blessings]. While I never heard it described as such in Zabid, it is the appropriate adornment for religious festivals.

should ideally be provided from the male domain.[39] On religious *ids* and special events, women are given clothes and money by their male relatives. This transfer of material wealth is understood as a demonstration of love [*hubb*]. Expensive adornment not only indicates that a woman's family is wealthy (and generous) enough to support her in style, but also indicates to her peers that she is in positive, loving relationships. One friend told me, 'A girl is always given gold, if she is married or not, because her father loves her. He wouldn't ask for it back when she married.'[40] In Yemen, 'Presentations of money, or of goods with precisely known monetary values, are essential for the initiation, maintenance and restoration of the full spectrum of human relations' (Weir 1985:152).

Women's adornment signifies more than the material wealth of the family. As Miller points out, fashionable consumption is more than the creation of distinction (cf. Bourdieu 1984), there is also 'a close relationship between possession, the construction of identity and the adherence to certain social values' (1987:205).[41] In Zabid, appropriate consumption of material goods is intrinsic to a construction of social personhood; there is a sense of moral 'rightness' to spending on adornment a sum commensurate with one's place in society and one's income. It is expected that a considerable portion of income will be devoted to conspicuous display. The existence of unkempt and poorly adorned family members implies that the head of the household is a miser [*bakhil*], and stinginess corrodes the reputation of them all. One man criticized the head of a *bayt kabir* for having badly dressed children.[42]

The issue of gold jewelry deserves special attention. In Zabid, gold represents economic status, and it is important in making invidious distinctions between families. However, it also signifies purity and value. Gold

---

39 Boddy notes this producer\consumer relationship in the Sudan (1989:96).

40 One woman, delighted with the fabric her husband brought her from a trip to Saudi Arabia, exclaimed, 'See how my husband loves me – this costs 800 riyals!'

41 Friedman (1990, 1991) discusses how strategies of consumption are related to the formation of the person; Heath (1992) discusses how dressing well is connected to the creation of social identity.

42 This is true all over Yemen. In Ibb, 'Extreme stinginess or miserliness are said to be accompanied by a lack of attention to one's personal appearance, neglect of one's house, a withholding of support from family members, and an unwillingness to give to the deserving poor' (Messick 1978:415).

is a part of a woman's person, and a token of her honour.[43] Like a dagger to a tribesman, gold means more to a woman's identity than a statement of her family's or her husband's wealth, although it certainly is that. The transfer of gold at marriage is a token of the bride's virtue, and her family's worth.[44] The fact that Western women are married without gold jewelry is consistent, in Zabidi eyes, with their lack of modesty and decency.[45] A groom must spend between 30,000 and 100,000 riyals on gold for his bride, a considerable sum by local standards.[46] To be married without gold is to make oneself cheap [rakhis], thereby disgracing one's family and exposing oneself to abuse.[47] Value is created through 'resistance' and 'sacrifice' (Simmel 1971:43–69). In the great expense of gold which a man must give to his bride, her value, and by extension that of her family, is created.

I mentioned earlier the case of a woman who was ostracized because she continued to live in her husband's family's home after she had been divorced. I met her with the one woman who was still speaking to her, Fawzia. Miriam told me the tale of how her marriage had started. When she was young she had fallen madly in love with her paternal cousin. He was

43 Dresch formulates the importance of rifles and daggers for northern tribesmen in a similar fashion (1989:374).

44 In this respect, Zabid differs from Morocco, as described by Kapchan, who writes 'The cloth she [the bride] wears, and the gold, are representative of economic status, not purity and honor' (1992:162). Kapchan argues that as commodity relations and capitalist values have permeated Moroccan society, material wealth has replaced the moral economy of honour (1992:160).

45 I was continually struck by the earnest concern which my friends had over my goldless situation. As noted earlier, Zabidi women were far more concerned with teaching me how to become a proper, modest woman than they were about my research. They were unsettled that my lack of gold implied I was a woman of questionable virtue. I did not feel justified in spending my grant money on jewelry, but when I returned home for health reasons in the middle of my research, I did beg some gold jewelry from my mother, to the relief of my Zabidi friends. Elizabeth Fernea records several similar incidents with Iraqi women's concern with the poor state of her jewelry collection (1969).

46 A woman receives at least eight to twelve gold bangles, a fancy necklace with matching earrings, a watch, rings, and a gold belt from her fiancé. The belts are often made from Swiss gold bars welded together with filigree, so the exact value is obvious. All gold must be at least eighteen karat, although twenty-two karat is preferred. Fourteen karat gold is considered *falso* as opposed to *asli*.

47 It would be hard to imagine that a Zabidi family would actually agree to marry their daughter without gold. This situation is only possible in the uncommon event of elopement.

already married, and her parents would not agree to her becoming his second wife. She finally married him secretly, but her parents, his parents, and his first wife were all scandalized. He soon began to treat Miriam badly, beating her and unjustly accusing her of infidelity; finally he divorced her. When I spoke with her, she had been demoralized by her ostracism in Zabid (even the neighbourhood children had begun to taunt her) and she was on her way to al-Hudayda, where her parents had moved. I was touched by Miriam's account of her love for and disappointment with her husband, and the hurt she suffered from the harsh judgment of Zabidi women. As Fawzia and I walked home, I expressed my sympathy for her. Fawzia, who was very fond of Miriam and more loyal than most, simply said that she had brought her troubles on herself by marrying the man without so much as a gold ring. She had made herself cheap, said Fawzia, and so the man did not value her, treated her badly, and accused her of misconduct.

Although I was surprised at the time by Fawzia's condemnation of her friend's comportment rather than that of her husband, Fawzia's attitude was perfectly consistent with a mode of behaviour which stands as much for relations between women as for those between man and wife: one must respect oneself and demand respect from others. And for a woman, one's self-respect is, in a certain sense, constituted by receiving (and demanding) gold. Fawzia was not only referring to the fact that if a man instigates the divorce the woman has the right to keep the gold, as a form of material insurance.[48] She argued that Miriam had in effect doomed the marriage from the start by not demanding the respect and recognition, in the form of gold, that she should have. She had devalued herself, and therefore could not expect to be treated with respect.[49]

48 Gold may not provide any security for a woman in an abusive marriage, given that the woman may have to compensate financially her husband and his family if she initiates the divorce. If a *kabir* woman is being badly treated by her husband, chances are her father will have enough clout to intervene positively on her behalf, and if her unjust treatment continues, he can afford to return the money and gold to the husband. A woman from a poor family is much more vulnerable to ill treatment: her father will be weak [*da'if*] and unable to intervene effectively on her behalf, may be unable to support her should she return to his house, or unable to return the money to her husband.

49 An example of an 'Amrani woman who had been married for a low bride price and was subsequently mistreated by her husband is cited in Dorsky (1986:107). Similarly, in the lower highlands, the bride price is considered a statement of the bride's honour and chastity (Myntti, cited in Gerholm [1985:141]). Mundy notes how important jewelry received at marriage is for Sar'ani women's identity (1983: 537).

The early presentations from husband to wife foreshadow a lifelong series of material transfers, at future religious festivals, and upon the birth of children, all of which are owed to the wife. As Haeri notes, 'An Islamic marriage is essentially a commercial mode of transaction superimposed onto the interpersonal marriage relationship' (1989:29). She importantly draws attention to the material obligations inherent in the relationship, particularly the obligations for material transfer in exchange for the production of children. However, she is less attentive to the process by which material exchange is infused with emotion. A husband who gives his wife presents of gold – on the 'id, for example – indicates his love for her in one of the two public demonstrations of affection which are sanctioned.[50] Not only are these transfers imbued with affect, but also with respect for her value as a person.

Appropriate Consumption

Adornment also provides an arena in which personal identity is created. A woman distinguishes herself by her choices; if she selects pleasing patterns and colours, she will be complimented on her taste [dhawq].[51] A woman who adorns herself beautifully and tastefully, who is clean, sweet-smelling, and graceful, will be known as an artist [fannana]. Women look for this quality when selecting brides for their sons or brothers.

There is a dual aspect to adornment, as Simmel (1950:338–9) notes: that of giving others joy through presenting a pleasing appearance to them, but also of the desire to distinguish oneself by receiving attention. In Zabid, these aspects are combined; a beautifully adorned woman not only distinguishes herself but also honours her hostess. She goes beyond merely pleasing the hostess; she recognizes that the hostess's party (and by extension her family) is worth the expense and time involved in adorning oneself properly. Appropriate grooming is a moral act, and therefore inadequacies in grooming practices provoke the same response as other moral failings: a great deal of criticism, from a great many people. Appearing at a formal party in an old or dreadful dress when one is known to possess better or to

---

50 The other is the time and expense a man will expend in getting medical care for his sick wife.

51 Or, alternatively, criticized. Zabidi women tolerate much more negative commentary on each other's grooming or taste than is commonly considered polite in North American society.

be able to afford better is an insult to the hostess's family.[52] Zabidis are quite conscious of how adornment honours the hostess: *khidhab* in particular indicates the closeness between the hostess and the guests who are wearing it. Women who are particularly close friends (or sisters) buy and wear identical dresses when they go out together, making a public statement of shared identity.[53]

Conclusion

Respect is granted to those who display a grand presence in public. One woman told me that the reason people were so concerned with the image they presented in public was that Zabidis had more respect for people who were rich and powerful. She acknowledged that as a good Muslim, one really ought to respect the good and weak as well as the rich, but not everyone remembered that. She told me a proverb which seemed to capture much of this dynamic of life in Zabid:

> God make us small in my own eyes
> But great in the eyes of others

As a good Muslim woman, one should be modest and humble before God, my friend explained, but one wants to be seen as great in the eyes of the *nas*.

In one respect, a woman strongly values personal humility and modesty; but, alternatively, she also wants her family to be distinguished, through the tasteful display of material wealth, in the eyes of her significant public. Her audience, her peers, usually have no difficulty ascertaining how much her outfit cost, nor qualms about making an aesthetic judgment of it. They are not shy about inquiring about the price of an object, and the questioned woman usually answers with pride rather than reluctance. After learning a price, however, the woman who made the inquiry is careful to add 'Whatever God wills' [*ma sha'llah*] to indicate that she does not intend to give the

---

52   The issue of what one can afford is key: poor people would not be criticized for appearing in an old gown, but wealthy people would be. The exception to this rather strict rule is at mourning, when it would show disrespect for the family if the guest showed up adorned. Mourning requires conspicuous non-consumption.

53   It is customary to marry two or three sons at one time, or sons and a paternal cousin. All the brides are given identical clothing, showing that the family of the grooms does not rank one of the bride's families above the other.

other woman the evil eye [al-'ayn al-hasad] by envying her good fortune.[54] This issue is central to the ambiguity which underlies visiting: while much of the practice of visiting is clearly aimed toward conspicuous display on the part of the hostess and the guests, it is in public contexts that one is most likely to receive the evil eye.[55] This fact constitutes the danger in visiting which underlies its pleasurable aspects.[56] When a woman displays wealth, she creates the greatness of her family or her husband's family, but she also makes it vulnerable by exposing it to envious eyes. Women who are already in a vulnerable state must avoid khuruj. Brides-to-be are not seen socially for at least the three months preceding their weddings. A woman who has a depressive mental illness [ikti'ab] cannot go out to any party until she is completely healed. Khuruj as a practice is understood as the finest quality of Zabidi social life, but it is also the site of danger.

54 As Simmel notes, 'The fashionable person is regarded with mingled feelings of approval and envy' (1957:548).
55 Women told me that, according to the Prophet Muhammad, they could receive the evil eye even from their own families, but they were most afraid of receiving it when out in public.
56 This dual aspect of sociability in Zabid is similar in this respect to Iteso beer drinking, which is highly prized as a form of sociability but also is the context in which one is most vulnerable to sorcery (Karp 1980).

6

Moments of Consequence: Weddings and Mourning Ceremonies

In 1880, 'Amir al-Zabidi, who was one of Zabid's merchants, celebrated the wedding of his son. The custom in Zabid involves the invitation of a great number of people from different social classes to the celebration, and the building of a *mikhdara* which is decorated with all sorts of embellishments and flowers. After lunch, the guests proceed to the *mikhdara* to chew *qat* and to be entertained. The groom is conducted in a procession, after which he sits on a high chair while the singers who recite Sufi chants sit in front of him. This is followed by the delivery of poems congratulating the groom, his father, and his family.

'Abd al-Rahman al-Hadrami, *Jami'at al-Asha'ir Zabid*

Weddings and mourning ceremonies are even more consequential for the status of families than is everyday socializing. Both are events which require recognition from a family's most wide-ranging associates, and they therefore provide a public representation of its network, part of the family patrimony. These events are notable for their distinctive patterns of consumption. Wedding celebrations involve the greatest conspicuous consumption and the most lavish, most widely extended, hospitality. Mourning ceremonies, in contrast, are marked by the conspicuous *absence* of consumption, and by a reversal of the everyday etiquette of hospitality.

Weddings: The Legal Ceremony

The wedding is composed of two essential elements: the legal ceremony [*aqd*] and the week of festivities [*farah*]. The *aqd* is a small ceremony held in the groom's home, during which the qadi, the judge, writes up the legal document of marriage – an agreement between the father of the groom and either the father of the bride or her legal guardian.[1] The groom then goes to the bride's house to exchange rings with his bride; a present of gold from the groom to the bride, usually a necklace and earring set is given at this time. *'Aqds* are often held in Ramadan, as it is considered an auspicious month [*shahr mubarak*]; the *farah* may be held the following summer or delayed until the family can afford to pay for the party. Although legally married after the *'aqd*, the couple does not cohabit until the *farah*.

The *Farah*

Zabid's wedding season occurs in the torrid Tihama summer; it is the most hectic social season in a community which is never quiescent socially. It coincides with school vacation, when teachers and students are free to participate in the work and pleasure associated with these significant events in communal life.[2] A family's honour is created and displayed to others during a wedding; it is a particularly important moment for the groom's family.

Weddings are the only events where the social lives of men and women coincide; both male and female family members must devote considerable time and effort if the wedding is to be successful. As the event approaches, a sense of how much is at stake is evident in the palpable tension which pervades the house of the groom. Emotions run high, as family members try to coordinate the complex series of events.

The wedding *farah* itself provides the significant opportunity for a family to create an honourable identity in the most public forum. The hospitality offered by the *bayt* can be seen as a 'glorious deed' which accomplishes honour through generosity.[3] Being '*kabir*' is more a process than a state, and throwing a grand wedding is part of that process. The wedding also may be part of the process of upward mobility through what Caton calls the 'dialectic of history.' The honour of the extant family members is constituted by the glorious deeds of past members and conversely, the deeds of present members can serve to glorify the past.[4] This section describes the

---

1 The qadi formally ascertains whether the girl assents to the marriage, by asking her either directly, or her father, as her proxy. It is unusual (and not approved of) for her to be married against her will.
2 Most of the wedding parties are held outdoors, either in the courtyards of houses or in the wedding tent. Zabidis consider the winter, when temperatures are 'only' 30°C to be too cold for sitting outdoors. Only small weddings are held during the winter.
3 The term 'glorious deed' is borrowed from Meeker (1976); he uses it to describe an act which serves to constitute honour. See also Caton's discussion (1990:27).

*farah*s of the *kibar* that are the ideal which less prominent families generate on a smaller scale.

Etiquette of Invitations

At weddings the extent of a family's social connections must be made concrete and publicly visible in the physical presence of *at least* one member of each family with whom the host family associates. The importance of social recognition at weddings is reflected in the formalized style of inviting guests. Issuing written invitation cards is currently in fashion; most great families extend them to the heads of the households they wish to invite. But invitations must also be issued verbally: a *muzayyin* and a member of the family must personally invite all the guests.[5] In addition, female members must be invited separately from male members, by verbal invitations extended by both a *muzayyina* and a female representive of the family. The bride's family and the groom's family usually issue separate invitations.

The formal lunch offered by the family must be attended: otherwise one risks gravely offending the host family. In the past, no one would attend a wedding lunch unless personally urged to come by a member of the host family on the day of the wedding feast itself. The *kibar* families would often not attend without being beseeched three or four times; the lunch could not start until the most notable families were in attendance. A few years ago a woman from a *bayt kabir*, who had lived in Saudi Arabia for several years, announced that invitations to lunch were going to be extended only once, with the general invitation, and that those who wished to come, should come.[6] All those invited came with the exception of the family that had been considered the most lofty in Zabid for most of the early part of the century. This innovation was followed with relief by the women, who remembered the hardship of having to traipse all over Zabid in the heat of the day, insisting their guests accept their hospitality.

Nonetheless, the tension between the hosts and the guests continues to be marked: the hosts closely monitor attendance, while the guests are stick-

---

4 'Present deeds can redeem the past as the past can validate present deeds' (Caton 1990:35). In Zabid, the agonistic exchange of hospitality, rather than poetry, as discussed by Caton, is the means by which honourable identity is created.

5 Out-of-town guests will be invited in person or by telephone as well as by mail.

6 Saudi Arabia is often the site of cultural transformation as Zabidis living in Yemeni neighbourhoods there reformulate their own practices as a result of contact with those from other regions in Yemen who have quite different practices.

lers for proper invitations. The obligation to attend, providing one has been properly invited (no self-respecting family would deign to attend otherwise), is particularly compelling in the case of weddings, and no excuse other than extreme illness or a sudden death in the family is valid.

The Events

A large tent [*mikhdara*], a wooden frame covered by cotton and lit by fluorescent lights, is constructed for the festivities; it is placed in a large empty space close to the groom's house.[7] It is decorated inside with brightly coloured carpets, bunches of bananas, and flowers. Tihama couches are arranged in a bleacher formation, affording all of the guests (between one thousand and fifteen hundred for a *bayt kabir*)[8] a view of the dais where the brides sit at women's parties and the grooms sit at men's parties.[9]

The parties which compose the *farah* take place during a week-long period. Tuesday evening the groom's family hosts a large, formal women's reception known as the *wusa*, after which the women of the groom's family go to the house of the bride and present a gold necklace. On Wednesday morning the bride's family host a reception. The bride sits with henna on her fingertips, veiled with a sheer green scarf, with a pan on her lap into which her family's associates put 5 or 10 riyals. These small cash gifts, similar to those at births, are based on the exchange relationships of the mother of the bride.[10] In the evening, a party [*zaffa*] is held for the bride at her house: a tray of eggs, candles, and rue [*shadhab*] is danced around her by dozens of wildly excited little girls.[11] At this party, guests contribute 5 riyals to the fee of the *muzayyina* who will accompany the bride to the home of the groom the following evening.

Thursday is the *dukhla*, when the bride enters the groom's house. The groom, adorned with a garland of jasmine, is the centre of a large, noisy

7 The *mikhdara* can cost up to 10,000 riyals to construct, including cost of materials and labour provided by the *akhdam*.
8 At the wedding of a respectable but less affluent family, there may be two to three hundred guests.
9 Given the great expense of wedding parties, most families try to marry at least two or three sons at one time. In addition, having more grooms and brides is thought to make the spectacle that much more impressive.
10 A similar practice takes place at elite weddings in Jiddah, Saudi Arabia (Altorki 1986:112).
11 Rue protects against the evil eye. My attempts to elicit the meaning of the eggs and the candles were not very successful: several women said, 'It's just like that' [*kidha bas*]. One suggested that the candles meant that the bride would become beautiful 'like light.' One might suppose the eggs are fertility symbols

procession, his *zaffa*. He is praised in poetry by a *dawshan*, a low-status musician, who may command high prices for his performance.[12] The groom's party is then taken by car to the bride's house. The groom enters the house, pays the *muzayyina* accompanying his bride, places his hand on his bride's forehead, and says the *fatiha*, the opening verse of the Qur'an. A carload of the groom's female relatives accompanies the bride, along with a maternal relative other than her mother and the *muzayyina*, to the groom's house. Sometimes this procession, especially for a *bayt kabir*, has as many as ten or fifteen cars.[13] A truck carrying floodlights and the sound system, over which the *dawshan* continues his poetic praise, leads the procession.[14] If the two houses are close together, the procession makes a slow detour around Zabid, to prolong the spectacle, followed by the male guests and a throng of children. Amid gunfire, the bride is carried by a male relative other than her father, usually an uncle, into the groom's house. The bride's entrance is followed by several *akhdam* who carry the possessions she is bringing into the groom's home. The bride and groom exchange juice and cake in their new house, and pictures are taken by the groom's family. Outside the room where the bride and groom are, pandemonium reigns; dozens of bechadored women and children crowd to see the bride, who is eventually brought out in the courtyard and seated on a platform.[15] When the guests leave, female neighbours and friends help the family of the groom prepare dozens of trays of a pastry called *bint as-sahn*, which will be baked the following day for the men's wedding lunch. (The women helpers often do not return to their houses until three or four in the morning.) After sharing juice with his bride, the groom returns to the *mikhdara*, still followed by the *dawshan* and his praises. Sweets are handed out to all the guests, who congratulate and bless [*tabarak*] the groom by kissing him and

---

12 One very prestigious wealthy family imported a famous *dawshan* from San'a', who praised the standing groom for two hours.

13 The *dukhlas* of the *akhdam* are done on camelback.

14 Wealthy families often have the entire procession videotaped, as well as the men's reception on the following day.

15 The bride is dressed in a white bridal gown and the gold jewellery given to her by her husband. She is often rendered virtually unrecognizable by heavy makeup, which in current Zabidi fashion includes a heavy white powder base and sparkly blue and pink eye shadow. In the past, Zabidi brides wore embroidered indigo gowns and an elaborate head dress. They also had their faces and chests decorated with *khidhab*, a custom now abandoned because it is said to evoke the pre-Islamic period. Now, only the bride's hands and feet are adorned with *khidhab*; the best experts in Zabid often charge up to 1,000 riyals for the application to a bride, as opposed to the 100–200 riyals for members of the groom's family. The groom's family pays for the *khidhab* of the bride.

shaking his hand. He returns to his home to spend the wedding night with his new bride.[16]

The main luncheon and reception for the men is held the following day. Approximately one hundred sheep are slaughtered for a thousand guests; the rice and meat are cooked in huge caldrons by low-status men. The male members of the groom's family, as well as neighbours and clients, help serve the meal, which is held in the largest available space closest to the groom's home.[17] The lunch is followed by an afternoon qat chew, during which the groom's family distributes expensive qat to their high-ranking and esteemed guests and also to the neighbours who have helped with the preparations.[18] Wealthy families also offer bottled soft drinks to their chewing guests. At sundown the men spit out their qat, perhaps pray in a nearby mosque, partake of a light supper, and prepare to chew again. This last party is known as the *sumra*, and it is held by only the *kibar*. Qat is chewed far into the night, and guests staying as late as three or four in the morning. A set of musicians may be hired to entertain them.

The women's party takes place on Saturday and a grand lunch is served. The guests then wash and change their dresses in the home of the groom or that of close neighbours in preparation for their party [*sub-hiya*], at which the groom's family proudly presents its new brides to the female public. This party lasts until ten p.m., although great families often have a late night *sumra* for the women, complete with entertainment.[19] The brides are drummed to the stage with great fanfare, accompanied by the women of the groom's family. They are seated on the dais, dressed in matching pink dresses, according to current Zabidi fashion. They are adorned with jasmine flowers and their wedding gold. Little girls, dressed in an imitation of their older relatives, complete with *khidhab*, and thrilled by the occasion, squabble over the right to dance on the dais. Like the male hosts, the women of the groom's family

16 The groom gives the bride 1,000 riyals when she first lifts her veil, and 2,000 riyals upon consummation. The blood on the bride's underskirt is privately shown to her mother by the mother of the groom as proof of her virginity. In the wadi, proof of virginity is publicly displayed, but this is considered crass in Zabid.

17 A courtyard or empty yard will be covered with cotton tenting to provide some shade from the mid-afternoon sun.

18 Other guests bring their own qat. The host family usually provides qat to those who help with overseeing the construction of the *mikhdara* the week prior to the *farah*. Qat prices vary daily, but given that the most expensive qat is usually bought for weddings, I estimate that the great families spent at least 50,000 riyals on qat during the wedding.

19 The musicians, from al-Hudayda or Ta'izz, are low-status *akhdam*, so the women can appear before them unveiled.

present qat to their esteemed guests, and to the neighbours, friends, and clients who helped in the preparations.

The wedding ceremonies are complete when, the following week, the bride is feasted by her own family at a party known as the *sab'a*.[20] Until this time, she should not leave her husband's house to visit another. This event is particularly important because it signals the acceptance of the bride's new status by her natal family, effectively blessing the union.

Creating Distinction

The prestige of the *bayt* is created in the pageantry of the *dukhla* procession, the splendour of the *mikhdara*, and the plenitude of the lunch. In the course of the *dukhla*, the prestige of the groom's family is trumpeted all over Zabid on loudspeakers and punctuated with celebratory gunfire. Reputation resides, at least partly, in the talk of others about the quality and style of wedding *farah*s; hosts talk of fearing that the *nas* will laugh at them if they are ill-prepared. Every effort is made to make the *mikhdara* appear as opulent and brilliant as possible. People comment on its size or decor: 'The *mikhdara* stretched for miles and was covered in jasmine!' A lavish wedding held thirty years earlier was still discussed: the men had *sumra* after *sumra*, one woman told me, and all the guests had received gifts of cardamom, cloves, and sweets to take away with them.

Comments on the lavishness (or stinginess) of the lunch are made. What is at issue is not the preparation of the cuisine itself, but the quantity; all guests should eat to their satisfaction.[21] There is little variation in the wedding lunch from house to house; it always includes boiled lamb, rice, potatoes, tomato and green onion salad, lamb broth, and pastry [*bint as-sahn*].[22] The only distinguishing feature of the cuisine, aside from its abundance, is the honey which is poured over the pastry.[23] Factors which affect

20 A few elite families send the newlyweds to spend a month abroad for their honeymoon [*shahr al-asl*]. The bride will be feasted by her family upon their return.
21 After one wedding lunch, my husband heard a low-status man loudly complaining that he was still starving, which was shameful as the host family is obliged to provide for all those who attend, be they high or low in status.
22 Any leftovers are distributed to the neighbourhood poor.
23 Yemenis are honey connoisseurs, and for a wedding, fine honey is part of the hospitality as conspicuous consumption. One *bayt kabir* spent 57,000 riyals on honey alone; some jars of the very finest were reserved for the most prestigious guests.

the outcome of the wedding, but are beyond one's control, like the weather, do not negatively affect one's reputation. After the initial upset is over, the trials are humorously recounted.[24]

The wedding, then, is the point at which ultimate difference is expressed, at which the family of the groom pronounces its distinctiveness and worth. This distinctive identity, as well as the hierarchy which emerges from this tournament of value, is made possible through a series of reciprocal exchanges. The production of a wedding, even of the richest family in Zabid, depends on the support of others in the community.

In the first place, one must have been keeping up one's social obligations to others in order for them to agree to attend one's own festivity. The grandest *mikhdara* would be without positive significance if not filled with guests to whom the host can be generous. Social omissions are noted and will be reciprocated in kind. If a man sends his son to represent his family at a wedding, his acquaintance would not admit inferiority by attending his peer's wedding himself; he would, in turn, send his son. If the host family has been remiss in social duties to the guest, the guest may not attend the host's *farah* in retaliation.

Wedding *farah*s require labour beyond what the family members themselves can provide. Ties of neighbour, kin, client, and friendship are drawn upon, but the successful mobilization of labour depends on some reckoning of reciprocity.[25] Those with upcoming weddings meticulously fulfil obligations to others in order to be sure of support at their own *farah*. This aid must be formally requested: the mother of the groom must personally ask the female heads of households for the assistance of their daughters in the inviting, and in the preparation of tobacco and pastry. These girls also act as surrogate hostesses, circulating at the wedding parties, asking guests if they would like a drink or fresh tobacco in the waterpipe. The groom's family provides long garlands of jasmine flowers for the girls who have

24 Rain turns the packed dirt of Zabidi courtyards and streets into a thick mud. One family had the misfortune of a downpour during the women's wedding lunch, further complicating the task of feeding the seven hundred guests. The women of this family said they were so exhausted at the end of the event that they had teased their younger brothers to elope. This was a particularly expressive joke – elopement is shameful.

25 Great families do not return labour to their clients or weaker neighbours, although they may to their equals. However, great families must recognize these weaker families by attending the life-cycle events if they wish to enlist their labour. For the weddings of weaker neighbours, great families may often contribute to the cost of the weddings or lend space in their houses for some of the parties.

assisted, which they usually string themselves. These girls are also obliged to wear *khidhab* and fine dresses to show their support for, and connection with, the host *bayt*.[26]

The furnishings (the beds, coverings, cushions, and carpets) for the *mikhdara* itself are loaned by connected families in the surrounding vicinity.[27] In addition, the host family must have wide connections to be able to borrow the accoutrements necessary for the comfort and enjoyment of the guests: waterpipes and large water thermoses, to be filled with cool water flavoured with incense.

Another important cycle of exchanges takes place between men. The men of the host family chew in their *mikhdara* on the days prior to the *dukhla*, and their associates bring in sheep or bags of rice or flour.[28] These gifts are formally recorded in writing so they may be reciprocated when the giver has a wedding. Great families usually receive between two and three hundred sheep. Those remaining after both the men's and the women's lunches can be sold, and the proceeds can be used for other wedding expenses. One man holding an influential government post received around five hundred sheep; in this way, people can use an upcoming wedding to establish a relationship with an influential man, who will be obliged to reciprocate the gift to the donor. The obligation to return these gifts is morally binding; not to give back is extremely shameful.[29] This gift is essentially a loan [*salaf*] in the guise of a gift, but this guise is essential to the exchange. The guests bring their 'gift' and are treated the following day to the wedding lunch.

I discussed in chapter 2 the fury of a family that had not been invited to the wedding of another *bayt kabir*. The shame inflicted by the omission of the invitation was made doubly hurtful by the fact that the men in the family were still obliged to return, the day before the wedding to which they had not been invited, the gift of sheep which they had received from the other family for their wedding. The gall of the insult was such that the offended family still refused to enter the other's home a year later when I

---

26 Their own families pay for their *khidhab*, but they can expect reciprocity for their future event
27 The *akhdam* are paid five riyals a bed to transport them from the houses to the *mikhdara*.
28 Bogary mentions a similar series of reciprocal gifts at weddings in his memoir of his boyhood in a quarter of Mecca (1991:85), as does Ibn al-Mujawir, a thirteenth-century traveller, indicating the breadth and historical depth of these practices (Smith 1993:163).
29 These debts contrast with those owed to bureaucratic agencies like the electric or telephone company. It is merely inconvenient rather than shameful to have one's electricity or telephone disconnected because of non-payment.

departed from Zabid. To give a gift when one is not invited to the party implies a subordinate position: a tribute-giver hoping to ingratiate a patron. Being forced into this position by an equal was a humiliation not easily forgiven.[30]

Another important, and binding, obligation between men is that of firing off a clip of bullets from their guns or automatic weapons at each other's weddings.[31] (A full clip costs 300 riyals.) The roar of guns is considered an essential aesthetic element for a successful *farah*; the obvious safety hazards are rarely mentioned.[32] Particularly impressive are the rounds fired in unison by the guests from tribal areas when they arrive for a wedding lunch.

To perform weddings properly according to Zabidi custom, the *nas* are dependent on the *mazayanah* and the *akhdam*, thus effecting a degree of complementarity between the estates. This remains so despite the grumbling of those resident in Saudi Arabia, who consider the fees to the *mazayanah* superfluous because the majority of the work is done by the family itself and its neighbours.[33] *Akhdam* and *mazayanah* families have client ties to the *bayts* in their neighbourhoods; the *bayt* holding the wedding must formally request their services and provide the standard recompense, which may include providing new dresses for the *akhdam* women employed, as well as cash.

The successful production of a great *farah* is a creation of a *bayt*'s distinctive identity. Prestige accrues to the family of the groom through their hospitality. Greatness depends on its member's peers – its audience – for the recognition which constitutes it. But its peers (those of roughly equal status) are not the only significant audience: all Zabidis, of every status, comprise the 'community of significance' in this instance. At the moment of the *farah*, the *bayt kabir* presents itself as autonomous, but the achievement of this autonomous posture depends on a series of exchanges, both symmetrical and assymmetrical, with others in the community. In produc-

---

30 The undercurrents of antagonism inherent in these exchanges, which create, on another level, solidarity and connection, is reminiscent of the Homeric Greeks: 'The mechanisms of sociability, as epitomized in guest-gift relations, appear as sources of abuse and danger as much as means to advantage or order' (Beidelman 1989:248).

31 Weapons are not an essential element of everyday dress for Zabidi men as they are for the northern highland *qaba'il*. Guns are evident only at Zabidi weddings.

32 It is illegal to fire off weapons in the city, but officials usually turn a blind eye or issue a fine after the fact. Sometimes the family requests over the loudspeaker that no guns be fired, a disclaimer that no one heeds.

33 Apparently, the *mazayanah* who work in Saudi Arabia no longer perform the traditional tasks for the Yemeni community there.

ing a fine *farah*, a *bayt kabir* is in agonistic competition with its peers, who are able to produce comparably fine *farah*s. But the production of a successful event depends on compelling one's peers to attend and one's subordinates to help. The production of weddings reproduces the relations of inequality in the community. Thus this posture of autonomy depends on domination.[34]

Zabidis sometimes complain about the town's less attractive features, primarily the weather, but claim that it is made beautiful by its *farah*s. They are extremely proud of the style in which weddings as performative events unfold. In a society where the styles of sociability come to represent a positive value at the community level, the wedding season is itself the apotheosis of this value. *Farah*s become the quintessential element of Zabidi civility, appreciated aesthetically beyond what they signify for the host families.[35] Their splendour and scale, embodied most impressively in *kibar* weddings, make them the cultural productions which best exhibit the finest qualities of Zabidi hospitality: gracious generosity in a fine and lavish setting. Thus the *kibar*, in their production of great *farah*s, are achieving – and defining – cultural value at a community level. Through producing these spectacular events, the *kibar* are embodying the cultural value which makes Zabid distinctive as a community. By hosting these events so valued by Zabidis, the *kibar* gain the prestige of the community, and also serve to define the community itself.

The Bride's Family versus the Groom's Family

The material objects given to the bride by her family or the groom's are part of the status competition between the two. The payment from the groom's family to the bride's on marriage is composed of two parts: the *nuqud*, which goes to the bride's father, and the *mahr* of gold jewelry and dresses, which is the bride's portion. Paid at the signing of the *'aqd*, the *nuqud* in 1990 was 15,000 to 20,000 riyals for elite families, and 5,000 for poorer families.[36] In Zabid, the *mahr* is the greater expense; in 1989–90

---

34 The connection between autonomy and domination is described by Eickelman for Morocco: 'The reason why dominance is so coveted in this system is that it allows a man to be autonomous, to assert his claim to be a full social person' (1976:143).

35 This aesthetic side to institutions of exchange is noted by Mauss (1970:77).

36 If the two families have a close relationship (kin, neighbour, or friend) they may agree to exchange the *nuqud* in regular instalments acknowledged with written receipts. Otherwise the payment is made in full. These payments have risen recently; in the early 1980s, 5,000 riyals was the highest payment.

between 30,000 and 100,000 riyals was spent on gold, depending on the status of the family.[37] The trousseau, delivered before the *dukhla*, includes cloth for forty fancy dresses (12,000 and 15,000 riyals), as well as elaborate makeup kits, head scarves, night gowns, brassieres, assorted perfumes, and some everyday clothing.[38] The gold and dresses are considered the bride's property, which cannot be alienated from her unless she wishes to instigate a divorce.

The tension between the bride's family and the groom's, which may be present during the engagement, revolves around the issue of confer- ring value and creating identity. The bride's family, if elite, is also concerned to make a statement of their own distinctiveness. When two elite families marry, there is much competition between them.[39] Although the weddings are generally more expensive for the groom's family than the bride's, in great families the bride's family spends a great deal on the wedding.[40] The entire *nuqud* received by the father of the bride is spent either on the parties for the bride or on gold and dresses for her.[41] The bride's family is losing a daughter, but for the sake of their own status, they have to appear not to need what they are given in compensation for the loss.

In marriages between two elite families or between an elite Zabidi family and one from out of town, the bride's family will be particularly concerned to supply tokens which indicate her (and its) value. One woman engaged to a man in al-Hudayda showed me the suitcases full of clothing, perfume, and gold provided by her father. Her younger sister said, 'My father loves

37 In Zabid, the bride's *mahr* is much higher than the portion which goes to her father, in contrast to the tribal highlands. In 'Amran, the bride's portion is between 3,000 and 7,000 riyals in contrast to the bride's father's portion, which is 50,000 riyals (Dorsky 1986:107).

38 The trousseau has become more elaborate in recent years. *Kibar* women married thirty years ago told me that they received between seven and ten dresses. However, these dresses must have been expensive, as they were elaborately embroidered and imported from India.

39 Some great families prefer to choose brides from respectable, but obviously less wealthy, households. In these cases, the groom's family shines without competition from the bride's.

40 Two Zabidi girls married into a *shaykhly* family from the wadi, one from a small *bayt* and the other from a *bayt kabir*. The weaker family held a small lunch for their closest friends and neighbours; the *bayt kabir* constructed a large *mikhdara*, and hosted not only the series of pre-wedding parties in the bride's honour but also male and female lunches and *sumras* after the wedding.

41 Gerholm notes that it is a matter of pride for men in Manakha to let the marriage payment be 'consumed by fire' (1985:139–40).

her a lot.'[42] Her possessions from her family, she said, would preclude the groom's family from thinking they were poor or pathetic [*miskin*].

The number of suitcases and possessions carried into the home of the groom is a public statement of her value as estimated by her own family.[43] The bride always brings a mattress and bed clothes, several suitcases, and in wealthier families, a perfume cabinet and perhaps a tape recorder. An elite bride's family not only tries to outdo the groom's family in quality of gold or gowns but may object to the trousseau offered by the groom's family. A bride of a prestigious and established *kabir* family repeatedly rejected the gowns presented by the groom's family, which the groom's family interpreted as an attempt to imply that her family was better than theirs.[44]

While the bride's family often tries to ensure their collective worth and her value through the possessions she brings into the marriage, the groom's family quickly establishes precedence. For the bride's first public appearances during and after the wedding, she wears the gold and dresses given to her by her husband's family. After a wedding a great family may host a two-week open house reception, when guests are invited to 'look at our brides' [*tatafarrag 'ala 'ara'is haqqana*]; the brides sit together on a couch, dressed identically. (Families who are marrying two or three sons may insist on giving identical gowns to each of the brides, to avoid any implication that one is valued more highly than the others.) The women of the grooms' family proudly ask their guests, 'How is our bride? Beautiful?' [*Kayf al-'arusa haqqana? Jamila?*]. The bride has been transformed into the social representative of the groom's family; every time she goes out in public for a year after the wedding, she should be adorned with a garland of jasmine flowers supplied by her husband's family.[45]

Significance for the Community

Women take pride in the fertility and affluence of the community as a

42 In the estimation of many of her friends, the gold she had received from her father was more expensive and nicer than that she had received from her fiancé.
43 I often heard women comment on the number of *akhdam* needed to carry a bride's suitcases.
44 This kind of controversy and competition does not always occur; many think it is demeaning to quibble over the dresses, especially since the quality of the dresses reflect the taste and generosity (or lack thereof) of the groom's family rather than the bride's family.
45 Hostesses often asked mothers-in-law, 'Where are your brides? Why didn't they come?' Brides continue to represent their natal families as well. In well-arranged marriages, the women of the groom's family adopt many of her family's associates, as she does theirs.

whole, by counting up the number of brides of the year, saying, 'Look at all our brides this year, *ma sha'allah*.'[46] This sentiment is expressed in social form through holding a series of parties in honour of all the Zabidi brides of the year, hosted in the two or three months which follow the wedding season. A relative of one of the brides will host a party, inviting all the new brides and their families of origin and their families of marriage. The brides sit together in their flowers, gold, and sparkly gowns. This is a moment when members of the community seem to take stock of themselves, when competition between individual families is muted, as women thank God for the continued viability of the Zabidi community.

Ceremonies of Mourning

The death of a family member is another occasion significant for familial status. Weddings require that one's associates recognize one's gain (at least from the perspective of the groom's family), and ceremonies of mourning require a recognition of one's loss. As during weddings, at death the treatment of women's bodies is central. At death, bereaved women are conspicuously unadorned. Unlike a wedding – the one Zabidi social event that male and female members of a family manage and produce together – a mourning ceremony is women's responsibility.

Deaths are announced on the mosque's loudspeaker immediately after they occur; the prayer caller is paid a small sum to announce the name of the deceased, along with the Qur'anic phrase which reminds the listeners that God created people, and that to God they will return at death.[47] The body is washed, incensed and perfumed, and wrapped in a plain white cotton cloth.[48] The affirmation of the faith [*shahada*], 'There is no God but God and Mohammad is his Prophet,' is written on the forehead of the deceased. According to the older women, this inscription is done because, when facing the afterlife, the most important identity of the individual is that of a believing Muslim. The body is carried on a Tihama bed to a graveyard [*majanna*] on the outskirts of Zabid. Male relatives and neighbours

46 The first year I was in Zabid there were between forty and fifty new brides.
47 Some families still hire the *mazayanah* to announce the death, although the mosque announcement is considered more efficient and less expensive.
48 As a meritorious charitable act, the rich often provide the poor with the expensive perfumed oils for burial. Specialists perform this task, although there is said to be only one man in Zabid now who does this work. Female corpses may be treated by a specialist or by an older woman in the family.

carry the body while the Qur'an is read out loud in a procession called the *jinaza*. Basil is placed on the grave by the mourners, who say the *shahada*; both these actions are thought to lighten the sins of the dead person. As Hertz noted (1970:48), death is more a transition than a destruction; for pious Zabidis, heaven is the desired destination. Chatting about heaven [*janna*] and hell [*nar*] and burial practices was not at all unusual. Several women offered information on death without prompting, motivated, it seemed, by concern for my fate after death as a non-Muslim. Two angels, Munkar and Nakir, are said to question the dead person; if she or he responds with the *shahada*, her or his destination will ultimately be heaven instead of hell. Until the day of reckoning [*yawm al-qiyama*], however, one can either be tormented in a dark and stuffy grave or be comfortable in a light and airy one. One's behaviour on earth affects this fate.

Men go to the mosque to pray for the soul of the deceased as soon as they hear the death announcement. The men in the family stay in the house for three days to receive visitors; on the third day after a death and again on the thirtieth day, they will pay for a ceremonial reading of the entire Qur'an [*khatim*] to be performed by a religious specialist in the mosque. Sometimes the young children in a family will perform Qur'anic readings by the grave.

Women do not attend the graveyard on the day of burial, but they may visit the grave, just before sundown, on the third and thirtieth days. They hand out food (dates and sorghum bread) to the poor or the neighbourhood children, which becomes blessed [*baraka*] through its dedication to charity. They may read the Qur'an or simply lay basil and palm fronds on the grave. Small luncheons are held on the third and thirtieth days after the death; only the immediate neighbours are invited. Neighbours gather in the home of the bereaved on the burial day, and the widest network of female associates attend the first formal gathering (the first or second day after the death), which is known as the *thalith*.[49] The kin of the deceased (both affinal and agnatic) sit together facing the guests who have come to offer condolences [*ta'azi*]. At the door, the mourners are given basil sprigs and perfume. The session proceeds in silence. Most mourners attend between the sundown [*maghrib*] and evening [*layl*] calls to prayer. After the *layl* call, especially on the *thalith*, the chief mourners sometimes burst into keening cries, inspiring

49 The *thalith*, which literally means the 'third,' refers to the three days that constitute the prescribed mourning period according to Muslim doctrine. However, in Zabid it signifies not the end of the three days of mourning but the beginning of at least thirty days of mourning. Zabidi women are aware that in this sense their customs are diverging from Qur'anic principles.

the condolers to join in.[50] Those more distant chastise the mourners, reminding them that death is God's will, and that crying questions his will, causing the dead person to be tormented [ta'dhabat] in her grave.[51] Some women seem harshly unsympathetic, hissing, 'forbidden!' [Haram, haram!] or 'God forgive this blasphemy!' [Istaghfar Allah].[52] After the thalith, it is most unusual for the principal mourners to cry in public.

What is notable about condolence visits is the reversal of the norms of hospitality. Generously sweetened tea, the icon of ordinary hospitality, is replaced with an unsweetened drink made from coffee husks [qahwa murra].[53] The cushions and cloths which cover the Tihama beds during ordinary receptions are removed; the bereaved and condolers sit directly on the twine with which the beds are strung, which can be quite uncomfortable.[54] An alternate seating posture is adopted. Guests ordinarily tuck their legs up underneath themselves, reclining against pillows; but during mourning, women sit with their legs dangling over the edge of the bed. Tape recorders or television, both of which regularly provide background entertainment, are forbidden in a house of mourning. The comfortable reception area is made austere for mourning.

For the first ten days neither the condolers nor the hosts chew qat or smoke the mada'a. A grave silence characterizes the mourning session, in contrast to the animated volubility of ordinary gatherings. The mourners may read from a book containing the Qur'anic verses or say prayers on their prayer beads [misbaha]. From the eleventh day until the end of mourning the family receives offical visitors on Sundays, Tuesdays, and Fridays [ayyam al-barahi].[55] Official visits can also be paid in the morn-

---

50 Although formalized, these cries are very moving.

51 Accepting the death without tears is thought to be exceptionally virtuous, indicating the possession of the self-control necessary to submit to the will of God; it is said to merit a reward [ajar] in heaven.

52 The mourning sessions seem to depend on those further away to issue these chastisements, to remind the mourners of the will of God and of standards of decorum and modesty. The issuer of chastisements at one mourning session may have them delivered to her in turn when she is mourning the loss of a loved one.

53 Sweet and spiced with cardamom and ginger, qahwa is a popular Yemeni beverage. But unsweetened qahwa or tea is considered unpleasant; if offered ordinarily, it would suggest miserliness or extreme poverty.

54 One family decided to dispense with this custom, and had cushions on the beds during the first week of mourning. We had no sooner left the house than the women I was with criticized the family for this indulgence.

55 Elite women in Jiddah have a similar practice of establishing official mourning days (Altorki 1986:107–8).

ings. All of those with whom a family has relationships must show up to mourn on one of these days, and often on the remaining days as well, to keep company with the bereaved. On the remaining days qat can be chewed and the waterpipe may be smoked.[56]

The bereaved forgo their usual adornment for the duration of mourning. They wear special mourning gowns of plain white cotton, fashioned in a simple style.[57] If a man has died, his wife has special mourning garb and prohibitions against combing her hair for four months and ten days. No gold, makeup, henna, *khidhab*, or jasmine flowers may be worn by the mourners. The prohibition on these kinds of adornment extends to guests as well as the bereaved. The obligation of others to show respect by abstaining from consumption at mourning visits is just as powerful as the obligation to show respect by donning a nice gown at a wedding. Guests who are not kin do not wear the formal mourning dresses, but wear darkish-coloured dresses.[58] All mourners and condolers must cover their hair during the visit.

One ought to go into mourning a year for a parent and siblings, four months and ten days for a husband, and one month for a more distant relative.[59] (Infants are not mourned in this formal fashion, although a mother may stay in for ten days to mourn a prepubescent child.) However, these times may be extended, especially if the head of a *bayt kabir* has died. The wife and female relatives of a great man, I was told, would not leave the house for at least a year, and possibly longer.[60]

As proper Muslims, women recognize that, at death, no matter what status people are in this life, they become equal Muslim subjects before God, judged by him. Any physical marking of the grave which would serve to distinguish the deceased is dismissed as '*haram*,' as are any audible public demonstrations of grief. Yet through the quiet withdrawal of the women,

---

56 Qat stalks may not be discarded on the ground as usual. The chewers pile the stalks up neatly beside them on the couch. The bereaved may chew as well as long as they do not clean and prepare the qat themselves. When I asked why this should be so, people said 'It's just like that – it's shameful' [*Kidha bas, 'ayb*]. I suspect that to have discarded qat stems all over the ground would detract from the self-consciously austere atmosphere.

57 Plain black cotton gowns are often favoured by younger women.

58 Dresses worn to mourning sessions should not be *asli*, but rather should be made of cheaper fabric.

59 The length of these mourning practices in Zabid are in accordance with Islamic law, and hence bear close resemblance to the practices of Muslims elsewhere.

60 The responsibility to mourn primarily falls on the elder women, both married and unmarried. After one to four months, the younger women may go out to represent the family in public, but should not wear gold, *khidhab*, or makeup.

this-worldly distinctions are created between families.[61] Women who go into mourning are said to be indicating their respect [ihtiram] for their families. One's respect for oneself and one's family is indicated by one's propriety, and mourning in this fashion is an element of propriety.[62] By withdrawing from society, and deliberately forgoing the daily pleasures and comforts of life, as well as the accepted styles of dress and adornment, women create the honour of their families. The longer they withdraw, the greater the claim to honour. It tends to be the kabir families who can withdraw into formal mourning for long periods of time, who are 'official' [rasmi] about mourning standards.

Some, influenced by life in Saudi Arabia, argue against this practice, which they see as designed solely for this-worldly competitive purpose; they claim that all Zabidi families care about in mourning is their honour [namusahum]. They argue that these families are distorting Islamic doctrine in favour of their own honour.[63] But for those who live in Zabid, adhering to, or transgressing, mourning customs does affect one's reputation. Fear that the nas will talk about transgressions of mourning customs is justified. One family was criticized behind their backs for their laxity in mourning. One woman said, 'Oh, they are running out of the door covered in gold and jasmine before the body is in the grave!' One grandmother was furious because three weeks after a paternal uncle had died, her granddaughter, recently married into a neighbouring family, had gone to another city to attend a wedding with her husband's sisters. The grandmother argued that the girl's gadding about so soon after a death reflected on her husband's family's honour [sharaf] as well as their own. After a tense interchange between the women of the family, the male head of the household had the girl (his younger half-brother's wife) recalled from the wedding.[64]

At death, the tension between equality and hierarchy is evident. As good Muslims, the family should not mourn the death, or admit that one Muslim

61 In the Tunisian village studied by Abu-Zahra, death, like other life-cycle events, was an 'arena for competing for social prestige' (1991:31).

62 A woman in mourning is often referred to as muhtashima, a word similar in meaning to istihya'. Mourning properly, like behaving modestly, is a matter of self-respect, which in turn creates the reputation of one's family.

63 The Saudi-residing relatives of a young girl whose mother had recently died urged her to decorate herself for their wedding, saying that the Zabidis were 'foolish' [mukharrifin] to put their honour [namus] before their religion.

64 This anecdote hints at men's attitudes toward women's mourning customs. Men only mourn for three days, but do not encourage women to abandon their more elaborate mourning. Men seem to share the idea that a family's value is created by the respect women show for the dead by withdrawing from society.

is better than another. Yet this value, one strongly expressed, is in conflict with the desire to mark the distinctive value of one's family. This conflict is uneasily resolved in mourning customs. The desire to mark one's family's continued viability and value is expressed through the dramatic reversal of the usual norms of hospitality and consumption, and marked by the withdrawal of women from society and from their ordinary styles of adornment.

The continuing viability of the family despite their loss is marked by the number of women who go into mourning along with the immediate kin. As noted above, all agnatic kin and affinal kin and close neighbours should go into mourning. The reproduction of social ties and the honour of the family of the bereaved are achieved through mourning as well as through marriage. An element of domination is also present here: the death of a member of a great *bayt* will ensure that those connected to them will delay their own festive social events. One *bayt kabir* delayed the weddings of several other families with whom they were connected through affinal ties: it was considered shameful for these others to hold their weddings during the first month of the mourning period. This was an expression of the influence of this *bayt*; a death in other, lesser *bayts* would not have such a disruptive effect on the social plans of others.

Formal mourning ceremonies are not the appropriate forum for the expression of grief or sadness. Women obliged to mourn for distant relatives' spouses or affines may not have met the person they are mourning, although they sympathize with the grief of those who did. Grief tends to be spoken of as anger [*za'al*] which may often cause illness; sadness [*huzn*] is used to refer to the state of mourning or mourning clothes rather than an internal emotional state. Public displays of grief are anti-Islamic; and, as will be discussed in the next chapter, a modest and respectable woman does not give way to grief in an uncontrolled fashion any more than she expresses anger in an unfettered form.[65] The style of Zabidi women's mourning can be contrasted to that in Inner Mani, Greece (Seremetakis 1990, 1991), where grieving as work becomes a form of resistance to male-dominated discourses. In Zabid, although mourning is labour (sometimes tedious), it is an institution which upholds rather than subverts or resists relations of status.

Most women of the *nas* exercise great restraint and cry little in public

---

65 Once again the *akhdam* practices are contrasted with those of the *nas*. The *akhdam* are said to scream and cry uncontrollably at death, beating themselves and the dead body passionately.

after death. However, narratives about death and grief, told in informal settings, convey pain and a longing for the loved one. These narratives are not told in the formal mourning sessions. When speaking of deaths of loved ones after the fact, women emphasize their distraughtness, saying, 'We couldn't stop crying for months.' Speaking of a young man who had been tragically killed in a car accident shortly after his marriage and university graduation, 'All of Zabid cried for that young man and his poor mother. Every house one went into people were crying, for months.' These narratives, often elaborately detailed and very moving, convey a sense of personal loss and a remembering of a distinct individual which is not expressed in the formal mourning ceremonies, where the identity of the *bayt* as a whole is at issue. These narratives frequently express the fact that anger and grief at a death may be somatized as illness; women often connect illness to the shock of the death of a loved one.

Death of a *Khadim*

The connection between mourning and social status was made particularly clear when a *khadim*, Ibrahim, who had lived as a servant and a permanent resident in a *bayt kabir*, Bayt Mahmud Hazimi, suddenly died, forcing them to take some action on how his life was to be recognized. His death was sudden and shocking to Bani Hazimi; although he had been growing thinner and weaker for months, no one had seemed to notice.

Ibrahim was a kindly old man, with an enormous smile, often on our street doing bits of shopping or odd chores for the family, asking all who passed, male or female, if their destination was 'our house.' He was famous in our neighbourhood for his gracious greetings at the door of Bayt Hazimi, where he would entreat guests to 'Enter among us!' [*Dukhuli 'indana*]. He had known no other home and took as much concern over the affairs and events of Bayt Hazimi as they themselves did. When the family had married their sons the year before, Ibrahim had been in the thick of the hectic wedding preparations.

I dropped by Bayt Hazimi by chance the afternoon of Ibrahim's death, just after his body had been taken to the graveyard. Everyone was in an uproar; the children were distressed. Ibrahim had often supervised the young children, who appeared to return his obvious affection for them. Layla, the sister of the head of the household, announced the effort they had gone to the night before when the seriousness of Ibrahim's illness had become apparent to them. She told how they had roused the pharmacist to administer medicines, worth, she said, 50 riyals. (When a son in the family had fallen sick a month earlier, he had been whisked to al-Hudayda in a taxi.) Layla also noted the few possessions Ibrahim had left behind, a few white loin cloths (a new one, she noted, they had purchased for him for their wedding), a few riyals which must have been frugally saved from his tiny daily salary of 3 riyals, and a few clay receptacles for tobacco, although he did not smoke. This meagre cache so carefully hoarded seemed poignant in the context of the wealthy family's finely decorated home.

As a neighbour, I was asked to join Bayt Hazimi in the evening of this death, because they were 'sitting in the house' for three days because of Ibrahim's death. (They did not use the word for formal mourning [ta'azi].) The older women of Bayt Hazimi were already in mourning because a distant paternal kinswoman's husband had died. This kinswoman attacked 'Umara, the wife of the head of Bayt Hazimi, and Layla, his sister, saying that Ibrahim was 'only a khadim' and that their duty was to mourn for her husband. 'Umara and Layla were offended, and told her that he had been 'their khadim,' and said, 'He was one of us' [huwa min 'indana].

The gathering that evening, however, was not a formal mourning session, which reflected the family's uneasiness about how, in fact, they ought to acknowledge Ibrahim's passing. It was the first time in our year-long association that I saw these women, who were usually so decisive in their judgment of what was appropriate, appear uneasy about anything. Despite their recognition of a certain shared identity based on their long life together, Ibrahim was not considered part of their bayt in its genealogical sense. They were flouting convention by recognizing him at all – in view of their previous mourning obligations – but they felt it necessary to recognize his death in some fashion. However, there were clearly limits: Ibrahim was granted the minimal mourning period owed a Muslim – three days – and no mourning clothes were worn, nor were the couches stripped of their cushions. Only the family's closest neighbours and clients attended, not the wider circle of associates who were present at their wedding the year before, and who would have been present had a 'real' member of the family died.

Ibrahim had lost touch with his own natal kin. Although his mother was alive, he had not seen her in years, and she did not come to acknowledge his death. She was a servant in another elite home. It seems their identities had been subsumed under the families they were servants for, at the expense of the maintenance of their own natal kin ties.

On the third day of mourning I went with the family and a few neighbours to visit Ibrahim's grave just before sundown. We squatted around the grave. The young boys and girls were reciting the Qur'an; the eldest trembled slightly as he saw his mother silently wipe her eyes, but he kept on reciting in a clear voice. All the children in the family were deeply disturbed by the death; the smallest boy, age three, wanted to stay at the graveside to wait for Ibrahim. The adults were troubled, too, about the fate of Ibrahim's soul; he had never prayed, which accounted, in their eyes, for his tremendous fear of death.[66] As dusk settled, we laid basil on the grave and slowly walked back to their house in unusual silence.

We gathered in the house again after the visit to the graveyard. Unlike formal mourning sessions, where silence reigns, those present reminisced about Ibrahim, recalling anecdotes about him and his kind invitations to them. It was because of his low status that all the neighbourhood women had been able to get to know Ibrahim and become fond of him. One neighbour noted that the death announcement from the mosque had referred to Ibrahim as 'The *khadim* of Mahmud Hazimi.' She wondered if perhaps they should have said 'slave' [*abd*] because it sounded nicer. To this another neighbour responded, 'We are all the *akhdam* of God,' changing the usual phrasing, which is 'We are all the poor [*masakin*] or slaves [*abid*] of God.' It was only after Ibrahim's death that his shared identity with them, as people equally subordinate before God, was belatedly acknowledged.

I relate this anecdote in such detail because it reveals a great deal about the way social categories and the value of persons are constructed and reproduced. I do not think any of Bani Hazimi would have contested Ibrahim's goodness as a person, and they obviously felt that at least he ought to be granted a proper Muslim burial, despite elite doubts about whether the *akhdam* are proper Muslims. I think they were also quite fond of Ibrahim, particularly the younger children; this closeness and familiarity, however, was not allowed to override fully the status distinctions between them. Although he defined himself in terms of Bayt Mahmud Hazimi, and their house as his house, they did not consider him 'one of the family.' Their provision of medicine for him, and his burial expenses, were considered charitable acts rather than the obligations of kin.

Ibrahim's death was problematic for this family; in a practical sense, they had to make adjustments to the loss of a member of their household. (And indeed, on the evening of his death, Layla was interviewing some

---

66 When one of the guests (implicitly critical) suggested that it had been their responsibility to teach him to be a good Muslim, Layla uneasily answered that in the past people did not teach their *khadims* how to pray, and that training had to begin young to be effective.

akhdam to take over Ibrahim's job of sweeping their courtyards.) But in another sense, this exceptional case also expresses a problem inherent in Zabidi ideas about hierarchy, probably not uncommon in hierarchical societies where servants and masters live together: how to mark the passing of one who is socially inferior, but affectively close, without undermining the relations of hierarchy. For a brief moment, I think that they were aware that their upholding of a system which excludes a certain class of people, and defines them as morally opposite, distant others, also constrains them in particular ways. This anecdote exemplifies some of the ambiguity of how hierarchical relations are lived in Yemen, where prejudices against a group may be undermined by knowledge and affection for an individual.

Conclusion

Both weddings and mourning ceremonies mark the transition of an individual from one state to another. Yet in these ceremonies the individual is less a focus than is the family of which he or she is a member. The hospitality and conspicuous consumption which characterizes weddings is dramatically reversed in mourning, as are practices of adornment. Yet both events are moments which are central to defining the identity of the *bayt*. The state of the family, whether celebratory or mournful, is evident in the comportment of women's bodies. At funerals the impact of women's practices on the men's is evident. Men only mourn publicly for three days, whereas the women's mourning periods rearrange the social schedules of their *bayt* and their affines, agnates, and often close neighbours.

Both mournings and weddings are moments when the host family essentially demands recognition from its associates. Failing to attend without just cause is grounds for severance of social ties. Familial identity and status are created in the process of exchanging formal recognition. The number of guests or condolers that come in person to pay their respects constitute the family's prestige in the public eye. This fact is perhaps more significant in mourning: at weddings, the obligation to recognize the other is bolstered by the desire to attend a performative event valued in its own right, whereas mourning visits, especially in the long later months after the shock of a death has passed, can be tedious and uncomfortable.

7

Personhood, Emotion, and Hierarchy

Emotional displays are intimately bound up in the practices of Zabidi sociability. One of the most obvious qualities which mark everyday interaction in Zabid is the frequent declaration of anger. I rarely witnessed a social occasion during which one woman did not say to another, 'I'm angry [za'alana] with you – you visited Bayt So-and-So instead of our house,' or 'Why didn't you visit me when my father was sick?' I received plenty of such accusing challenges myself, and I was at first mystified by them. After a few weeks in Zabid, I had the uncomfortable feeling that the entire female population was angry with me, for omissions that I neither intended nor even fully understood.

The meanings assigned to emotions in Zabid are related to the specific nature of the competitive, hierarchical society. Following Myers (1988:591-2), I view the enactment of emotion as a semiotic practice, which involves evaluations of particular situations. Myers suggests that the universal logic of emotions is related to the 'existential situation of human subjects in a socio-moral order,' but also that the meanings of emotions in a particular society are related to its social structure. This chapter considers one particular emotion, anger [za'al], as it is understood and commonly enacted in Zabid. Anger in Zabid, as elsewhere, is a moral assessment of transgressions in the context of particular social relationships (Harre 1984:123), or a definition of the relationship between oneself and something or someone valued (Myers 1988:594). Emotional displays are part of the form and style of sociability; individuals among the Zabidi *nas* try to ensure that their family receives the recognition they consider their due. I discuss how displays of emotions are related to the nature of the competitive social structure and how anger is dialectically related to other emotions such as love [hubb]. The less-negotiable distinctions between the estates are marked (and justified) by differing styles of emotional displays. The final section discusses some of the ways in which anger is enacted within families.

Identity and Emotion: The *Nas*

As previously noted, the social structure, particularly the ranking between *nas* families, is emergent, inherent in the practice of visiting. An agreed-upon premise of life in Zabid is that the social world is hierarchically structured: the subordinate position of the *akhdam* to the *nas* is unquestioned. What is not agreed upon (and potentially malleable) is the place of *nas* families in relation to each other. In his discussion of honour, Meeker notes: 'One's sharaf cannot be simply accomplished, it must be recognized' (1976:250). The mutual recognition of each other's honour which is accomplished by this exchange of hospitality is required to establish one's place within the hierarchy of Zabidi society. Distinctions between families are continually created and contested in this process of exchanging visits, at the same time as people try to maintain equal, balanced relationships with those whom they consider of the same standing.

This centrality of forms of sociability to the status of one's family is related to the way in which anger is shown by the Zabidi *nas*. The negotiation of attendance at each other's social functions is the context in which displays of anger most often occur. A 'moral judgment' is required to identify what one is feeling as a particular emotion. Anger as a concept, Harre suggests, 'requires the grasp of a quite definite social fact, for instance, a specific social relation between persons, assessed within the local moral order. Anger requires the assessment of an interference with oneself or some other with whom one has bonds of care and responsibility as a transgression.' (1984:123)

In the context of the Zabidi moral order, exclusion to visit or invite constitutes a threat to one's person and family, which results in justifiable anger. Because the standing of one's family in Zabid depends so greatly on public respect created by the recognition implicit in the act of visiting, women are quick to act on any snub. Slights are perceived as challenges to one's position which have to be answered, usually through anger.

Given the fact that most families have fairly wide-ranging ties, a family's social obligations inevitably conflict. Whether or not a deliberate slight was intended, the neglected party expresses anger. Neglect suggests that another family is valued over one's own; one's family has been given less recognition than another, therefore implying that one's family is somehow less significant. That Zabidis explicitly make this connection between visiting and hierarchy is evident in the accusation commonly hurled at someone who has not visited in a while – that she is snobbish [*mutakabbira*]. This accusation is often delivered sardonically, revealing the fury of a woman who would not admit that the other families her family has been neglected in favour of are any better than is hers. Others read connections, relative status, and the quality of relationships from presences or absences, so very public statements are made at each social event. If a particular family does not make an appearance at a formal, invited party, the members will be asked by mutual acquaintances why they were not present. If they have been overlooked by the host family, they will say bitterly they were not invited. Conversely, host families take careful note of who among those invited did not show up.

Failure to recognize key life-cycle events – in visits or invitations – is interpreted as an offence. At Ramadan, every family which has connections to one's family must be visited: not to do so is a strong insult. Neglect suggests the family has been dropped entirely from one's social network. Not visiting in times of grave illness will seriously compromise a relationship.[1]

Another serious transgression is negative gossip. Women often claim that Zabid must be the most gossip-ridden place on earth, and great care is made to ensure one's family does not become the focus of negative talk. Topics of gossip which are considered inflammatory include any slander that suggests a moral failure. This can range from hints of sexual impropriety, allegations of stinginess, or assertions of failure to honour obligations to kin or neighbours. To be identified as the source of negative gossip is to open oneself to extreme anger from those gossiped about. Women do gossip, but most are very circumspect about it and are reluctant to reveal their sources. They say merely that they heard it 'from the people' [*'ind al-nas*] instead of naming the particular person. As much as failure to recognize one socially through visits or invitation, negative gossip threatens one's place in society by besmirching one's reputation.

Anger is not only a response to an offence. It can also be used as a strategy or tactic. Everyday displays of anger are very much a part of how women attempt to manipulate each other and to manage their relationships with other families. To face one's insulter directly is appropriate; allowing

---

1   Altorki (1986:102–9) provides a detailed account of similar practices in Jiddah, Saudi Arabia. Breaches between women are often mediated by others; in Zabid, a serious affront may require extensive mediation to mend the relationship

people to snub one without redress is not, nor is grovelling for attention.[2] This expression of anger is the appropriate response of a self-respecting person who demands respect from other people. It is considered a duty to one's family to demand respect, although this sentiment is closely intertwined with a sense of offence against one's self. Since personal identity is so closely tied to familial identity, the treatment of each individual member has implications for all: an insult to one will result in the other members displaying anger on his or her behalf. Small children (under the age of ten) took umbrage if we had not visited their families, even at this tender age reacting to a perceived threat to their families. Anger is a reaction to insult to self, and it also implies an obligation. One only gets angry with someone who 'ought' to visit one, with whom some tie exists, or ought to exist. If one does not receive an invitation to a social event held by a family with whom one does not have an actual or potential relationship, there is no anger involved. One merely says, without anger, 'I'm not invited' [*Ana mush ma'azuma*].

In contrast, when an omission has been committed by one with whom one has a relationship, a Zabidi woman faces the offending woman directly. However, the style of declaring anger is very formalized, without any indication of loss of control. Anger is expressed by a declaration in a sharp tone of voice stating the alleged wrong committed by the other and demanding a response from the offender. The wronged woman makes every effort to insist that the transgression was entirely the other woman's fault, that she and her family have been snubbed without cause. While attempting to pin fault on the other, the woman also emphasizes her own goodness and loyalty, saying, for example, 'We always visit you when you have a special occasion [*munasaba*],' which, combined with the veiled threat of severance of ties ('Why should we visit you if you don't visit us?'), is usually enough to convince the offender to offer appropriate excuses, make amends in the form of a swift visit, or even, very occasionally, apologize. Should the offender provide adequate mollification, the incident will likely be forgiven if not forgotten.

Excuses which are considered valid are: sickness of oneself or a family member; a death of someone close; or obligations to work or school, although the latter are accepted only grudgingly, particularly by older women, who consider the 'work' of visiting more important. A woman also uses the anticipated anger of others to whom she is close as a way of

2   I knew one woman who would not get angry but would sulk and snivel in order to get attention, which most other women found laughable and silly.

getting out of another, more distant social obligation. A diplomatic woman frequently excuses herself by claiming obligation to those who are known to take precedence, like agnatic kin, affines, or neighbours. For instance, a woman may state: 'I had to attend a party at my paternal uncle's home' or 'My mother's sister's daughter had a baby,' or 'My neighbours have a wedding.' The neglected woman may grumble that her friend could have spared a little time, but she would have to agree that it would be shameful [ʿayb] not to fulfil obligations to kin and neighbours. Justifiable anger can only result when a woman is free to fulfil an obligation, and *chooses* to do something else instead.

A legitimate excuse offered by the offender undercuts one's right to be angry; however, it must be plausibly delivered in order to save the 'face' (Goffman 1967:5–45) of the injured party. Therefore, the process of juggling one's obligations to avoid angering others requiries considerable diplomatic skill.[3] One woman explained an absence by exaggerating the amount of time she had stayed in her house due to illness. By apologizing and offering the legitimate excuse of serious illness (along with a dramatic rendition of her gruesome symptoms), she conveyed that she had not been trying to snub them. They in turn, by not pushing her with inquiries about how long her illness had lasted, by expressing sympathy, and by ceasing their reproaches, indicated that they accepted the excuse. Another tactic employed to handle angry inquiries diplomatically is the 'polite lie.' Women quickly lie about the whereabouts of their kin when questioned by the hostess, saying, 'My sister is at home,' when in fact she is attending another party. Lying [kidhb] is considered a sin according to Islam, but women never referred to these statements as lies but rather as something one says to avoid angering people.[4] Diplomatic lying is constantly employed in the daily management of social relations.[5] Diplomatic strategies have to be employed by everyone, rich or poor. Unless relations are mended, any self-respecting family will adamantly refuse to enter the home of those who have insulted them. There is no *bayt* so *kabir* that they can

---

3   At first, when I was asked why I had not turned up at a social event, I would baldly state that I had accepted another invitation from Bayt So-and-So, implying to my hostesses that I preferred another family over theirs, which is both impolite and naive. I soon learned the error of my ways.

4   Gilsenan's (1976) discussion of lying in Lebanon includes the linguistic strategies designed to control the flow of information, especially that which would be harmful to the reputation of one's family.

5   When I learned how to 'lie' quickly and convincingly, a friend laughed and said, 'Anne, now you know Zabid!'

afford to antagonize others recklessly by refusing to acknowledge them, because any large-scale social event requires the cooperation of other families, a point noted in the last chapter on weddings.

Part of the emotional intensity which infuses the negotiation of visiting has to do with the fact that respect is granted through the physical presence of another in one's own home. Between neighbours, there is often inequality in visiting, but poorer neighbours will often try to gain a minimal recognition from wealthier neighbours by angrily asserting their right, in terms of the egalitarian ethos of *jiran* relationships, to receive at least a minimal acknowledgment of their respectability through visits from their loftier neighbours.

Love and Anger

Anger is closely connected to love [*hubb*]. A few months into my stay, I asked a friend why everyone in Zabid always seemed to be angry. She laughed and said, 'If people don't love you, they would not be angry with you for not visiting them. They would not care where you had been or who you had been with.' In Zabid, having people angry with one is infinitely preferable to indifference, which implies that one's presence is not desirable or even necessary. The relationships by which one's position in society is achieved are managed through expressions of anger but also of love. People do not, of course, talk about 'reproducing relationships' (*cf.* Fajans 1993) but they constantly talk about how they 'love' some people and are 'angry' at others. Of the two, love, indicating positive social relations, is preferable; but both are better than the alternative – insignificance. People often complain of the burden [*ta'ab*] of the continual conflict over obligation and the wearisome aspect of having to go out, lest someone get angry, when one really would rather stay at home. However, the merest hint that one's presence is not desired or valued is far worse than any anger or inconvenience. This state of affairs would clearly indicate one's exclusion from the 'community of significance.'

Anger and love presuppose each other.[6] This connection between love and anger is such that people often say they are angry when a loved one is temporarily absent. Visiting is often talked about as indicating love. Often two families with a close relationship may say, 'We love them and they love us. We always go to their house and they come to ours.' Acknowledgment

---

6   This structuring of emotions is similar to the dialectical relationship between anger and compassion among the Pintupi (Myers 1988:597).

of one's significance, through visiting, is fused with the sentiment of love, which contributes the warmth and delight which sometimes characterize women's visits. Lack of acknowledgment, in contrast, is fused with anger, hence contributing the bitter tension that also inflects the practice of visiting. Meeker's interesting discussion of honour suggests that love represents unity and connectedness, and is associated with femaleness. Maleness, in contrast, signifies the honour of the family (or clan), therefore structuring the distinctions between families or groups. He states: 'Maleness is active and structures, while femaleness is a formless overarching unity of "love"' (1976:386n). While the visiting practices of Zabidi women do serve to unite the community, they also serve to create distinctions. Visiting, recognizing each other's worth, is often talked about as love. But love, far from being formless, distinguishes between those who are loved (and valued) and those who are not. Meeker's assertion that maleness equals significance and femaleness equals unity seems overdrawn; in Zabid, women's work in visiting serves to both unify families and signify distinctions between them.

Politeness

As may be expected, the closer the relationship, the more intense the anger at a slight or insult. But in the course of any social occasion, declarations of anger are often so common as to constitute a category of greeting in themselves. In this case, anger will be declared in a light and friendly tone, as a woman playfully exaggerates her abject misery at the absence of the other. In this usage, anger is employed as a 'play frame' (Bateson 1972:177–93), with the frame 'this is play' being established by the tone of voice. Through this kind of statement of anger, women politely demonstrate their connection, their love of the other. It is part of the aggressive welcoming that hostesses extend to guests. It is a form of honouring the guest by stressing how much her presence is valued. The hostess says, 'I'm mad at you – where have you been? We never see you!' The guest routinely replies, 'I've only been in my house' [Fi al-bayt bas], an implausible claim. The exchange usually stops there. These exchanges can be distinguished from those described earlier not only by the tone of voice but also by content. For instance, when an insult has been registered, the offended party explicitly states the nature of the omission and demands a convincing excuse. While polite declarations of anger are playful, they are not meaningless flattery. Having no one ask where one has been, or claim anger at one's absence, is something of a worst-case scenario in Zabidi social life. It indicates that one's presence is merely tolerated. Since one cannot withhold hospitality without damaging one's own reputation, omitting these kinds of polite declarations of anger implies that the guest is not truly valued.

Inculcating Appropriate Emotion

As in every society, Zabidi children are trained in the appropriate expression of emotion. Being angry at a child under the age of five or six is viewed as pointless, because it is thought that children have no sense [*aql*]. Women who are provoked into slapping their children are criticized by whomever is around. (I never saw an adult beat a child seriously.) An unrestrained temper in an adult is seen as a sign of a shameful lack of self-control or even of craziness. If a child has a wild tantrum, adults do not try to control the child: rather, they let the tantrum run its course. The child is not punished afterward, although it may be mocked and teased, especially if she or he is older than five or six. Control of emotions must be achieved by the person, as reason is gradually acquired. It is not a capacity which can be engendered through a display of force.

Although very little effort is expended in controlling the misbehaviour of children, occasionally children are taught how to direct anger appropriately. If the child is provoked in some way, the women instruct the child as to where to direct anger. One girl hit her younger brother; his mother held the girl and instructed the brother to hit her as she had hit him.[7] A child who had hit his head on the edge of a bed was given a sandal and told to hit the bed that 'hurt' him 'with heat' [*bil hami*]. One evening I visited my friend Jamila, who was very sick with malaria. She greeted me with the news that her son Muhammad, aged five, was angry because she was sick. After a few minutes of conversation, she reclined on the bed, exhausted, closing her eyes. Jamila's friend Samira, also present, said to Jamila's little boy, 'Your mother is dead, look at her, her eyes are closed.' Muhammad started to scream in horror. His grandmother quickly intervened, telling Jamila to sit up for a moment, and saying to the child, 'She's not dead! Look at what a liar Samira is! Hit her for making you angry!' She grabbed a stick, instructing her grandson to give Samira a tap on the hand to punish her for her offence. The child was taught to react to his 'injury' (in this case, the needless fright) by directing his anger at its cause, Samira.

---

7 Older children are supposed to defer to younger children. There are no obvious differences in how male and female toddlers are treated. Differences are much more evident after the child acquires '*aql* and training in modesty begins in earnest.

Children gradually learn to focus anger toward its source, and as they age, they learn how to channel anger into the stylized form of adult Zabidis. While demonstrations of anger because one has been insulted are ubiquitous, any uncontrolled display, like the hurling of insults or physical violence, is considered base and incompatible with decent adult social intercourse.[8] Standing up for oneself and one's family in the face of a slight is laudable, but trying to provoke another woman to anger is not. While registering complaints about neglect are part of every social interaction, personal and acrimonious attacks on another woman are not acceptable. Others play a supportive role in making sure that unrestrained anger is suppressed. When an exchange between two women threatens to become vituperative, silence ensues, indicating that someone has gone too far. The other women withdraw verbal support from one or the other. Someone introduces a new (and neutral) topic of conversation, and any attempt to revert to the earlier conversation is ignored. At a wedding lunch, one neighbor, Ishraq, flew into a temper, accusing another, Magda, of laziness and unwillingness to help with the preparation of the meal. Magda said nothing to defend herself during Ishraq's lengthy and acrimonious attack, nor did any of the other women present, who merely tried to distract Ishraq. When the hostess of the lunch arrived belatedly, Magda quietly requested that she tell Ishraq of her contributions to the chores earlier in the morning. While Magda did not ultimately let Ishraq's accusations go unchallenged, she did not allow herself be drawn into argument. Ishraq shamed herself with her uncontrolled anger, especially since her accusations against Magda were unfounded. Those who are not able to express anger appropriately are considered childish, crazy, or low status, lacking modesty and respect for themselves.

Emotion, Modesty, and Hierarchy

The preceding section discussed the appropriate style of display of emotion in the everyday negotiation of social life among the Zabidi *nas*. In many societies, emotion discourses are related to power relations (Abu-Lughod and Lutz 1990:13–14); in Zabid, hierarchical relationships are connected to display of emotions. While the restraint the Zabidi *nas* show around conflict is not as extreme as it is in Oman, as described by C. Eickelman (1984) and Wikan (1982), it is still marked in comparison to the *qaba'il* and the *akhdam*. In Zabid, the differences in emotional expression between the *nas*

---

8 Physical violence between Zabidi men in public interactions is also uncommon.

and the *akhdam* are discussed both as an expression of hierarchical relationships, and as a justification for this hierarchy.[9]

The concept of modesty guides the development of a sense of personhood in reference to a code of morality that stresses containment of physical needs or desires, as evidenced by control of body and demeanour in public. Modesty also underlies the demonstration of all other emotions: having a sense of shame means that one would be embarrassed to express anger (and grief) without restraint. Thus the emotional dimension of modesty – shame or embarrassment – functions as a regulator of other emotions (see Myers 1988:605).[10] Display of emotions is thought to be related to both sense [*'aql*] and modesty, both of which are linked to the formation of mature persons and to social status.

The *Akhdam*

The hegemony of modesty is such that those who do not display it are thought to be inferior as a result. The *akhdam* are said to lack control over their emotions of anger and grief as a consequence of their lack of modesty. Metaphors of 'hotness' and 'coolness' are drawn upon in emotion discourses, as in the discourse of honour and modesty. Ideally, Zabidi women are supposed to be cool [*barid*] in their display of emotions: crying in public is discouraged, excessive giddiness is deplored, and extreme 'hotness' in the display of anger is associated with low status. As noted in chapter 4, hotness is also used to describe sexual passion; women are cooled through circumcision. The hotness of anger ought to be controlled by the exercise of self-control, as must any intimation of sexual interest. The *akhdam* appear not to share the evaluation of the hotness of anger as negative. At one social gathering, Latifa, a woman from a *bayt kabir*, inquired of a *khadima* as to why there is so much fighting, not only verbal but physical, at *akhdam* weddings. (Fighting at a non-*akhdam* wedding would, I imagine, be seen as shameful, although no one even mentioned the possibility to me. I saw no violence at any of the social events I attended.) The *khadima* replied, laughing, that anger made a party good because it was hot [*hami*]. This evaluation of anger as hot or burning [*haraq*] is shared by the *nas*, but

9 Studies of hierarchical societies in West Africa reveal a similar relationship between status and emotion: Riesman (1983, 1992) on the Fulani of Burkino Faso and Irvine (1990) on the Wolof of Senegal note how those higher up in the status hierarchy exhibit emotional restraint, while those lower are emotionally expressive.

10 As Myers notes for the Pintupi Aborigines of Australia (1986:120), 'shame' is a 'metasentiment' defined in relation to other emotions and an encompassing sense of personhood.

in contrast to the *akhdam*, the quality of hotness is perceived by them as negative, dangerous, and shameful.

Violent confrontations between women on the streets provoked by quarrels between their children are unthinkable for most Zabidi women. In contrast, *akhdam* women, while arguing on the streets, may hurl insults and lift their skirts or grab their crotches as a way of cursing each other.[11] I never saw this behaviour myself, but I heard a Zabidi woman tell of her shock and embarrassment upon witnessing this style of presenting anger. Her audience collapsed with laughter at this tale and some even hid their faces at the thought. A non-*akhdam* woman may get angry if she thinks her child is being unfairly bullied by another child, but even raising one's voice on the streets is considered a shameful loss of control by the *nas*. Anger arising from conflict between children is frowned upon because it is widely held that, as one woman told me, 'Children have no sense and they always fight, but a few minutes afterward they forget about it, so why should we [women] enter into the problems between *juhhal*?' (a common word for children which literally means 'the ignorant'). To take conflicts between children seriously is to lower oneself to their minimal level of self-control.

Relationships within *akhdam* families are reputed to be more violent than those in *nas* families. The *khadima* who helped out daily at my friend's home frequently complained that she and her co-wife were constantly beating each other over disagreements about the division of the housework. (The co-wife is younger and stronger than she and hence came out the better in physical conflicts.) Contentious women in a non-*akhdam* *bayt* will be asked, 'Why are you behaving like *khadimas*?' in hopes of shaming them into behaving in a fashion appropriate to the family's perceived or desired status.[12] The *akhdam* and the *nas* do not intermarry; one informant cited not only their lack of modesty as a reason why this should be so, but also the reputed *akhdam* propensity to anger and violence, which is thought to be incompatible with the familial solidarity and cooperation so essential to prestige and status in Zabid.

Another distinction in displays of anger is that the *akhdam* are said to channel anger into spirit possession. A consultant from a *bayt kabir* said that one should always be polite to the *akhdam* because when they get angry they become possessed by *zar* spirits and can become 'crazy.' The

---

11 A similar practice among the *akhdam* was noted by Ibn al-Mujawir in the thirteenth century (Smith 1993:166, 170 n48).

12 Among the *nas* disputes between family members should be hidden.

nas claim to be afraid of the *zar* ceremonies and never attend them, although the woman who performs *zar* exorcisms (an ex-slave) was treated with awe and a fearful respect. I never saw or even heard of a *zar* ceremony while I was in Zabid, and as social events they are even more marginal to mainstream Zabidi society than are the *akhdam* themselves. When my husband brought home two unusual iron and silver ankle bracelets from the suq, my landlady became alarmed, saying that they are used in the *zar* cult. She warned me not to wear them lest they attract the *zar* spirits and make me crazy.[13]

The *Qabaʾil*

In hierarchical societies, it is common for ideas of personhood to be linked to hegemony, and therefore emotional expression is understandably a location of significant differences between persons. While the *akhdam* provide an ever-present contrast to the *nas*, the tribespeople reside outside of Zabid and are encountered primarily at large social events like weddings. The *qabaʾil* also have a quite different attitude toward the display of anger and confrontation. While their comportment is not morally opposed to that of the Zabidis, it has different emphases. The Zabidis are in awe of the propensity of the *qabaʾil* to retaliate over slights swiftly and sometimes violently. I was advised to use caution with the *qabaʾil* because they 'get very angry.'

I accompanied my Zabidi friends to several *qabaʾil* weddings outside Zabid. The tribeswomen appeared to be impatient with the Zabidis and their pretensions to superior sophistication. At one wedding, my friend Samiya began teasing them by saying that I was her sister. When they demanded to know what *bayt* 'we' were from, Samiya refused to tell them. As the name of one's father's *bayt* is how one is primarily identified, refusing to tell the name of one's *bayt* is considered disingenuous and therefore suspicious behaviour. The tribeswoman, annoyed by Samiya's refusal, and unconvinced I was Samiya's sister, angrily asked why she was lying to them, glaring furiously at us. A more diplomatic Zabidi woman intervened, saying that Samiya was a tease, and that she just called me her sister because we were friends; anyone, she said, could see I was a foreigner. Samiya told her the name of her father's *bayt* and the tension was diffused, although the tribeswoman still appeared unappreciative of Samiya's sense of humour.

13 Perhaps the *zar* cult, if it is in fact a central practice for the *akhdam*, may comprise some sort of counter-hegemonic discourse, as Boddy suggests for Sudanese women (1989:5). The horror with which the *nas* discuss the *zar* suggests that it may form a source of power for the *akhdam*, albeit one which is disparaged and dismissed as anti-Islamic by the majority of the Zabidis.

I had the opportunity to witness discussions about the nature of these distinctions between the qaba'il and the Zabidis through my friendship with Jamila, who was raised in Zabid, and her paternal cousin, Tayyiba, who lived in the wadi. Tayyiba often visited Jamila's family in Zabid, staying a few weeks at a time. For the most part, Tayyiba was very sweet-tempered, but at a party, a Zabidi woman, showing the common Zabidi chauvinism, teased Tayyiba, saying that Zabid was far superior to the wadi. Tayyiba said heatedly that the wadi was 'heavenly' [jinan] and that the qaba'il had honour [sharaf], implying that the Zabidis did not. The Zabidi woman, still teasing, asked her why she did not leave the party and go straight back to the wadi. Tayyiba assumed that the woman was implying she was not welcome at the party. Tayyiba was enraged and retorted that if she were at her adversary's house, she would certainly leave, but as she was an invited guest at another woman's home, she, Tayyiba, would stay as long as she pleased.

Tayyiba explained to me that she was a tribeswoman and did not suffer insults lightly, and that if anyone insulted her, she was obliged to return the insult with one ten times as scathing. Tayyiba was applauded by some of the women for standing up for herself, but her cousin Jamila said to me later that she would prefer to go home and cry in private if insulted rather than make a scene. After Tayyiba had calmed down, she announced that for Jamila's sake she would try to be patient with these women from Zabid, as Jamila became visibly upset at harsh words.

Jamila's reaction to Tayyiba's display of temper illustrates how most of the nas in Zabid perceive the appropriate response to unjust provocation. Several women explained to me, Jamila among them, that if one were provoked, it would be far better to maintain one's dignity and control through silence rather than answer heatedly, as Tayyiba had done. Jamila explained that in Zabid, people would think she was bad [mush tamam] if she reacted as Tayyiba had done, while noting that Tayyiba's anger was neither exceptional, nor unacceptable, for the qaba'il. For the nas, being angry is not an excuse to be out of control. Physical violence, screaming, or even scathing verbal exchanges are not acceptable ways of expressing anger in public contexts. This difference between Zabidi and qaba'il shows of anger was often explained to me as a key distinction by which their different identities were constituted.[14]

14 Zabidis are particularly in awe of the reputation of highland tribesmen for violent anger. A Zabidi proverb says, 'Hit a jinni [demon], but don't hit a Jebali [person from the highlands].' Caton's (1990:29–31) discussion of the way anger is expressed by highland qaba'il suggests that their form of displaying anger is not uncontrolled either. However, the tendency for angry confrontations among the qaba'il to escalate at least into a symbolic form of violence is a difference held to be significant by the Zabidis.

Tayyiba invited Jamila and myself to the wadi the day after *'id al-kabir*, and we accepted, but in the face of pressures from neighbours, we spent the day in Zabid. Jamila forgot to telephone Tayyiba to cancel our engagement. We faced Tayyiba's wrath on her return to Zabid as well as a long lecture on how the *qaba'il* kept their word, and one could never trust the Zabidis to show up when they were invited, she said. This last accusation was a little unfair, although it is true that in Zabid, a certain amount of prevarication is necessary in order to juggle conflicting invitations.[15]

Anger within *Nas* Families

The discussion so far has focused on anger and love as they are enacted in relations in public. Such expressions within the family have a different tenor. As previously noted, violence or anger within families of the Zabidi *nas* is considered shameful and people try to conceal it if it occurs. Although most families have quarrels, of course, incessant conflict makes the family appear weak and divided to outsiders. Given the proximity of houses in Zabid, and the fact that much activity takes place in courtyards, altercations are easily overheard by the neighbours. Families try to hide truly acrimonious fights about shameful topics, with varying degrees of success.[16] Fathers and husbands, however, do have the acknowledged right to beat or discipline recalcitrant dependants, but what is shameful is the necessity of doing so.

As discussed in chapter 3, relationships between natal family members are ideally characterized by love. If they are instead characterized by cruelty or neglect, a woman will be struck at her most vulnerable point. A woman is loathe to complain about her natal family to outsiders, as this generally tarnishes the reputation of the family as a whole, and her ultimate security depends on them. An unmarried woman may be particularly vulnerable after the death of her father, if her brother resents supporting her.[17] When the household is taken over by her brother, who will usually be married with children at this point, conflicts may arise.

One friend, Latifa, an unmarried woman, described to me the subtle

---

15 Several ethnographic accounts of visiting in urban contexts in the Middle East (e.g., Aswad [1974] and Dorsky [1986]) note how prevarication is necessary to avoid conflict. This may not be necessary or possible in the small villages where the *qaba'il* live.

16 Generally, the *kibar* are more successful at this than the weaker families.

17 Bonds between brother and sister are ideally (and often in practice) very strong and affectionate; an unmarried woman does have the right to stay in her natal home. Any transgression of this norm is considered a hurtful betrayal.

transformations in her family after the death of her father. Her elder half-brother became the head of the household which at that point comprised her half-brother's wife and their children, Latifa, her sister and brother, and her mother, their father's second wife. After her father's death, her elder brother became very grudging with money for gold and dresses for his younger sisters and their mother, although he was more than generous with his wife and daughters. Latifa's mother said to her, 'He encroaches on our rights' [*Akl min haqqana*], and confronted him angrily. She reminded him that they were not mere charity cases, but in fact had rights in the estate which he managed.[18] Latifa was very angry over her brother's treatment of them, particularly because she had always been very fond of him. Latifa concluded that it was this situation, compounded by her grief over her father's death, that caused a serious illness which struck her shortly thereafter.[19] Latifa astutely noted she was far more secure than unmarried women in poorer families, whose families had no land.[20] I was privy to this information because of my close friendship with Latifa; the family as a whole presented a seamless face of harmony to the community.

Married women can manage their relationships with their husbands through an institutionalized form of anger. The mistreated wife leaves her husband's home for her natal home, not to return until he goes after her [*yaruh ba'dha*] bearing gifts and apologies. The wife is said to be angry or fed up [*ghadbana*].[21] One woman was angered by her husband's failure to supply the presents owed to her on the occasion of the 'id: money and a new dress. She left in a fury when her husband decided to invite men to chew qat the same evening she had invited her friends. Their house was built in such a fashion that the women would have to walk through the men's *mabraz* to reach the interior of the house, where the female guests are received. She argued that her friends would be embarrassed [*musti-*

---

18 In fact, according to Islamic inheritance laws, Latifa's brother had inherited an equal share to his half-brother; she and her sister had each received half as much as the brothers; and her mother had received an eighth. This amounted to a considerable amount of land; the total land of the family made them one of the largest landholders in Zabid.

19 Long-term anger as a consequence of mistreatment by a family member is thought to be very injurious to one's health.

20 Although women do not control the land themselves, the fact that they have a recognized right of inheritance gives them a stronger bargaining position in the family. Women are very attuned to the material bases of influence. Mundy (1979), in her study of a highland community, discusses this issue at length. Women in Zabid may choose to inherit a room in the natal home instead of land, ensuring the security of a place to live in case of divorce.

21 This is similar to a wife being *mughtaza* among the Awlad 'Ali Bedouin (Abu-Lughod 1986:101) or *hanaga* among 'Amranis (Dorsky 1986:141).

hiyyat) at the thought and would not attend her party. Her husband paid her no heed. This last inconsiderate act on the part of her husband was enough to make her return to her mother's *bayt*, where she stayed for three months, until her husband came to fetch her. Zabidi observers told me that the husband was likely spurred on to quicker action because the wife was pregnant for the first time in thirteen years. When she had returned to her mother's house previously, her husband did not go after her for a year. By declaring that she is *ghadbana*, a woman declares righteous anger at her husband and puts the onus on him to reconcile. This process provides an opportunity for the woman to declare her anger formally; and it gives the husband time to calm down, reconsider his behaviour, and signify his willingness to rectify the situation without resort to the extreme step of divorce. A woman whose natal family is too poor or is unwilling to support her may not have this option. She may therefore have to turn to neighbours or kin to convince her husband to behave properly toward her.[22]

Another problematic and painful circumstance in which anger may occur is when the husband decides to take a second wife. While women hestitate to condemn the institution entirely – as it is allowed in Islamic law – it is generally unpopular, particularly if a man's first wife is fertile. Although some households where one man had two wives operated quite smoothly, a few women cited a proverb, 'The new makes the old mad.' Some women were said to bear their anger and hurt (literally, burning [*haraq*]), with patience [*sabr*]; others could not, especially if the husband did not disguise a preference for the new wife. These households were characterized by constant fighting and bitterness. The first wife of a man in our neighbourhood was said to be virtually paralysed with illness after years of conflict with her contentious co-wife.

Much of the anger within families centres around the issue of marriage. As in many patrilineal, patrilocal societies, the new bride's entrance into the household is a time of tension. In Zabid, much of this tension seems to revolve around the bride's relationship with her husband's sisters and his mother. The typical areas of conflict concern the distribution of resources and the domestic labour. Usually these problems are ironed out within the

---

22 I heard an unusual story about a woman whose natal kin were in Aden, though she, her husband, and children lived in Zabid. She was very angry with her husband, who persisted in drinking his salary away, leaving insufficient funds for feeding and clothing the family. In her rage, she poured kerosene over herself, and lit it. She was quite badly burned, although she survived. She succeeded, through this startling strategy, in shaming her husband. Her neighbours pressed the man to reform his habits. Most Zabidis were horrified by her actions.

first year of marriage, and in many families what was notable was not the discord but the affection and cooperation between the brother's wife and her female in-laws. However, this is not always the case. Ahmad, of Bayt Sulayman Fadhal, married his father's brother's daughter, Hannan, of Bayt Abdullah Fadhal. She had born him five sons and was pregnant with her sixth child when the trouble which had been brewing for many years came to a head. There had been tensions between the two families for some time: Ahmad's and Hannan's fathers were embroiled in an inheritance dispute. Their mothers, who were also sisters, were no longer on speaking terms. Ahmad's sister, Nowal, and Hannan had a particularly hostile relationship. A fierce fight broke out between Nowal and Hannan over a petty issue, the distribution of jasmine flowers. (Ahmad had bought enough for all the women in the family to attend a formal party, but Hannan accused Nowal of taking more than her share.) Hannan complained to Ahmad, who hit Nowal and sent Hannan back to her natal home, saying that he was sick of the continual fighting in the household.

In Hannan's absence, Nowal managed, practically single-handedly, to arrange an engagement between Ahmad and a young woman from another Zabidi neighbourhood, hoping Ahmad would divorce Hannan. When the wedding was announced a month later, Ahmad's two paternal aunts complained to him about his unjust treatment of his cousin, and their niece, Hannan. In a fury, Ahmad told them to leave his house. The aunts had a right to stay in their natal home; the insult was made even more galling by the fact that these two aunts had fondly helped care for Ahmad's children since their birth. They both took up residence in a neighbour's house which was temporarily vacant and ate with Hannan's family.

The wedding party took place with the notable absence of these paternal aunts, so these further problems in the family became public, and the topic of much speculation. The party itself was small, as is common for a man's second marriage, but it was made smaller by the fact that several of the invited guests did not attend out of sympathy with Hannan's family or the paternal aunts. After the wedding, Ahmad installed his new bride in a new house he had built some distance from the main household. Hannan, fiercely bitter over Ahmad's marriage, remained at her father's house, where she bore her child, another son. I heard before I left that he planned to take her back, although I cannot imagine that relations between her and Nowal would have been improved. The paternal aunts returned to Ahmad's household after he agreed not to divorce Hannan and had formally apologized to them.

This crisis is illustrative of how anger generated within families, if unchecked, can reverberate out into the community. The wider social networks of both families were affected; those who had close ties to both were forced to choose, or face the wrath of one or the other. The situation was made even more complicated by the fact that the two houses were in the same neighbourhood. Their mutual neighbours, regardless of their opinions about who was right and who was wrong, tried to maintain relationships with both, but remaining neutral was a difficult chore. To this end, the immediate neighbours all claimed to know nothing about what was going on, although the rest of Zabid was abuzz with gossip about the affair. The reputation of the family as a whole suffered greatly with this very public display of disharmony. None of the individuals came off looking very good. Hannan was criticized for stirring up trouble between her husband and his sisters. Nowal's arrangement of the marriage was condemned as malicious intervention,[23] while Ahmad's shameful treatment of his paternal aunts, and his marriage to a second wife, when his first had born him several sons, was considered appalling. The most discreet observers merely said this incident was an example of the drawbacks of marriage between paternal cousins, as relations between the two houses were irreparably damaged.

Conclusion

Displays of emotions are related to ideas of the person and the social hierarchy in Zabid. Among the *nas*, the way anger is displayed is clearly related to the agonistic competition between *bayts*. To ensure one's honour, one must be recognized by others in the community. The display of anger may be a reaction to a slight, or a strategy by which one attempts to ensure the deference one thinks one is owed from others. Slights must be repaid or addressed in order to protect the place of one's family. This kind of exchange of anger is to be expected in an agonistic society where the identity of one's family depends on recognition from the community. Among Zabidi women, this competition is played out in the exchange of hospitality; anger, or threat of it, is often a tactic by which women attempt to ensure the place of their families in society. But the display of anger by the Zabidi *nas* is highly stylized: any hint of lack of control implies a lack of reason [*'aql*]. Control over one's emotions is underpinned by modesty. The lack of modesty of the *akhdam* is seen as a significant deficiency in moral personhood. As a consequence, they are said to lack control over

23 Some even referred to her as a devil [*'afrita*].

their emotions. This difference is both a sign of, and justification for, their subordination. The *qaba'il* are not necessarily considered deficient as persons. However, the difference in style of emotional presentation between the *nas* and the *qaba'il* is a quality by which their respective identities are defined.

Relationships within families ought to be characterized by love and respect, signified by the fulfilment of obligations owed to each other. Infringements of these obligations often lead to the anger and divisiveness that ought not to characterize relations between *bayt* members. It is within families, the site of the strongest obligations and the closest ties, that passions sometimes run high. When tensions generate such anger that disputes gain attention outside of the family, the reputation of the family, up until this point carefully guarded by its members, inevitably suffers. It is at this point that relationships within families, and with those outside the family, may be dramatically reworked.

8

Moral Worth and Piety in Everyday Life

The services due from one Muslim to another are six: If you meet him, greet him; if he invites you, accept his invitation; if he asks your advice, give him advice; if he sneezes and thanks God, tell him 'God bless you'; if he falls sick, visit him; and if he dies, walk in his funeral.

Hadith of the Prophet Muhammad

At the bottom of all our mystical states there are techniques of the body.

Marcel Mauss, *Techniques of the Body*

Muslim piety, as the hadith of the Prophet cited above indicates, underpins relationships between persons. Styles of sociability are governed in part by ideas of how good Muslims should behave toward each other. Religious feasts are themselves sociable events when recognition is due to family, neighbours, and friends. And moral personhood is constituted through religious observances and demonstrated to others through comportment. I discuss here the distinguishing features of Islam as it is practised by Zabidi women: how pious identities are constructed through practices of the body, primarily the performance of daily prayers and the Ramadan fast; how these identities are enacted in the course of sociability; and how Islam is used to imagine the world.[1] The latter topic is discussed in reference to the performance of the *mawlid*, a ritual recitation of an account of the life of the Prophet Muhammad. Prayer and fasting are rites common to Mus-

---

1 These practices are the most important to *nas* women's everyday life, regardless of their level of literacy. There are, of course, several other ways in which one could approach the study of Islam in Zabid, especially given its long history as a centre of Islamic learning.

lims everywhere, whereas the *mawlid* is only found in particular communities.

A problem in the anthropology of Islam is how to account effectively for universalistic aspects (common to all Muslims) and particularistic ones (acceptable only to specific Muslim populations). The analytical distinction between the 'great' and 'little' traditions as a way of accounting for the diversity of Muslim beliefs and practices has been questioned by many. The equation of the great tradition with the orthodox and literary (specifically the sacred texts of the Qur'an and the Hadith), and the little with the more popular, but also less correct practices, distorts more than it reveals.[2] Asad (1986:6) persuasively critiques Gellner's study *Muslim Society* (1981), which links the great/little distinction in Islam to social formations (towns versus tribes). Another problem with the great/little distinction is the assumption that the pillars of Islam – the five basic requirements of all Muslims (affirmation of faith, prayer, fasting, alms, and pilgrimage) – can merely be assumed to be fulfilled in roughly the same manner by Muslims everywhere, in contrast to more idiosyncratic practices such as saint veneration or spirit possession, which are thought to require an exploration of cultural context (Eickelman 1989:258). Some anthropologists have suggested that the practices of a given community inevitably combine elements which are both popularistic and orthodox (Tapper and Tapper 1987:70). Status and prestige may be accorded not only because of mastery of the sacred texts but also as a result of fulfilment of local concepts of pious comportment (Lambek 1990). Bowen's insightful examination of everyday prayer ritual in three Indonesian contexts shows how the performance of prayer obligations, incumbent on all Muslims (thereby part of the great tradition), can be as influenced by local understandings of (and debates about) the nature of community and society as more idiosyncratic practices (1989).

Following these studies, I examine those practices which are thought to constitute piety as understood in Zabid. These practices are essential to identity and adult respectable status. According to Asad (1986), within a given Islamic discursive tradition, individuals are instructed in appropriate practices as established in a particular community. I draw upon three of his ideas to understand Islam as practised in Zabid: how an Islamic tradition is related to the formation of 'moral selves'; how practitioners situate them-

---

2   The shortcomings of this approach are apparent to the analysts of other world religions as well. For instance, Stirrat (1984) criticizes the often undisguised elitism of this kind of analysis.

selves in the present in terms of an Islamic past and future; and how it is practitioners' understandings of 'apt performance' which will specifically relate present practices to the past, and potentially transform them (1986:7–14).[3]

Submitting the Body to the Will: Learning How to Pray and Fast

Pious comportment is essential to identity as a respectable and responsible member of the Zabidi community. Piety is demonstrated regularly through the public performance of prayer. Along with the practice of gender segregation, the prayer obligations provide a fundamental organizing principle which structures time and social practice. Many have noted how the prayer calls serve to orient time (for example, Eickelman 1977 and Delaney 1991); I mentioned earlier that the visiting periods are structured by the prayer calls.[4] Not only do the calls structure sociability and social life in general: they also serve as continual reminders of the obligation to submit oneself to God.

The proper performance of daily prayers is intrinsic to both male and female adult social identity. Most Zabidis perform all prayers, although they may combine a few so they pray three times a day instead of five. At the sundown prayer, unless menstruating, women either pray at the home of their hostess or return to their own homes to do so. The women ask each other if they have prayed, and often encourage the younger girls to do so. Although women do not pray in mosques as men do, their piety, as demonstrated through prayer, has this public dimension in which the performance of prayer obligations is supported and encouraged by elders and peers.

For the most part, little effort is expended to control the behaviour of young children; however, some attempt is made to instil appropriate religious dispositions. Babies are often dandled on a woman's knee as she chants the affirmation of the faith in a playful tone: 'There is no God but God and Muhammad is his Prophet.' After children are two or three, adults tend not to play with them, leaving them to the company of their peers and

---

3 Eickelman notes three specific elements which should be considered as well: *time* or the historical contexts in which practices are introduced and reproduced; *scale*, the extent to which practices are universal or particularistic; and *internal debate*, discussions within and outside the community as to what constitutes correct practices (1989:262).

4 Each of the mosques in Zabid has a prayer caller, each with his distinctive style. Five times a day, from any given point in Zabid, one can hear several calls, not in exact unison, but overlapping each other.

the casual supervision of their older siblings. An exception, along with training in modesty, is made with training in prayer. Older children may mould the bodies of younger siblings into the posture of prayer or lay out prayer mats for them. This training is neither formal nor particularly consistent, but older siblings and adults delightedly encourage children who are willing. Little children of this age often spontaneously produce a 'prestigious imitation' (Mauss 1973) of adult prayer postures. One precocious three-year-old threw himself on a couch with his arms extended, crying, 'God is great' [Allahu akbar], much to his family's amusement. (His little feat was repeated to all guests the family hosted that evening.) One Friday, a grandmother proudly dressed her small grandsons in miniature replicas of adult garb – spotless white gowns and caps – and perfumed them in preparation for their first trip to the mosque with their father. She said, 'They are too young to understand fully but we dress them up and send them off so they will learn little by little.'[5]

The movements of the body involved in the process of prayer (standing, prostrating, kneeling, and sitting) are essential for the efficacy of prayer. I was often asked when and how Christians prayed; when I replied that no particular time or position was mandatory, although often people clasped their hands and knelt, people were inevitably shocked and doubted whether such an ad hoc approach could possibly be adequate.[6] Being able to pray is thought to be related to the development of reason in a child. As with the development of a sense of modesty and control of emotions, it is not a capacity which can be coerced from a child through a show of force, but one which develops gradually. However, encouragement and physical training, coupled with shaming through comparison with others of a similar age, are employed to instill proper comportment in children.

Bourdieu's discussion of 'bodily hexis' by which social values are 'made body' seems not to be relevant to religious principles. While I agree that techniques of the body structure subjective experience, his suggestion that embodied principles are necessarily 'beyond the grasp of consciousness' (1977:94) is not apt for prayer or fasting. Although the performance of prayer obligations is so engrained in adults as to appear natural, a conscious effort to concentrate on the intent [niyya] of the act, fulfilment of obliga-

---

5   The development of religious dispositions through training of the body is of course not exclusive to Muslim societies. Jackson argues that everywhere bodily awareness is connected to ethics: 'Bodily self-mastery is thus everywhere the basis for social and intellectual mastery' (1983:337). Beidelman has a nice account of etiquette of the body and morality among the Kaguru (1986:60–5).

6   Caton describes a similar reaction in the highlands to Christian prayer (1990:312 n17).

tions to God, rather than an unthinking performance, is necessary for prayer. This was the reason given for turning off the television or tape recorder when praying – to allow the devotion of one's full attention.

Associated with the performance of the bodily movements are the preparations for prayer, the purifying ablutions: one must wash after defecation, urination, sexual congress, menstruation, and sleep. Rienhardt suggests that the principle underlying Islamic purity rules is to negate the effect of the loss of will involved when the body releases, as it must, defiling substances (1990:19-20). He argues that ablutions are above all concerned with a 'reconsecration' of the body to the will, a persuasive point given the prominence of the role of will and intention in the submission to God embodied in the daily performance of prayers. Although children are taught the prayer postures first, they eventually learn that a prayer is not valid unless preceded by the proper ablutions and an effort of dedicate oneself to God instead of worldly concerns, both of which are necessary to an efficacious act of devotion.

This process of encouraging the development of the will through physical training is involved in another technique of the body intrinsic to proper Muslim comportment: fasting. During the month of Ramadan, Zabidis, like other Muslims, fast from sunrise to sunset. Children are said to be unable to perform the fast because they have neither the physical strength nor the will required, but as they are often quite enthusiastic about trying, they are given little exercises [tamrin]. The smallest will fast between meals; if the child becomes cranky or listless, she or he is fed without chastisement. Another exercise is fasting from food but not water for half a day or a day. Children who are eight or nine may fast properly for four or five days out of the month, with the goal of increasing the number of days the following year until, like adults, they can fast properly for the entire month of Ramadan.[7] Like training in prayer, training in fasting is thought to strengthen the will, which eventually develops until it is perceived as controlling the desires of the body in a fashion appropriate to devout adults.

Piety and Community Identity

Piety is at the foundation of the identity of the moral individual as a subject before God, but also at the foundation of familial identity and the identity of the Zabidi community. The history of religious learning is fundamental

---

7 By the age of thirteen or fourteen, most Zabidis keep the entire fast unless ill or menstruating. Although not obliged to keep the fast when pregnant, most women try to do so.

to collective Zabidi identity, a heritage which establishes Zabid as a place of worth in their own eyes and constitutes fame in the estimation of other Yemenis. However, piety and religiosity have implications beyond identity: they are thought to affect the well-being of the community as a whole. A connection is made between the correct fulfilment of religious observances and the welfare of the community. Prayers and fasts are owed to God; their neglect is said to anger him. The anger of God at neglect of recognition in the form of prayers which are owed to him seems structurally consistent with the anger individuals in families show at neglect by others who owe them social recognition. Dust storms and the drought in the Tihama region during my stay were said to be a result of God's anger at the people's neglect of their religious obligations.

Piety and Social Status

Piety is often cited as a criterion which distinguishes Zabidis from the *qaba'il* and the *akhdam*. While the *qaba'il* are recognized as devout, Zabidis question their interpretation of practices such as veiling; many don't wear chadors unless they are in Zabid. Ignorance of Islam and laxity in religious obligations indicate and justify, in the eyes of Zabidis, low status.[8] The *akhdam* are said to be ignorant of Islam, not to pray or fast, and not to conform to standards of modesty which are understood as expressions of piety. The *akhdam* do consider themselves Muslims, but may not be as informed about religious observances as the *nas*.[9] They still have far fewer educational opportunities, religious or state, than the *nas*, because of poverty and prejudice.

Piety and Familial Identity

Piety is related to social status not only in terms of the *nas\akhdam* distinction but also in distinctions between *bayts*. The effort to inculcate religious dispositions in children indicates the importance of pious comportment for the reputation of the whole family. Well-raised children, an achievement which Zabidi women value highly, are those with correct comportment

---

8   Messick's interesting discussion of the *shari'a* texts notes the hegemony of the learned over the unlearned: 'The position of the learned to the unlearned was implicitly fused to the whole dialectic of the God to human relation' (1993:158).

9   In chapter 6 I discussed the *khadim* whose fear of death was thought to be related to his neglect of prayer. I saw one old *khadima* pray, but without performing the proper ablutions beforehand. She achieved only a 'non-prestigious' imitation which was mocked by her employers.

[adab]. Adab connotes religious piety as well as social propriety – a sense of moral being in the world in which practices of the body are inextricably linked to the foundation of a pious self. Metcalf, commenting on Lapidus's illuminating discussion of works of classical scholars on adab, notes:

Knowledge ... is not true knowledge unless it is realized, for there is no concept of the detached intellectual. Nor can one's inner self be untouched by what one knows and hence by what one does. Consequently, adab may 'mean' correct outer behavior, but it is understood as both cause of and then, reciprocally, fruit of one's inner self. Knowing, doing, and being are inescapably one. (1984:9–10)

Children with adab reflect their rearing and indicate they come from a good home, where religion is taken seriously.

A certain degree of piety is necessary for respectable status in Zabid. As noted throughout, prestige and status in Zabid are granted within the rubric of Islamic beliefs and practices. It is untenable to claim prestige based solely on secular achievements, publicly implying a dismissal of Islam. The discourses of 'people' [sha'b] and 'nation' [watan] propagated by the central government are to a certain extent in competition with Islam. Zabidis are aware of the importance of the central government as the mediator of material and cultural capital in contemporary Yemen. Still, piety should accompany wealth and political influence. Although education in state schools and universities (or those abroad) is the primary means for social mobility in Yemen now, religious education still has cachet. Many of those families famed in the past for religious scholarship still remain among the elite today; the current members of these families are no longer involved in scholarship, but the 'glorious deeds' of their ancestors affect their reputation. (These two bases of prestige are often combined in the study of Islamic history at the university.) The head of one upwardly mobile family studied Islamic history at the San'a' University, returning to Zabid to teach in the high school, where he has established a reputation as a religious scholar. Another was appointed to a state legislative body in the capital based on his local reputation as a learned religious shaykh; when in Zabid he continues to teach Islamic studies to young Zabidis and give the sermons to the community on the 'ids.

Pious Actions and the Afterlife

Pious comportment affects the reputation of one's bayt in the community and it is essential to a sense of moral self. In addition, charitable acts in this world, as well as the fulfilment of one's obligations to God, affect one's fate in the afterlife. Goodness is created through actions in the world; a worthy soul is developed through pious acts.[10] Giving alms is one of the pillars of Islam; wealth without generosity is denounced in Zabid.[11] Ramadan in particular is a time for charitable acts; even families of relatively modest means try to provide small food gifts to their most destitute neighbours. At the end of Ramadan, wealthy families distribute sorghum to the poor (a kilo for every member of the poor family). In the past, on 'id 'arafat [the religious festival during the hajj], wealthy families would slaughter a bull and distribute the meat to the poor; some families still distribute meat from a lamb or sheep to the neediest in the neighbourhood. Reluctance to help those in need seriously damages one's reputation.

Stinginess or avarice is thought to be punished in the next world; I was told that a woman who thought only of her possessions, without charity to the needy, would spend the afterlife in hell with her gold burning on her neck.[12] Good, generous actions, in contrast, are rewarded. One day, as I sat with a friend, a young boy came in with a petition for contributions to the blood wealth [diyya] which a murderer owed the family of the man he killed. My friend immediately contributed 50 riyals. I asked if the man had really committed the murder, and she assured me he had. When I asked why she was helping a murderer, she said, 'He is poor and cannot pay the diyya himself. If you give to someone, God gives to you.' God is said to give a reward [ajar] in heaven to those who are generous in this world.[13] (Of course, the wealthy are the ones who have the means to be most generous.)

10 Individuals also gain merit in the afterlife by performing pious acts such as reciting the names of God and fasting on special days other than Ramadan.
11 Sometimes inconsistencies in the behaviour are obvious. One woman told me of a man who made a considerable amount of money by distilling and selling liquor. She noted that while his means of employment was haram, he was very generous in distributing food to the poor regularly. She laughed, saying, 'How can we understand this man? God will judge him.'
12 If women are independently wealthy, which some women in elite families are, the obligation to be generous holds for them as well as male members of the family.
13 In tribal areas, diyya is usually paid by the extended kin group; I presume this man's kin group was unable to raise the sum required. Because this woman had no obligation to contribute to it, it was seen as a charitable act. Many religious acts are performed with the understanding that God will give a reward, in this life or the afterlife, in return for pleasing him. Haeri discusses the extent to which the idea of 'contract' is embedded in Islamic thought, encompassing not only relationships between person and God but between husband and wife (1989:28-30).

Countering Hierarchy

While piety is at once a prerequisite of, and a basis for, prestige, an aspect of piety is humility before God and an awareness of the fact that it is God who will judge between people on the basis of their good deeds rather than their wealth. This fact seems at odds with the emphasis on establishing one's superiority over the other families in the community. However, part of the competition includes how well one lives up to one's obligations to others; value is accorded in part by generosity. The forum where competition and judgment takes place, the visiting circuit [*khuruj*], is also a basis for the formation of a moral community. In addition, the recognition of the significant life events of others is recommended as a pious virtue.[14] However, Zabidis are aware of the divisive aspects of *khuruj* and often draw on Islamic concepts of equality to mitigate the harsher aspects of the competitiveness in their community. Those who are exclusively concerned with rank in their selection of visiting sites are criticized. A 'good' woman treats everyone with respect and does not shun the poor in favour of the rich. A friend, in a discussion about the *kibar* families in Zabid said, 'Some of them are so snobby they won't sit beside a poor woman. We are not like them, we love all good people, rich or poor, as the Prophet said we should.' To a certain extent, Muslim criteria can be used to assert moral superiority over the criterion of wealth.[15] Individuals may deny others' claims to superiority if they display an unbending arrogance unmitigated by a sense of obligations to others. Criticizing a *kabir* family with a reputation for haughtiness, a poorer neighbour said, 'The Prophet wants us to remember that we all walk on this earth – none is higher than the next.' When speaking of a *kabir* woman who remembers to treat everyone with kindness and grace, a woman commented, 'She is from the greatest family in Zabid but she is generous [*karima*] and humble' [*miskina*]. (In this context, one often hears the word *miskina* [poor or pathetic] used in a positive sense, as the opposite of snobby [*mutakabbira*].)

The *Mawlid*

This tension between distinguishing oneself and one's family in the eyes

---

14 The moral obligation to acknowledge others is particularly pronounced during Ramadan.
15 This tactic was almost inevitably used in comparisons between Yemen and the Western world, whose material wealth and political might does not compensate for its moral depravity, I was often told.

of the community while maintaining an unassuming attitude of submission to God is always present in Zabidi social life. It is particularly addressed in another important religious practice in Zabid, the recitation of the *mawlid*, which describes the life of Muhammad. Aside from the pillars of Islam, equally shared by both men and women, *mawlids* are now performed almost exclusively by women. Why men rarely perform *mawlids* now, although they have in the recent past (within the last twenty years), is not clear.[16] What is clear, however, is that even though *mawlid* ceremonies are not performed by all Muslims, they are considered part of the authoritative religious tradition as established in Zabid.[17] Women are no less concerned than men with avoiding practices which are *haram*, and discussions of appropriate practices are common.[18] However, the appropriateness of *mawlid* performances is questioned by none, and they provide the contexts in which women collectively express their faith in Islam. In contrast, men's collective rituals consist of reading sections of the Qu'ran aloud during Ramadan. Ceremonies celebrating the completion of the entire Qu'ran [*khatims*] are held on the twenty-seventh day of Ramadan by the men of several Zabidi families to celebrate the anniversary of the revelation of the Qu'ran to Muhammad [*laylat al-qadr*].[19]

In *mawlid* poems, significant aspects of the Prophet Muhammad's history are brought together. There are several versions of the *mawlid* text; common to all are introductory phrases praising God, the announcement to Muhammad's mother that she is pregnant with the Prophet, his birth, and significant events in his life, including his night journey [*mi'raj*] to heaven where he is established as the most illustrious of all the prophets, and receives instructions from God for the daily prayer obligations for

---

16 I hope to clarify this point in future research.

17 In this respect, *mawlids* can be contrasted with celebrations for a saint [*ziyaras*], a practice which is a topic of internal debate not yet fully resolved. Educated young Zabid women and men, influenced by the literature of the Muslim Brotherhood, are critical of the practice, as are Zaydi government officials, who denounce it on television as polytheism [*shirk*]. (The highland Zaydi sect does not approve of saint veneration, although the practice was widespread in Shafi'i communities.)

18 In Zabid, young women, able to comprehend the Qur'an and the hadith, sometimes provoke generational conflict by criticizing their older relatives. One daughter sharply reprimanded her mother's hairstyle (parted at the side instead of in the middle, as a hadith of the Prophet recommends). Eickelman (1992) considers the impact of mass education on religiosity in Oman and Morocco.

19 Men also regularly pray collectively in the mosques. Most perform the noon prayer at Zabid's Great Mosque on Friday and listen to the sermon of the *shaykh*.

Muslims.[20] In *mawlid* poems, all of these facts about Muhammad's birth and life (described in various places in the Qur'an and the hadith) are brought together in one panegyrical text.[21]

In Zabid, the recitation of the *mawlid* concerns, at different times, both the temporal aspects of social reproduction and one's fate in the afterlife. I have made an analytical distinction between two kinds of situations in which *mawlid*s are performed.[22] The *mawlid*s held on these two types of occasions vary in intent and in emotional intensity. On the first occasion, *mawlid*s are held by certain families, in fulfilment of vows designed to ensure the health or well-being of family members. These are held at any time of the year, depending on the specific events or crises in a family which are thought to require God's aid. Other *mawlid*s are held on certain dates of the Islamic calendar which commemorate and celebrate key events in the Prophet's life. In these contexts, women use *mawlid*s to imagine the life of the Prophet and make it meaningful as an example to follow in their own lives. The next section provides a brief account of the ceremony itself.

The Event

Mawlid ceremonies are formal, invited events; women don new or fancy dresses, their nicest gold jewelry, and jasmine flowers. The woman in whose honour the *mawlid* is held, such as the new mother, the recovered patient, or the hajja, will be specially adorned with a long garland of jasmine flowers, in the fashion of brides in Zabid. Their hair (which is frequently left uncovered in women's gatherings) must be covered, if only with a tissue.

20 There is more than one version of the *mawlid* poem in Zabid, but all the recitations I participated in included similar elements. Several families had old hand-written copies, while some had store-bought copies of the *mawlid* of Barzanji. I am not certain of the authorship of the hand-written copies; I was told it was not important. I assume it *is* rather important to some, especially the descendants of the religious scholars who compose *mawlid* poems; the woman's point was that knowing authorship or even being able to read the text was not a prerequisite for women participating in the *mawlid* and partaking of its benefit.

21 *Mawlid* ceremonies are held in many places in the Muslim world and have different forms and meanings. In Lamu, *mawlid* ceremonies become a vehicle by which the *sharif*s [descendants of the Prophet] maintain their right to mediate between ordinary people and the Prophet (al Zein 1974:345–9); in Morocco, the *mawlid* functions to uphold the legitimacy of the monarchy (Combs-Schilling 1989:160–74). Recent anthropological studies in Turkey suggest that *mawlid*s there, most frequently held at deaths, focus attention on other-worldly salvation through the creation of a significant link between the participants and the Prophet (Tapper and Tappper 1987:84; Marcus 1987:126).

22 The word *mawlid* refers both to the text honouring the Prophet Muhammad and to the event at which the *mawlid* text is recited.

The *mawlid* has a crescendo-like structure. It begins, like any women's social gathering, with women greeting each other, exchanging qat and news, and smoking the waterpipe. The room is scented with a special incense known as *fauh*. Although the special incensing serves to transform the reception room into sacred space and the gathering into a sacred time, differentiating it from the everyday gatherings it much resembles, it is performed with little pomp. The professional reader begins the recitation of the text.[23] The guests gradually become more drawn in until all are participating at one point, as the text recounts the sequence of Muhammad's birth. During the next passage of the text, women chant a refrain which welcomes the newborn Muhammad into the world. The participants hold out their hands to receive the blessings of God. At this point, the hostess circulates with a commonly used incense, 'ud [aloewood]. However, instead of incensing their hair and dresses as they usually do, women bring the burner under their chins and inhale the smoke, or cup their hands over the burner and draw their hands lightly over their faces.

The reciter continues; the guests may retreat into their own conversations, but they continue to participate in the refrains. During the recital of the *mawlid*, lids are taken off the water jugs so the blessings [*baraka*] of God will descend into them. After the recital, the hostess passes out glasses of this water along with candies or toasted sesame seeds, also described as *baraka*. The *mawlid* often does not have a clearly marked ending; instead it casually begins to resemble other social gatherings. However, the indication that something special has been created is that everyday items such as water, candies, and sesame seeds have been infused with *baraka* as a result of the recital of the *mawlid*. The entire reading takes between forty-five minutes and an hour.

Moments of Vulnerability: Healing and the *Mawlid*

Concern over health is as much a part of daily life in Zabid as is religion. Despite a certain influence of Western scientific theories of infection and prevention of disease – presented on television, in the local clinic, and in school books – the idea that God is responsible for sickness and healing, for life and death, predominates. Vowing to read a *mawlid* is a woman's chance to contact God directly and respectfully attempt to influence her

23 There are a few professional readers in Zabid who receive money for their recitals; these women are much in demand because their style of reciting is aesthetically appreciated. If a professional reader is not available, any literate woman will read. Illiterate women have memorized the responses as a result of years of participation in past *mawlids*.

own destiny and that of her family. Women do so in times of vulnerability, on the occasions of sudden serious illness and birth. *Mawlids* performed in these contexts are attempts to ensure the health and safety of their families in everyday life, through proper contact with God and Muhammad.

A vow is made to God by an individual, without ceremony. A pregnant woman will often vow to read a *mawlid* if she delivers safely, or one of her family members will make the vow on her behalf. Women's narratives about birth are full of descriptions of their fears during the delivery which were assuaged by their vow to God; they gathered strength and courage from their belief that their requests to God for aid would be answered. After a successful birth, the *mawlid* is held to fulfil the vow and thank God for his mercy.[24] Vowing to read a *mawlid* is thought to be particularly efficacious for a woman who has had difficulty getting pregnant; the *mawlid* will be held after she gives birth.[25]

Women essentially establish a 'contract' relationship with God wherein favours such as health are granted in exchange for the offering of the *mawlid*. In these contexts, women, while acknowledging that all things are from God, implicitly contest this accepted truth by using the *mawlid* to try to manipulate their own and their families' fates. The *mawlid* ceremony, then, constitutes a potential domain of influence, by which women entreat God and Muhammad to intervene positively in their lives.[26] While it is important to remain humble before God and treat these vows as requests rather than demands, Zabidis clearly connect the request for aid (the vow), the 'gift' of health or well-being from God to person, and the person's 'return' by reading a *mawlid* which praises God and Muhammad. The reading indicates a positive outcome of an exchange relationship; that God, in his generosity, saw fit to fulfil the request.[27]

---

24 *Mawlids* are frequently performed on the eleventh day after birth, known as the *shadhba*, when the mother washes her hair for the first time after the birth. The *mawlid* is performed regardless of the sex of the baby. On the fortieth day after a birth, a *mawlid* may be held during the large invited party that is held by her husband's family.

25 Those vows designed to elicit God's blessings are used in tandem with drugs prescribed by doctors, pharmacists, or traditional healers. In this sense, the *mawlid* has to be seen as an integral part of a maintenance of health, fertility, and well-being, which involves regular religious observances, proper diet, and Western-style medical care, where available.

26 *Mawlids* of this sort are pledged to achieve a positive outcome in school or a safe return from a journey. Women pledge and perform *mawlids* on behalf of male family members as well as female.

27 Discussions of relationships between person and saint in Iran (Betteridge 1985:197–8) and Turkey (Tapper 1990:247–8) indicate that these kinds of exchanges are similar in structure to the exchange relationships Zabidi women establish between person and God through the *mawlid*.

Announcing Good Fortune

In Zabid, the *mawlid* ceremony develops a sense of moral self in that using it to announce good fortune expresses appropriate humility before God. Holding a *mawlid* to announce success also indicates a recognition of the fact that it is from God that all blessings flow. This tension between the ambition to be successful and recognized as such in the community, and the desire to act in a manner consistent with a concept of a modest, pious self is a central dynamic of Zabidi social life.

The woman in whose honour the *mawlid* is held is reincorporated into the community and her new status is announced in a religiously appropriate fashion. Hosting a *mawlid* not only presents good fortune to the community but also creates, or reinforces, a family's reputation for piety, an important basis of prestige. Further, *mawlid* ceremonies resolve, at least temporarily, the tension between equality before God and the ranking based on worldly fortune. A *mawlid* is a public tying of worldly success to the grace of God, and proclaims success without risking the wrath of God due to failure to show respect. Success can be displayed without attracting the evil eye from others in the social world. Punctuating social interaction in Zabid is the phrase *ma sha'llah* [whatever God wills], which indicates that the witness of the good fortune of another does not wish to cause the evil eye through envy. By holding a *mawlid* to announce success, the members of the family themselves preempt the evil eye, by publicly recognizing that their own good fortune is a result of the grace of God.[28] The guests, by participating, indicate that they, too, join the family in celebrating the grace of God. The *mawlid* is beneficial not only for the family which holds the ceremony but for all the participants. By reciting a *mawlid*, a meritorious act, women cultivate pious selves and partake of the blessings [*baraka*] of God that are brought down upon all the participants.[29]

Mawlids Celebrating the Life of the Prophet

The *mawlids* discussed above are planned by individuals to elicit and

---

28 This interpretation of how hierarchy and competition are understood and conveyed in a religiously appropriate fashion in Zabid can be contrasted to Tapper's (1983) analysis of sociability and religiosity in a Turkish town. She contrasts formal receptions, when hierarchy is established, with *mawlids*, where equality between women is emphasized. In Zabid, the tension between hierarchy and equality, and unity and competition is continually negotiated in every social interaction.

29 The *baraka* which descends while a *mawlid* is being read is said by women to be particularly efficacious for conceiving a child.

announce success in a religiously and socially appropriate fashion. There is, as well, another class of *mawlid*. Those held on three religious holidays celebrating key events in the life of the Prophet are concerned with the religious imagination, in that people, by participating in the *mawlid*, make the life of Muhammad the Prophet meaningful and evocative in their daily lives. I use 'imagination' in Beidelman's sense, as something that 'relates to the ways people construct images of the world in which they live' and which 'relates to the ways in which people picture a world different from that which they actually experience' (1986:1). It is the stuff of imagination, symbols and metaphor, which sustains faith and allows participants in differing places and times to make a longstanding, and purportedly unchanged, system of beliefs and practices relevant to their daily lives (Eickelman 1990:4).

During the recitation of the *mawlid* on these three religious holidays, women focus attention on the life of Muhammad as an example to follow in their lives. The intensity of these *mawlid* celebrations is greater than that of those performed in response to worldly benefits; participants are more drawn into the *mawlid* and tend to pay attention to the recitation all the way through the performance.

*Mawlid*s on the Prophet's birthday [*Mawlid al-Nabiyy*], and the Islamic religious festivals, the Mi'raj and Bahjah (fifteenth of the month of Sha'ban), are held by many houses. They commemorate and celebrate key events in the life of the Prophet.[30] The *kibar* houses in Zabid hold *mawlid*s which are attended by immediate neighbours and invited guests. Those whose families are not holding a *mawlid* themselves, but who have many social connections to other families in Zabid, will visit several houses in one evening. On these occasions the *mawlid* is held at night, after a meal at sundown, as during Ramadan.

During the recitation of the *mawlid*, women imagine the life of Muhammad, from his birth onward. Like many Muslims, Zabidis find Muhammad's life a beautiful example to follow. Women described to me afterwards how his life showed them the way to avoid hell. On these occasions, as they read the *mawlid*, women often cry as they reflect on the tribulations Muhammad faced in the course of delivering the word of God to people on earth. The latter passages of the *mawlid* outline Muhammad's night journey to heaven [the *mi'raj*], describing how he met the preceding proph-

---

30 There is no public procession in Zabid, as there is in other parts of the Middle East (Eickelman 1987:292–3).

ets in each of the seven heavens and was recognized by them and by God as the pre-eminent prophet. In discussions after the *mawlid* on the Mi'raj, several women told me how moved they were by the Prophet's intercession with God on behalf of mankind to reduce the daily prayer obligations from fifty to five obligatory prayers a day.

The *mawlid* allows them to imagine the life of Muhammad as the most significant period in the history of Islam – which remains meaningful for them, as Muslims, now, centuries afterward. As Asad argues, 'An Islamic discursive tradition is simply a tradition of Muslim discourse that addresses itself to conceptions of the Islamic past and future, with reference to a particular Islamic practice in the present' (1986:14).

Through participating in a *mawlid*, Zabidi women situate themselves in their Islamic past. Following the example of the life of Muhammad in one's present life is central to one's fate in the afterlife. Zabidi women often stated that God will weigh one's sins against one's good works and pious acts on the Day of Judgment [*yawm al-Hisab*]; reading the *mawlid* is a itself a pious act.

Mawlids for the Hajj

*Mawlid*s held before a woman departs on the hajj are the most emotionally evocative *mawlid*s. They are important in two ways: like those held on the Bahjah and Mi'raj, these *mawlid*s stimulate the religious imagination. Those who are not going on the hajj pray that some day they, like the soon-to-be hajja, will have the opportunity to see the sacred places of Mecca and to take part in the pilgrimage, retracing the steps of Muhammad. An extra poem [*qasida*] is added to this *mawlid*, describing sacred places such as the Well of Zamzam; all the women stand up, face Mecca, and recite it together.

There is a certain recursiveness inherent in Islam, which is highlighted at the time of the hajj: a notion of returning to the centre of Islam, the place of the revelations from God to Muhammad (Delaney 1990:516). Through the hajj, Muslims create connections to this past Islamic history and return to Mecca, the true home of Muslims. Yet by returning to the centre of Islam, the pilgrim also moves closer to a future in the afterlife. It is this bringing together of an Islamic past, present, and future that participants focus on while performing the *mawlid* before someone leaves on the hajj.

The poem sung in conjunction with the *mawlid* before the hajj is interrupted frequently by ululations of the sort common at weddings; this section of the *mawlid* celebration is referred to as a *zaffa*, a word also used to refer to the party for the bride before her wedding. My informants explained to me that the hajj, along with marriage and death, is the most important rite of passage a woman will experience.[31] This connection between bride and hajja is made even more explicit by the fact that on the occasion of a woman's first pilgrimage, her friends come to bring her presents, as they bring presents to the new bride. At the *mawlid* before the hajj, these three rites of passage are symbolically unified: the prospective hajja is treated like a bride, who is about to undergo a life-transforming experience, one which she hopes will ensure a positive fate after death.[32]

While this is a very happy celebration, almost everyone is crying. Participants infuse this *mawlid* ceremony with affect from their own experiences – either memories of their own pilgrimages or their desire to perform the hajj in the future. The relatives of the prospective hajja entreat God, by their *mawlid* and the accompanying *qasida*, to allow the woman to perform the hajj with a clear mind, concentrating only on her religious duties. The prospective hajja uses the *mawlid* to bolster her resolve to become a sincere pilgrim. Her inner state [*batin*], which only God can see, should be pure; she should focus only on the religious duty at hand, not on the cares of this world.[33] After completing the hajj in good faith, all the pilgrim's sins to date will be forgiven.

The fact that crying in public during these recitations is condoned is noteworthy. As noted in the previous chapter, at death, if the bereaved cry, others immediately try to stop them, often by harshly reminding them that it is *haram* [forbidden] to cry, because it indicates displeasure with the will of God. When hurt arises from neglect or temporary partings between loved ones, the most common and appropriate reaction is anger. The only time I ever saw women cry in an unselfconscious fashion was during *mawlids*; being moved to tears over the life of Muhammad is

---

31 This was the only context in which I heard death referred to as a 'rite of passage' and as a potentially joyful transition.

32 Women who had performed the hajj inevitably described it to me as one of the most significant and beautiful events of their lives. Metcalf (1990) has a nice account of how the hajj can be essential to the development of a Muslim identity.

33 This aspect of singularity of purpose is very important. Trips to Saudi Arabia to perform the hajj frequently are coupled with shopping or seeking medical treatment. At one *mawlid* I attended for a prospective hajja, her friends brought presents. Her mother intercepted the presents, explaining that since the girl was also travelling to see a doctor, this particular hajj could not be treated as a pure pilgrimage, which constitutes a rite of passage.

acceptable; publicly crying in other situations is not.[34] The *mawlid* is explicitly concerned with contemplating the performance of a religious duty essential to a positive future in the afterlife, but the relatives of the hajja are also concerned to entreat God that she return safely from the arduous journey. Upon the safe return of the relatives, another *mawlid* is recited in thanksgiving.[35]

The celebration of the Zabidi *mawlid* differs from the Turkish one analysed by the Tappers (1987). They argue that, through the recitation of the *mawlid* poem, Turkish women exalt childbirth and motherhood to a spiritual level, granting Muhammad a superhuman status through this process. Turkish women overcome what the Tappers call the 'salvation paradox' – that is, how ordinary people become immortals in heaven (1987:86).[36] I did not find any evidence to suggest that the theme of the birth of Muhammad per se was identified by Zabidi women, as life givers, as having transcendental import that would lead to salvation. In a more prosaic fashion, Zabidis claim that *mawlid*s are especially efficacious for fertility and birthing problems and are the appropriate means for thanking God for a safe delivery. In Turkey, *mawlid*s are held at death but never at birth; the reverse is true in Zabid. Zabidi women focus on the miracles of Muhammad's birth and significant events of his life not only to reaffirm their belief in their religion, but also to constitute themselves as Muslims who follow the 'beautiful example' of Muhammad.[37] This orientation toward the re-

34 While women do not cry uncontrollably, a certain slippage of the usual restrained comportment is evident. Their close monitoring of their own comportment, and that of others, so evident in ordinary life, is less apparent during the *mawlid* ceremony. Women clearly find the vision of their Islamic heritage and future, presented in the *mawlid*, moving and beautiful. When I queried them about their crying, women said, 'Our religion is beautiful' [*Din haqqana jamila*], and would urge me to convert so I could fully understand.

35 For a woman's first hajj, a lunch is hosted by her family to which the family's closest friends, neighbours and relatives will be invited. Money is distributed to the neighbourhood poor before the luncheon.

36 Similarly, Marcus (1987:126) argues that by holding a *mawlid* at death, women, as 'life givers,' through the exaltation of the birth of the Prophet Muhammad celebrate the 'flow of life processes' which transcend death.

37 I suspect that Zabidis would find the Tappers' (1987:85) suggestion – that granting Muhammad a superhuman status is made possible by an implicit transformation of the Christ paradigm – both unpersuasive and blasphemous. This may reflect ethnographic differences. Empirically, there is no basis for proposing Christian influences on Zabidi practices as the Tappers suggest for the Greek Orthodox on the practices of Egirdir Turks. See Abu-Zahra for a critique of the Tappers imposition of Christian concepts and influences onto the Islamic ritual of the *mawlid* (1991:11–17).

creation or imitation of the life of Muhammad is particularly prominent in the *mawlids* before the hajj.[38]

I think it is also likely that the aesthetic aspect of the recitation of the text, with its stylized vocalization and antiphonal refrains, is appreciated for its own beauty, conveying a non-discursive meaning which is prior to, or co-exists with discursive understanding.[39] The oral presentation of the *mawlids* means that even if not fully comprehended discursively at first (as it probably is not by young participants), all women, literate or not, have potential access to this religious experience.

Conclusion

Religious dispositions are cultivated through training of the body in prayer and fasting; as Delaney notes, 'The meaning of Islam is mediated through the meanings and comportment of the body in everyday life' (1991:25). The will is strengthened through bodily techniques; prayer, including appropriate ablutions, serves as a constant resubmitting of the body to the will in the service of worship.

Piety is a quality by which Zabidis define their identity, serving as one more point by which to differentiate themselves from the *akhdam* and *qaba'il*. It also remains a foundation of prestige which provides, to a certain extent, a discourse within which to assert moral superiority over those so presumptuous as to forget their obligations to others and to God. I have argued that the *mawlids* held in fulfilment of a pledge designed to elicit some benefit implicitly address the central issue of the importance of achieving worldly success without losing sight of the fact that it is God who grants blessings and success. *Mawlid* ceremonies in this fashion mediate the ever-present contradiction between equality of Muslims before God and the hierarchy of families so evident in everyday life. By presenting their good fortune to the community in the context of a *mawlid* performance, they preempt the evil eye by tying their good for-

---

38 The pilgrim must 'hone himself to the prophetic model, the person of the Prophet Muhammad, in whose footsteps on this occasion he can literally walk' (Metcalf 1990:100–1).

39 I am influenced here by Graham's discussion of the recitation of the Qur'an, which seems equally applicable for the recited *mawlid* text. He argues, 'There is also a nondiscursive understanding or meaning that is part of the experience of overt encounter with the text itself – an encounter that is primarily oral\aural in character, rooted as it is in the recitation, or listening to the recitation, of the text' (1987:111).

tune to the grace of God, and they enhance their families' reputations for piety.

I have also argued that the *mawlids* performed on the anniversaries of key events of Muhammad's life provide means for women to situate themselves in terms of Islamic history and a reminder of how to live morally in this world in preparation for the next. The *mawlid* held before the hajj is focused toward this link with the Prophet, as all the participants, not just the prospective hajja, imagine retracing the steps of Muhammad and fulfilling this important religious obligation, which will mean forgiveness of sins, and hopefully, positive future.

Conclusion: The Rise and Fall of Families

This book describes the style of life in a small but ancient town, in which the elite families have the income and leisure – derived from their ownership of most of the land in the surrounding region – to engage in competitive hospitality governed by a refined etiquette.

I have argued in favour of the premise that among the *nas* the hierarchy of *bayt*s in Zabid is one in which the position of families in relation to each other is perceived as mutable. Because individual identity is inextricably linked to the identity of one's *bayt*, the comportment of one member affects the reputation of all. Several forms of behaviour which have consequences for this competition between families for status have been discussed: modest comportment, the exchange of hospitality, conspicuous consumption, and piety.

Hierarchy in Zabid cannot be taken for granted because it must be continually re-enacted or altered through the process of recognition inherent in the exchange of hospitality. The issue of recognition is central. The standing of one's *bayt* in the community depends not only on one's wealth, but also on having one's *bayt* recognized as significant by others. Reputation exists, at least partially, in how 'known' one is – in the breadth of one's social ties. In the process of exchange of hospitality, a *bayt*'s distinctive identity is created.

Family fortunes do change in Zabid, and an individual member can affect the future standing of his or her family and its descendants through financial and moral actions. This fluidity in social ranking is why the self-monitoring of one's own comportment and the surveillance of that of others is so important. Comportment, hospitable and modest, is related to material wealth. Wealth obviously affects one's ability to maintain other honour-creating practices, but this material wealth must be properly maintained and deployed. The ability to manage wealth and reputation varies within kin groups bearing the same patronym, and, as may be expected, fortunes change over time. I have argued here that women's practices are central to the long-term management of a family's reputation and standing. To illustrate the connections between consumption, sociability, and status, I present in conclusion a couple of stories describing the changing fates of two Zabidi families in the twentieth century. One family has experienced a distinct decline in their social position, while the other has managed to effect an obvious rise.

The first story takes as its focal point an old woman, 'Aysha, who in the course of her lifetime had seen a great transformation in the material fortunes of both her natal and marital families. 'Aysha was a woman of great energy and wit, if not tact. She had a rather inclusive notion of what constituted her business, which encompassed the business of all her relatives by blood or marriage, most of her neighbours, and the tenants who lived in her house in the latter part of her life. This vignette is informed by what she told me about herself and her family, by my observations during my close relationship with her, and by what neighbours told myself or my husband about the vagaries of her life and that of her son.

Although 'Aysha did not know the day or year of her birth, judging from the age of her children and grandchildren, she must have been at least sixty. Age showed in her lined face, but her constant commentary, ceaseless movement, and wiry frame gave her a durable air which convinced me she would bury us all, and chat all the way to her grave. Her appearance of indomitability was undermined only during her periodic bouts of malaria, when, too weak for her usual loquacity, the slightness of her form became apparent, betraying a physical frailty usually subsumed to her forceful personality.

She had been born into a weak branch of a prominent trading family. In the style of her youth, she was married before puberty; her husband was a wealthy man, who owned both land and slaves. He and 'Aysha had three children, two of whom survived until adulthood – a son, Adil, and a daughter, Fatima.

'Aysha lived well for the first years of her marriage, enjoying the luxuries of life. Earlier in the century, qat was transported by camel to Zabid from the highlands only every second day. 'Aysha's husband, like other wealthy men, purchased enough qat for two days, putting aside the second day's portion in banana leaves, so they would not have to go without. 'Aysha's son Adil acquired young the taste for qat when daily chewing was still a province of the elite. When his father died, Adil quickly sold off much of his considerable landholdings for qat. He also spent lavishly on his marriage to the daughter of a friend of his father, from an old and prominent family. To house his new bride, he built a second-story addition, a *khilwa*, to the already imposing structure of the original house. When he had run through his inheritance, he went to Saudi Arabia, as did so many Yemeni men in the 1970s, hoping to make a fortune. He left his young wife, who had not yet conceived a child, with his mother. While he was away, his wife's father died, and her brother, less fond of Adil than her father had been, recalled her to her natal home and arranged their divorce.

This was a time of great stress for 'Aysha. She told me that in this time her eyes had exhausted their capacity to produce tears because for three years when Adil was away she heard nothing from him and she used to cry every day. She was terribly upset by the dissolution of Adil's marriage and twenty years later still bitterly condemned the woman's brother for breaking up the marriage, as she said the bride had loved Adil. 'Aysha's positive relationship with this woman contrasted with her hellish relationship with Adil's next wife, from a far lesser family than the first. No children resulted from this short-lived match either. 'Aysha fought relentlessly with this young woman, perhaps because she still missed Adil's first wife, of whom she had been so fond, or perhaps because the second wife's lowly origin reminded her of how far their own status had slipped in recent years. (Despite her later years of near penury, 'Aysha was proud, fiercely protective of the shards of their reputation, and a bit of a snob.) 'Aysha never even referred to the existence of the second wife, whereas she told me of the first wife at great length. A neighbour introduced me to the second wife; even though she had remarried and had six children, her memories of her fights with 'Aysha had still not faded.

'Aysha's daughter, Fatima, proved her strongest supporter, more loyal and trustworthy than her son. Fatima was married to the son of another wealthy landowner and had two children. Instead of taking another wife when it was discovered that Fatima could have no more children, her husband married off their teenaged son to a young bride from a prominent neighbouring family. This young woman had five sisters, all beautiful, charming, and devoted to each other. They were all married into Zabid's most prominent families, providing affinal connections of which 'Aysha was very proud. By 1990 the young couple had nine lovely children, who were constantly at their great-grandmother's house, delivering fruit, treats, or messages to her. The older girls helped 'Aysha with her housework and the precocious younger children provided her with entertainment and anecdotes. Fatima and her family ensured that 'Aysha need not fear, ultimately, for her welfare, as they would always take her in if Adil's fortunes fell still further. However, a certain refuge in times of need was not exactly what 'Aysha wanted. Her ambition, thwarted by her feckless son, was to be a matriarch like many of her peers, wives of powerful men who presided over their unmarried daughters, married sons, their wives, and children, for all their sentient days. However well placed 'Aysha may have been in her earlier life to have had this sort of career, it was not to be.

Although an intelligent and literate man, Adil had little ambition and no business sense; he had undermined the family's position in society by squandering their resources. He had to rely on his nephew to get him a modestly paid job at the Local Development Council, which he occasionally attended despite his penchant for sleeping late. 'Aysha told me that she and Adil could perhaps have scraped by on this meagre salary were it not for qat; although she herself chewed only a bit each day, Adil's consumption continually threatened their small budget. He made himself look foolish by trying to borrow money from wealthier neighbours who knew perfectly well that in terms of the resources he commanded and his profligacy he was unlikely to pay them back.

Their house, in size and its elegant interior and exterior carving, attested to their former prominent status. Instead of a large and influential family, which one could easily imagine inhabiting their large complex, they were left with the pathetic shards of a kin group: an old woman and a divorced middle-aged man. When we met them, Adil had been living without a wife for several years, an unusual and certainly unenviable state in Zabid. His once splendid *khilwa* that he had built for his first bride had been rented out for years to army officers and Egyptian schoolteachers. Poorly maintained by them and the renters, it had decayed in Zabid's heat and dust into a rather mangy-looking place, too dilapidated to attract any more tenants.

Another vestige of their lost wealth was the row of waterpipes which adorned the centre of the table in their sitting room. They were kept brightly polished, as if 'Aysha still hosted large parties which would require several waterpipes to be lit at one time. Her house was kept as if she could expect a deluge of guests at any moment, although her visitors were not frequent. They had more or less slipped out of the competitive exchange of hospitality that characterizes the social life of other great families; indeed, they were no longer of the 'great' and even if their material resources had not been so depleted, she did not have the labour to stage the great Zabidi social events, which require several female family members, nor did she in her later years have the energy to visit more widely than she did. Adil was not well regarded in the male community; he was almost a client of the wealthy family next door, chewing with them almost daily and never hosting them in return. What notable connections they had were maintained by 'Aysha.

Her sister's granddaughters were among her most prized social connections. Her sister's daughter had married into one of Zabid's wealthiest trading families. In her dotage, 'Aysha's sister lived with them. Her niece and grandnieces treated 'Aysha with the respect due a grand lady, and she was at her gentlest when with them. I accompanied her on a visit to their house, and caught a glimpse of what she might have been like had her life gone the way she wanted: gracious, dignified, and charming with an incisive wit. This contrasted with her everyday persona, when she, forced into parsimony by her son's extravagance, was quick to quibble over a riyal or two with a local tradesperson in a fashion less than dignified. The kind of comportment which would have seemed powerful in a matriarch toward her younger kin was interpreted as meddlesomeness when exercised with neighbours over whom she had no claim.

Scurrying about in the mornings in only the brief top and skirt worn by older Zabidi women, dishing out free advice to all, male or female, 'Aysha at first appeared heedless of gender segregation, although older women's reputations are not as vulnerable as those of younger ones. At night when going out, however, like other Zabidi women, 'Aysha donned a chador. Her strong allegiance to modest practices was evident in her fierce protection of the reputations of her grandchildren and great grandchildren. She would not hide from a man who came looking for her son, but she would chase them off quickly enough if her granddaughter was visiting. As a neighbour, I too received my share of lectures from her on appropriate comportment.

Some described her as a miser [bakhila]. While her frugality was out of necessity sometimes aggressive, she often showed a generosity that seemed to come from another life. During Ramadan, she distributed portions of meat and a yogurt dish to her poorest neighbours; the quantities were small, but delivered with noblesse oblige. Although charitable and kind on these occasions, when she was out in the evenings in our neighbourhood, the difference between her family's origin and that of the poorer neighbours was not one she let anyone overlook.

'Aysha was old and tired and despaired of her son ever recouping the family fortune, marrying, and producing a herd of children she could oversee. Her energy went into maintaining her most notable family connections. What she was able to save from the meagre providings of her son she devoted to offering hospitality to them at least a few times a year. She differed from her poor neighbours not in income, but in the social recognition she could still reel in.

The first party I attended at 'Aysha's house was held after the evening call to prayer and as her capacious courtyard was lit only by a dim fluorescent bar, the disrepair of the couches, riddled with termite tracks, was disguised. The cushions on the couches had long passed their capacity to cushion anything, compressed as they were into thin boards, their fabric worn and tatty. But although 'Aysha and Adil were unable to afford the outlay for a new set, everything was spotlessly clean. The guests, although far too few to fill the courtyard, numbered among them at least one representative of the notable families to whom 'Aysha was still able to maintain connections. 'Aysha offered them perfume and incense from her carefully hoarded supply. Her offerings, like the guests, were few. But what she had was offered and accepted graciously.

The only positive thing that the neighbours could say about 'Aysha's son Adil was that he loved children (too bad he'd had none of his own, they would add). 'Aysha was troubled by this; she told me that her last bit of work that remained to her before she died was marrying Adil off. Just before we left Zabid, 'Aysha had finally manage to arrange for him to marry a divorced woman with a child from a previous marriage, who at thirty was rather old by Zabidi standards. Although poor and of humble origin, she was deferential enough to meet with 'Aysha's resigned approval. 'Aysha announced as she introduced her to me that since it was Adil's third marriage, they would not be making much of a fuss – 'just the neighbours,' she said, would be invited. Adil's fiancee said quietly that it would not be appropriate to have a big party, since she was 'so old.' No one mentioned the obvious, that their social circle had shrunk so markedly since Adil's first splendid wedding, and they could now afford to host only a few guests anyway. When she dictated – she never learned to write – a letter to me a few years later, it was not Adil's wedding she proudly mentioned, but the grand wedding *farah* of her daughter's granddaughter, the likes of which, she said, 'Zabid had never witnessed before,' with singers from Aden and al-Hudayda entertaining all the guests.

'Aysha could not read the Qu'ran, but she was a pious woman who never missed her daily prayer obligations. Although she often firmly stated that 'all is from God,' she did not exactly accept her fate with resignation. She clearly voiced her opinion of nefarious human agents that she considered responsible for thwarting her or her family. That which she did not manage to bend to her will, she accepted sometimes with grace, but more often with bitterness, understandable perhaps in a life as disappointing as hers had often been.

The next vignette describes a family, Bayt Muhammad Khalid, whom 'Aysha had known since birth, whose fortunes had improved as hers had fallen. Like 'Aysha's story, this narrative is based on my association with various members of the family, as well what their neighbours and friends told me about how their reputation had changed.

The deceased father of Muhammad Khalid had worked in the past as the overseer of the large estate of their neighbours, Bayt Bassam. He had orga- nized the selling of the produce from the Bassam estate, and managed his employer's money, investing in land and trade goods for him. Muham- mad's father was himself a poor man, and his parents were dead, and he could not afford to marry. Out of kindness and charity, his employer paid for his wedding to Iman, also an orphan.

Iman had been abandoned by her parents; she was raised as a charitable act by a woman in one of the families in 'Aysha's neighbourhood. (After the woman who fostered her died, Iman had no close connection with the family.) 'Aysha and Iman were of the same generation; like many in this neighbourhood, 'Aysha condescended to Iman, who loathed her in return. Because they inhabited the same quarter, they invited each other to their larger social events such as weddings, but they never visited informally. 'Aysha may have looked down upon Iman's stigmatized origin as an aban- doned child, but Iman's son Muhammad was as careful a manager as Adil was profligate. Iman's family's current material position, while still far from the wealthy *kibar* families, was much more promising than that of 'Aysha's.

Bayt Khalid was currently headed by Iman's eldest son Muhammad, who had acquired local respect through his religious learning. He was among the first in Zabid to receive a university degree in Islamic law [*qanun*]. He was influenced by the new Islamist trends; his young female students, who attended his classes in their chadors, brought home to their mothers his teachings on correct Islamic behaviour, which often differed quite markedly from what the older generation considered appropriate. He made quite a show of not chewing qat with the other men in the afternoon. According to his sisters, he thought the custom kept Yemen backward and wasted time. This radical departure from the norms of Zabidi consumption practices (I heard of only two other men who abstained from qat), left him open to charges of miserliness. His family denied that frugality or lack of money was the reason for his not allowing them to chew qat or chewing himself; his sisters fiercely claimed that he would rather pray and read holy books and said that, anyway, qat did not please them. Whatever the reason for this abstention, it did mean that they were not spending considerable daily sums on qat as are most Zabidis. His pompous 'holier-than-thou' attitude meant that he was not unreservedly popular. However, he was an influential teacher in the high school, widely respected for his learning, and he had allies among those prominent families who shared his style of religiosity.

Muhammad's mother, Iman, had little patience with snobby Zabidis looking down on her and tried to avoid large parties. Muhammad's wife, a woman from a tiny village in the wadi, was on her tenth pregnancy in fourteen years, and had neither the energy nor the requisite Zabidi savoir faire for *khuruj*. It fell to Iman's daughters to uphold the family's social connections and forge new ones. Three sisters were married into respectable if not wealthy Zabidi families in other quarters, so they had connections in several other neighbourhoods. Two unmarried sisters remained in the household, Muhammad's older sister, Hanan, and a younger sister, Anhar. They were fiercely loyal to their natal family; they venerated the memory of their father and spoke of their brother Muhammad in reverential tones. Anhar gave her schoolteacher's salary to her brother for the household budget and Hanan was constantly sewing clothes for Muhammad's children, to whom she devoted as much time as their mother did. Hanan almost single-handedly hosted the visitors every time Muhammad's wife had another baby. Their visiting and entertaining made them the driving force behind the family's rise in the female social world, although they were viewed with some ambivalence. While Anhar was bright and gregarious, she had alienated some with her bitter attacks on those she suspected of snubbing her. Some of her most devoted friends, her teaching colleagues at the local elementary school, however, were from Zabid's best-known families. She shared her brother's style of religiosity, and, in order to be particularly modest, she often donned gloves and stockings before she went out, a step most Zabidi women considered excessive and uncomfortable in Zabid's heat.

In 1989, when Muhammad had decided it was time to marry off his younger brother Walid, the bride desired was Amira, the granddaughter of the patriarch of Bayt Bassam, their father's former employer. The current head of Bayt Bassam was not as strong a figure as his father had been, according to Hanan, nor had he any business sense. Bayt Bassam, once a wealthy, notable family, had been weakened by a very public dispute between the two branches of the family who still inhabited the same family complex but refused to speak to each other. Both had few children and this complex always seemed deserted compared to others similar in size. Their energies seemed to go into fighting with each other rather than entertaining; I attended only one social function there, a birth reception, and the guests, like family members, were few.

Amira, Walid's fiancé, had no siblings aside from one sister. Neither of the sisters, unlike most Zabidi women of their age, had received a scrap of education. Yet the older one was married to a foreign-educated man, whose mother and father were among the foremost supporters in Zabid of the education of women. This match always puzzled me, especially since the mother-in-law claimed to have had nothing to do with the arrangement of the marriage, saying that her son had arranged the marriage himself with the girl's father. A reason for this unusual match was implied by Hanan, when they had announced the engagement of Walid to Amira, the younger daughter. Hanan told me how Bayt Bassam's family fortunes had so dwindled that they had virtually no money and few social contacts, but that they still had a great deal of land. Since there were no sons, the daughters could expect to inherit the majority of the land, which their husbands would manage and their sons would inherit. Perhaps the inheritance spurred the engineer to marry Amira's sister, braving the tangible disapproval of his strong-willed mother, with whom his illiterate bride uneasily lived.

I suspect that in the match between the second daughter and Bayt Khalid, the material factor of eventual land inheritance was not irrelevant either. But in Hanan's telling of the arrangement of the engagement, her brother Walid had always loved Amira, whom he had watched growing up. (He was twenty-five and she fifteen when the engagement was arranged.) Implicitly referring to the difference in status between the two families, she said that Amira's father had only agreed to the marriage because of the close relationship between Muhammad's father and his father. They could not afford the entire payment to Amira's father, but because the two families were close, the money was paid in small instalments, according to an agreement formalized in writing.

Bayt Muhammad Khalid was not a wealthy family, but they were particularly united in achieving their upwardly mobile ambitions. The production of this wedding was a project the family had worked collectively on for a long time. Anhar had wanted to go to university in the capital the year before. Muhammad had agreed and she was set to go, but then he decided that they would still need another year of her salary to finance her brother's wedding. Although bitterly disappointed, because her best friend was due to start that year, she never mentioned it in public.

They had been working for months on the construction of the *bayt* for

Walid within their family complex, doing a bit of work whenever they had the cash for supplies and labour. Finally, as the wedding approached in the summer of 1990, when the *akhdam* were mostly busy with other people's weddings, the entire family pitched in to help with the construction. This was the first time I heard of a *nas* family doing their own physical labour, and I doubt I would have heard of it from anyone but Hanan, who was so proud of the fine house they had built she could not resist bragging about it to me, even though many would consider it demeaning to have done the work themselves.

They had still not set a final date for the wedding until a month before the event occurred, dithering about whether they would actually have enough money to pull it off. Another sister, who had arrived from Saudi Arabia where her husband was working, finally convinced them to go ahead and throw the wedding during her visit. She and her husband contributed to the money needed for the purchase of the rest of the bride's gold jewelry a few days before the wedding. She had also brought fancy dresses from Saudi Arabia for her sisters to wear for the wedding festivities, saving Muhammad the expense of outfitting them. She and her older daughters threw themselves into the last-minute wedding preparations, as did their neighbours, one of whom volunteered their house so the female guests could change and relax before the wedding lunch.

The resulting *farah* was by no means as lavish as those thrown by the *kibar* that summer, but the *mikhdara* was decorated in the best style that they could manage, and they invited as many guests as they possibly could afford, about three hundred. The festivities were well attended by the school staff, both female and male, at their separate events. Even Zabid's governor came to the men's party.

The weddings in this family showed the changes in their fortune over the years: the father had been married to an orphan, on the charity of his employer, and the eldest son had married fifteen years ago to the daughter of a poor rural family. Their status had improved so much in the intervening years that the second son could be married to the granddaughter of their father's employer, whose family had declined as theirs had risen. Hard work and the wholehearted cooperation of both male and female members helped to effect this dramatic transformation. They were also one of the first families to take advantage of the possibilities of modern education and the school system to gain respect and influence as well as income. Although they were not considered a *bayt kabir*, and to some were still upstarts, they were a family to be reckoned with and acknowledged in contemporary Zabid.

The vignettes offered here illustrate, in the untidy detail of everyday life, the themes discussed in this book: the process of becoming *kabir* or sliding from that status; the cooperation between male and female spheres; and the shifts of material resources and prestige which occur over generations. Status is not static, it is emergent, inherent in the process of recognition, which gives the constant whirl of social interaction its frenetic edge.

This book suggests the wider significance of women's sociability for the standing of their families in Zabid. The women in a particular family are collectively responsible for upholding their family's social connections – part of the family patrimony – through hosting social events and attending those held by others. In Zabid, formal relationships exist between families as a whole; both men and women, in their respective public spheres, ensure the continuing viability of these ties. The honour of a family does not exist without continual recognition, and this recognition must be granted through the physical presence in one's home of a representative of another family. The *bayt* is a moral space, and by entering it, one allows oneself to be encompassed temporarily by the host family. To enter another's house is to acknowledge that one's reputation will not be tainted by one's presence there: it is a recognition of respectability. Hence not visiting is an implicit challenge. Given this significance for social standing within the community, it is not surprising that visiting is taken as very serious business.

Women are responsible for the everyday maintenance of the family's wider ties within the Zabidi community. They visit each other's homes more frequently than do men, and consistently host larger parties. The *kibar* households are those most able to afford the time and material resources that such events require. However, *kibar* women also pay visits to poorer kin, neighbours, and clients, which minimally acknowledge their respectability. This acknowledgment is essential if the members of the *bayt kabir* want to draw on the support of weaker neighbours and clients in the production of their own social events. In addition, there is a moral ethos that suggests that all Muslims, regardless of material wealth or social status, deserve recognition.

The social and economic position of the elite in Zabid is based on the domination of others both outside and inside the community: the rural people who work on their land as sharecroppers and, within Zabid, the *akhdam*. Relationships of dominance and subordination come to seem commonsensical as they permeate lived identities through the most everyday practices. What is significant is how the comportment of women, particularly the practices of modesty which structure interactions between

men and women and presuppose expressions of emotion, become the ratio-
nale – from the perspective of the elite – for the continuing domination of
the *akhdam*. The practices of female modesty are a locus for both personhood and hierarchy, embodying personal virtue and piety, as well as the
moral worth of families. It is in this context that the extreme measures to
control women's sexual comportment, such as female circumcision, have to
be understood. Women's modesty practices become a basis for self-esteem
and social superiority, but women themselves are constrained by these
practices. The failure of the *akhdam* to uphold the dominant standards of
comportment connotes flaws in moral personhood, implicitly justifying
inequalities in society. Modesty underpins the expression of emotions;
therefore, according to the Zabidi *nas*, the *akhdam* also lack restraint in the
display of emotions, particularly anger and grief. The fact that the moral
values of personal worth, piety, and family honour are embodied in appropriate comportment serves to lend persuasive force to these hierarchical
relationships.

From an analytical perspective, it is clear that more than morality is
involved. Claims to *asl*, respectable descent, which, along with appropriate
comportment, is a basis for acceptance among the *nas* , would be difficult
for *akhdam* to establish in a community such as Zabid where most people
are known, if not personally, at least by reputation and social identity. The
elite do not overtly recognize that the *akhdam* have few other economic
options but to engage in activities – begging, physical labour, and domestic
labour in the homes of others – which to them are shameful. Although
most of my field research was done among the *nas*, there were indications
that the *akhdam* were not as morally distant from the *nas* as was claimed,
especially in terms of Muslim identity.

I have argued that the ways in which emotions are enacted in Zabid are
related to the nature of the social structure and ideas of personhood. Anger
as a response to slights, and as a strategic display, is mobilized to manipulate, defend, or negotiate the recognition of one's family. One has to
demand respect and challenge insults through controlled confrontation.
However, these displays of anger are very stylized. Any intimation that
one has lost one's head is shameful. For the *nas*, modesty – the capacity to
submit passions to will – underpins the display of emotions as it does sexual desire.

From a man's perspective, his female kin should be concealed, behind
chadors and the high walls of his home, from the eyes of his significant
community – other adult males. The interior of his home and the adorned
bodies of his women can be witnessed only indirectly by other men,

through their female kin. However, I have suggested that this indirect display of wealth is significant for the status of families as a whole. A woman exhibits the wealth of her family in the quality of her adornment, but it is also testimony to her family's moral qualities such as generosity. The fulfilment of the moral obligation to provide for one's dependants, in a style appropriate to one's means and position in society, is made materially evident. Further, the transfer of material goods from a man to a woman is understood subjectively to indicate love and respect. Women indicate their respect for their families through their modest comportment, and male family members indicate their respect for their female kin by fulfilling their material obligations to them. Thus adorned women in public display how their families value them as persons. Adornment signifies the material means and moral qualities of a man; while for a woman adornment is affectively charged as an indication of her personal value.

The transfer of gold at marriage exemplifies this general point. To marry without it is to make oneself cheap – to devalue oneself and debase one's family. The transfer of gold indicates a woman's virtue and the value of her family. Particularly among the *kibar*, a woman's natal family endows her with material possessions to indicate their value of her as a person and their worth as a family. To make oneself cheap is to open oneself to abuse and danger: one must demand respect to be treated with respect.

Piety is the foundation of identity, for both men and women; in this respect, local Zabidi practice is in perfect accord with the teachings of the Prophet Muhammad. Training in prayer and fasting inculcates in children a primary principal of personhood: the capacity to submit one's body to one's will, and the obligation to submit one's will to the will of God.

Piety is not only the foundation of appropriate persons but also an important basis for status. Pious acts not only positively affect the future of the individual in the afterlife, they also affect the reputation of one's family within the community. But pious acts are more easily within the reach of the great families; piety is one of the most significant elements of prestige. Zabidis make a connection between modest comportment of family members – which is understood to be a function of piety – and piety itself. Together they constitute respectability and honour.

Considerable resources are expended in the pursuit of sociability in Zabid: for appropriate attire, hospitality, and the qat which is consumed daily. As has been shown in several chapters, material wealth is a necessary basis of social status in Zabid. However, material wealth alone is not enough: it has to be consumed, distributed, and displayed in appropriate ways, converting material wealth into cultural capital. Zabidis are aware of some of the contradictions inherent in their consumption practices. A woman told me a proverb, part of a popular song, which she guaranteed would make any Yemeni laugh in recognition:

Qat and meat
One's legacy deplete

The central economic problem which every landowning family faces is how to maintain the expected standards of consumption without having to liquidate one's land, thereby undermining the long-term security of one's family. Land ensures not only continued income, but also that one's family will continue to be considered one of the *kibar*. Whereas prestige is constituted in part by consumption practices which require considerable expenditure, the material base of a family must be safeguarded in order to ensure the continued viability of one's family over time. There are several families who retain only vestiges of their once-*kabir* status due to mismanagement of their estates, providing examples to others of the delicate balance which must be maintained between consumption and preservation of the material base.

The practice of women's sociability, *khuruj*, is highly valued. It defines social identity on several levels. The enthusiasm with which this practice is pursued provides an evocative identity which is said to offer integration at the community level and distinguish Zabid culturally from other communities. Yet *khuruj*, the finest quality of social life of Zabid, is also the site of danger and divisiveness. One's family's reputation is put on the line, open to the evaluation of others. A family's affluence is displayed on the bodies of women in the context of public visits, but it is also made vulnerable to the evil eye. The envious eyes of others are a danger that exists in sociability.

The tensions inherent in social life in Zabid are essentially unresolvable. A *bayt* presents itself on social occasions as autonomous, but this autonomous stance is only a moment in a series of exchanges. As in so many other societies where honour is a value, an audience is necessary, as honour does not exist without recognition. Competition with one's peers is necessary to define one's own identity. But one must fulfil one's obligations to others in order for those others to give one the recognition one is due. As much as modesty, hospitality creates honour for families, and the exchange of hospitality distinguishes as well as maintains bonds between families. Through the process of the agonistic exchange of hospitality, *bayts* define themselves in opposition to other *bayts*. Generosity is a positive quality, but by being generous, one is attempting to encompass, at least temporarily, those to whom one is being generous. Standards of consumption must be maintained without undermining future security. And finally, one must balance the desire to be a member of a distinguished family in this world with the obligation to be a humble, pious person before God. One can never remain at rest or relax one's vigilance in comportment.

Glossary

This is a short glossary of words commonly used in this text. The words are here fully transliterated. Those which appear more than once, and are not glossed within the text each time, are included. The 'a' in brackets indicates the feminine form of the word.

'abīd, sing. *'abd*   slave, also used to refer to ex-slaves
adab   correct comportment, good breeding, manners
Aden   former capital of South Yemen
akhdām, sing. *khādim(a)*   servant, lowest social status in Yemen
'aqd   legal ceremony of marriage
'aql   reasın, sense, will
'arb'ayīn   fortieth, party held to honour a woman who has given birth
'arūsa   bride
aṣl   deep-rooted
aṣlī   genuine, original
'aṣr   afternoon prayer, earlier visiting session
'ayb   shame
banāt, sing. *bint*   girls
baraka   God's blessings
bayt, pl. *buyūt*   family, house
bayt kabīr, pl. *al-kibār*   notable families, the notables
bukhūr   incense
chador   black modesty garment, covering women's bodies (also known as a *sharshaf*)
da'īf   weak
dukhla   evening of the wedding festivities when bride enters the groom's house

*dur*ʿ   finely woven, patterned cotton dress
farah   wedding festivites
farash   pillows and couch coverings
fashaʾi   relaxation
fūta   sarong
ghaḍban(a)   angry, fed up
hadīth   saying of the Prophet Muhammad
ḥajj   pilgrimage
ḥajj(a)   one who has made the pilgrimage
ḥarām   forbidden
al-Hudayda   port city on the Tihama
ḥubb   love
ʿīd   religious festival
istiḥyāʾ   modesty
istiḥī!   (imperative) behave properly!
iḥtirām   respect
jahil, pl. *juhhāl*   child, ignorant person
jīrān   neighbours
kabīr   great, big
khādim(a), pl. *akhdām*   servant
khidhāb   an ornamental pattern decorating women's hands and feet.
khātim   recital of the entire Quʿran
khazzan (verb)   chew qat
khilwa   second-story room
khunna   face veil
khurūj   going out
kibār (pl.)   elite, notable families
layl   evening prayer, second visiting session
mabraz   male entertaining space
madāʿa   waterpipe
madhhab   legal school
maghrib   sundown, sundown prayers
majanna   graveyard
majnūn(a)   crazy person
mawlid   ritual recital of an account of the life of the Prophet Muhammad
mazāyanah, sing. *muzayyin(a)*   butchers, barbers, circumcisors
maʿazūm(a)   invited
mikhdara   large tent constructed for wedding festivities
miskīn(a), pl. *masākīn*   poor, but also (in Yemen) nice, not arrogant
murabbaʾ   room in Zabidi house

murtaḥ(a)   comfortable
mustaḥīy(a)   embarrassed
mutakabbir(a)   snobby, presumptuous
nafs   passion
nās   people, used in Zabid to refer to ordinary and elite people
qabā'il   tribesmen, rural folk
qabal   courtyard
qāt   plant, *Catha edulis*, chewed in sociable gatherings
sādah, sing. *sayyid*   descendant of the Prophet Muhammad
San'a'   capital of Yemen
sha'b   people
Shafi'i   school of Sunni jurisprudence
sharaf   honor
shilla   clique
sumra   late evening qat-chewing parties, often held at weddings
ta'abān(a)   tired, worn out
Ta'izz   city in Lower Yemen
Tihama   coastal plain along the Red Sea
tujjār, sing. *tājir*   merchants
'ūd   aloewood
wājib   duty
wilāda   birth, birth reception
za'al   anger
za'alān(a)   angry
zār   spirit possession ceremony
Zaydi   school of Shi'i jurisprudence
zumalā', sing. *zamīl(a)*   colleagues

Bibliography

Abu-Lughod, J. 1987. The Islamic City – Historic Myth, Islamic Essence, and Contemporary Relevance. *International Journal of Middle East Studies* 19:155–76.

Abu-Lughod, L. 1985. A Community of Secrets. *Signs* 10:637–57.

– 1986. *Veiled Sentiments: Honor and Poetry in a Bedouin Society.* Berkeley: University of California Press.

– 1990. Anthropology's Orient: The Boundaries of Theory in the Arab World. In H. Sharabi, ed., *Theory, Politics and the Arab World*, pp. 52–131. New York: Routledge.

– 1993. *Writing Women's Worlds: Bedouin Stories.* Berkeley: University of California Press.

Abu-Lughod, L., and C. Lutz. 1990. Introduction: Emotion, Discourse, and the Politics of Everyday Life. In C. Lutz and L. Abu-Lughod, eds., *Language and the Politics of Emotion*, pp. 1–23. Cambridge: Cambridge University Press.

Abu-Zahra, N. 1970. On the Modesty of Women in Arab Muslim Villages: A Reply. *American Anthropologist* 72:1079–87.

– 1974. Material Power, Honour, Friendship, and the Etiquette of Visiting. *Anthropological Quarterly* 47:120–38.

– 1991. The Comparative Study of Muslim Societies and Islamic Rituals. *Arab Historical Review for Ottoman Studies* 3–4:7–38.

Adra, N. 1982. Qabyalah: The Tribal Concept in the Central Highlands of the Yemen Arab Republic. Ph D thesis, Temple University, Philadelphia, Pennsylvania.

Altorki, S. 1977. Family Organization and Women's Power in Urban Saudi Arabian Society. *Journal of Anthropological Research* 33:277–87.

– 1986. *Women in Saudi Arabia: Ideology and Behavior among the Elite.* New York: Columbia University Press.

Altorki, S. and D.P. Cole. 1989. *Arabian Oasis City: The Transformation of 'Unayzah*. Austin: University of Texas Press.

'Amri, Husayn b. Abdullah al-. 1985. *The Yemen in the 18th and 19th Centuries: A Political and Intellectual History*. London: Ithaca Press.

– 1987. Slaves and Mamelukes in the History of Yemen. In W. Daum, ed., *Yemen: 3000 Years of Art and Civilization in Arabia Felix*, pp. 140–57. Frankfurt/Main: Umschau-Verlag.

Anderson, B. 1991. *Imagined Communities*. New York: Verso Press.

Anderson, J. 1982. Social Structure and the Veil: Comportment and the Composition of Interaction in Afghanistan. *Anthropos* 77:397–420.

Antoun, R.T. 1968. On the Modesty of Women in Arab Muslim Villages: A Study in the Accommodation of Traditions. *American Anthropologist* 70:671–97.

Appadurai, A., ed. 1986. *The Social Life of Things:Commodities in Cultural Perspective*. Cambridge: Cambridge University Press.

Asad, T. 1986. *The Idea of an Anthropology of Islam*. Occasional Papers. Washington, DC: Center for Contemporary Arab Studies, Georgetown University.

– 1993. *Genealogies of Religion*. Baltimore: Johns Hopkins University Press.

Aswad, B.C. 1974. Visiting Patterns among Women of the Elite in a Small Turkish City. *Anthropological Quarterly* 9:9–23.

– 1978. Women, Class, and Power: Examples from the Hatay, Turkey. In L. Beck and N. Keddie, eds., *Women in the Muslim World*, pp. 473–81. Cambridge, Mass.: Harvard University Press.

Baldry, J. 1984. One Hundred Years of Yemeni History: 1849–1948. In J. Chelhod, ed., *L'Arabie du Sud: Histoire et Civilisation*, tome II, pp. 73–111. Paris: Editions GP Maissonneuve et Larose.

– 1985. The History of the Tihamah from 1800 to the Present. In F. Stone, ed., *Studies on the Tihamah*, pp. 45–50. Salt Lake City: University of Utah Press.

Balfour-Paul, J. 1990. The Indigo Industry of the Yemen. In R.B. Serjeant and R.L. Bidwell, eds., *Arabian Studies*, pp. 39–62. Cambridge: Cambridge University Press.

Barakat, H. 1985. The Arab Family and the Challenge of Social Transformation. In E. Fernea, ed., *Women and Family in the Middle East*. Austin: University of Texas Press.

Bateson, G. 1972. *Steps to an Ecology of Mind*. New York: Ballantine Books.

– 1988. Play and Paradigm. *Play and Culture* 1:20–7.

Beeman, W.O. 1986. *Language, Status, and Power in Iran*. Bloomington: Indiana University of Press.

Behnam, D. 1985. The Muslim Family and the Modern World. *Current Anthropology* 26:555–6.

Beidelman, T.O. 1972. The Kaguru House. *Anthropos* 67:690–707.

- 1983 [1971]. *The Kaguru: A Matrilineal People of East Africa.* Prospect Heights, Ill.: Waveland Press.
- 1986. *Moral Imagination in Kaguru Modes of Thought.* Bloomington: Indiana University Press.
- 1989. Agonistic Exchange: Homeric Reciprocity and the Heritage of Simmel and Mauss. *Cultural Anthropology* 4:227–59.
Benedict, P. 1974. The Kabul Gunu: Structured Visiting in an Anatolian Provincial Town. *Anthropological Quarterly* 47:28–47.
Betteridge, A. 1980. The Controversial Vows of Urban Muslim Women in Iran. In N.A. Falk and R.M. Gross, eds., *Unspoken Worlds: Women's Religious Lives in Non-Western Cultures*, pp. 140–55. San Francisco: Harper and Row.
- 1985. Gift Exchange in Iran: The Locus of Self-Identity in Interaction. *Anthropological Quarterly* 58:182–202.
Bidwell, R.L. 1983. *The Two Yemens.* Boulder, Colo: Westview Press.
Boddy, J. 1988. Spirits and Selves in Northern Sudan: The Cultural Therapeutics of Possession and Trance. *American Ethnologist* 15:4–27.
- 1989. *Wombs and Alien Spirits: Women, Men, and the Zar Cult in Northern Sudan.* Madison: University of Wisconsin Press.
- 1993. Aesthetics, Politics, and Women's Health in Northern Sudan and Beyond. Paper presented at the annual meeting of the American Anthropological Association.
Bogary, H. 1991. *The Sheltered Quarter: A Tale of Boyhood in Mecca.* Trans. O. Kenny and J. Reed. Austin: University of Texas Press.
Bornstein, A. 1972a. Al Zohrah – An Agricultural Village in the Tihama. FAO Food and Nutrition Program – Yemen 13.
- 1972b. Al Homrah and Ibn Abas: Two Fishing Villages in the Tihama. FAO Food and Nutrition Program – Yemen 71/513.
Bourdieu, P. 1976. Marriage Strategies as Strategies of Social Reproduction. In R. Forster and O. Ranum, eds., *Family and Society: Selections from the Annales*, pp. 117–44. Baltimore: Johns Hopkins University Press.
- 1977. *Outline of a Theory of Practice.* Richard Nice, transl. Cambridge: Cambridge University Press.
- 1979. The Kabyle House. In *Algeria 1960*, pp. 133–53. Cambridge: Cambridge University Press.
- 1984. *Distinction: A Social Critique of the Judgement of Taste.* Cambridge, Mass.: Harvard University Press.
Bowen, J.R. 1989. Salat in Indonesia: The Social Meanings of an Islamic Ritual. *Man* 24:600–19.
- 1992. On Scriptural Essentialism and Ritual Variation: Muslim Sacrifice in Sumatra and Morocco. *American Ethnologist* 19:656–71.

Bujra, A. 1971. *The Politics of Stratification: A Study of Political Change in a South Arabian Town*. London: Oxford University Press.

Burrowes, R.D. 1987. *The Yemen Arab Republic: The Politics of Development, 1962–1986*. Boulder, Colo.: Westview Press.

Butler, J. 1990. *Gender Trouble: Feminism and the Subversion of Identity*. New York: Routledge.

Campbell, J. 1964. *Honour, Family, and Patronage*. Oxford: Clarendon Press.

Carapico, S. 1988. Autonomy and Secondhand Oil Dependency of the Yemen Arab Republic. *Arab Studies Quarterly* 10:193–213.

Carapico, S., and C. Myntti. 1991. A Tale of Two Families: Change in North Yemen 1977–1989. *Middle East Report*: 24–9.

Caton, S.C. 1986. Salam Tahiyah: Greetings from the Highlands of Yemen. *American Ethnologist* 13:290–308.

– 1990 *'The Peaks of Yemen I Summon': Poetry as Cultural Practice in a North Yemeni Tribe*. Berkeley: University of California Press.

Chelhod, J. 1978. Introduction à l'Histoire Sociale et Urbaine de Zabid. *Arabica* 25:48–88.

Clark, H.B. 1947. Yemen – South Arabia's Mountain Wonderland. *National Geographic Magazine* 42:631–72.

Combs-Schilling, M.E. 1989. *Sacred Performances: Islam, Sexuality, and Sacrifice*. New York: Columbia University Press.

Daum, W., ed. 1987. *Yemen: 3000 Years of Art and Civilisation in Arabia Felix*. Frankfurt/Main:Umschau-Verlag.

Delaney, C. 1986. The Meaning of Paternity and the Virgin Birth Debate. *Man* 21:494–513.

– 1987. Seeds of Honor, Fields of Shame. In D. Gilmore, ed., *Honor and the Unity of the Mediterranean*, pp. 35–48. Washington: American Anthropological Association.

– 1988a. Mortal Flow: Menstruation in Turkish Village Society. In T. Buckley and A. Gottlieb, eds., *Blood Magic: The Anthropology of Menstruation*, pp. 75–93. Berkeley: University of California Press.

– 1988b. Participant-Observation: The Razor's Edge. *Dialectical Anthropology* 13:291–300.

– 1990. The Hajj: Sacred and Secular. *American Ethnologist* 17:513–30.

– 1991. *The Seed and the Soil: Gender and Cosmology in Turkish Village Society*. Berkeley: University of California Press.

Dorsky, S. 1986. *Women of 'Amran: A Middle Eastern Ethnographic Survey*. Salt Lake City: University of Utah Press.

Dresch, P. 1984. Tribal Relations and Political History in Upper Yemen. In B.R.

Pridham, ed., *Contemporary Yemen: Politics and Historical Background*, pp. 154–74. London: Croom Helm.

– 1989. *Tribes, Government and History in Yemen*. Oxford: Clarendon Press.

– 1990. Imams and Tribes: The Writing and Acting of History in Upper Yemen. In P.S. Khoury and J. Kostiner, eds., *Tribes and State Formation in the Middle East*, pp. 252–87. Berkeley: University of California Press.

ECWA/FAO Joint Agricultural Division. 1978. The Transfer of Technology and Investment Policy Design: A Case Study in Rural Poverty. In *Technology Transfer and Change in the Arab World: The Proceedings of a Seminar of the United Nations Economic Commission for Western Asia*, pp. 325–31. New York: Pergamon Press.

Eickelman, C. 1984. *Women and Community in Oman*. New York: New York University Press.

– 1988. Women and Politics in an Arabian Oasis. In F. Kazemi and R.D. McChesney, eds., *A Way Prepared: Essays in Islamic Culture in Honor of Richard Bayly Winder*, pp. 199–215. New York: New York University Press.

Eickelman, D.F. 1976. *Moroccan Islam: Tradition and Society in a Pilgrimage Center*. Austin: University of Texas Press.

– 1977. Time in a Complex Society: A Moroccan Example. *Ethnology* 16:39–55.

– 1978. The Art of Memory: Islamic Education and Its Social Reproduction. *Comparative Studies in Society and History* 20:485–516.

– 1979. The Political Economy of Meaning. *American Ethnologist* 6:386–93.

– 1987a. Mawlid. In M. Eliade, ed., *The Encyclopedia of Religion*, pp. 292–93. New York: Macmillan.

– 1987b. Rites of Passage: Muslim Rites. In *The Encyclopedia of Religion*, vol. 12, pp. 398–403. New York: Macmillan.

– 1987c. Changing Interpretations of Islamic Movements. In W.R. Roff, ed., *Islam and the Political Economy of Meaning*, pp. 13–30. Berkeley: University of California Press.

– 1989. *The Middle East: An Anthropological Approach*, 2nd ed. Englewood Cliffs, NJ: Prentice Hall.

– 1992. Mass Higher Education and the Religious Imagination in Contemporary Arab Societies. *American Ethnologist* 19:643–55.

Eickelman, D.F., and J. Piscatori. 1990. Social Theory in the Study of Muslim Societies. In *Muslim Travellers: Pilgrimage, Migration, and the Religious Imagination*, pp. 3–25. Berkeley: University of California Press.

Elias, N. 1978. *The History of Manners*. New York: Pantheon Books.

Fajans, J., ed. 1993. *Exchanging Products: Producing Exchange*. Oceania Monograph, 43. Sydney: Oceania Publications.

Fayein, C. 1957. *A French Doctor in the Yemen*. Trans. D. McGee. London: Robert Hale.

Fernea, E. 1969. *Guests of the Sheik: An Ethnography of an Iraqi Village*. New York: Anchor Books.

Fischer, M.M.J. 1980. Competing Ideologies and Social Structure in the Persian Gulf. In A. Cottrell, ed., *The Persian Gulf States*, pp. 510–38. Baltimore: Johns Hopkins University Press.

Fleurentin, J., C. Myntti, and J.M. Pelt. 1986. Traditional Medicine and Traditional Healers in North Yemen. *Sonderband* 5:133–44.

Friedman, J. 1990. The Political Economy of Elegance: An African Cult of Beauty. *Culture and History* 7:101–25.

– 1991. Consuming Desires: Strategies of Selfhood and Appropriation. *Cultural Anthropology* 2:154–63.

Gause, F.G. 1987. The Idea of Yemeni Unity. *Journal of Arab Affairs* 6:55–81.

Geertz, C. 1973. *The Interpretation of Culture*. New York: Basic Books.

– 1983. *Local Knowledge: Further Essays in Interpretive Anthropology*. New York: Basic Books.

Geertz, C., H. Geertz, and L. Rosen. 1979. *Meaning and Order in Moroccan Society*. New York: Cambridge University Press.

Gerholm, T. 1977. Market, *Mosque and Mafraj: Social Inequality in a Yemeni Town*. Stockholm: Stockholm Studies in Social Anthropology 5.

– 1985. Aspects of Inheritance and Marriage Payment in North Yemen. In A.E. Mayer, ed., *Property, Social Structure and Law in the Modern Middle East*, pp. 129–51. Albany: State University of New York Press.

Gellner, E. 1981. *Muslim Society*. Cambridge: Cambridge University Press.

Giddens, A. 1979./ *Central Problems in Social Theory*. Berkeley: University of California Press.

Gilsenan, M. 1976. Lying, Honor, and Contradiction. In B. Kapferer, ed., *Transaction and Meaning*, pp. 191–219. Philadelphia: Institute for the Study of Human Issues.

– 1977. Against Patron-Client Relations. In E. Gellner and J. Waterbury, eds., *Patrons and Clients*, pp. 167–83. London: Duckworth.

– 1982. *Recognizing Islam*. New York: Pantheon Books.

Goffman, E. 1959. *The Presentation of Self in Everyday Life*. New York: Anchor Books.

– 1967. *Interaction Ritual: Essays on Face-to-Face Behavior*. New York: Pantheon Books.

– 1974. *Frame Analysis: An Essay on the Organization of Experience*. Boston: Northeastern University Press.

Graham, W.A. 1987. *Beyond the Written Word: Oral Aspects of Scripture in the History of Religion*. Cambridge: Cambridge University Press.

Greenman, J. 1978. A Sketch of the Arabic Dialect of the Central Yamani Tihamah. *Al-'Arabiyya* 11:20–34.

Grunebaum, Ch.E. von. 1970. Ramadan. In A.M. Lutfiyya and C.W. Churchill, eds., *Readings in Arab Middle Eastern Societies and Cultures*, pp. 224–34. The Hague: Mouton.

Hadrami, Abdul-Rahman al-. 1985. *Jâmi'at al-Ashâ'ir Zabid*. Beirut: Dar Azal.

Haeri, S. 1989. *Law of Desire: Temporary Marriage in Shi'i Iran*. Syracuse: Syracuse University Press.

Handler, R., and D.A. Segal. 1985. Hierarchies of Choice: The Social Construction of Rank in Jane Austen. *American Ethnologist* 4:691–706.

Harré, R. 1984. *Personal Being: A Theory for Individual Psychology*. Cambridge, Mass.: Harvard University Press.

Heath, D. 1992. Fashion, Anti-fashion, and Heteroglossia in Urban Senegal. *American Ethnologist* 19:19–33.

Hertz, R. 1960 [1907]. A Contribution to the Study of the Collective Representation of Death. In R. Needham, trans. *Death and the Right Hand*. Glencoe, Ill.: Free Press.

Herzfeld, M. 1980. Honour and Shame: Problems in the Comparative Analysis of Moral Systems. *Man* 15:339–51.

– 1987. 'As in Your Own Home': Hospitality, Ethnography, and the Stereotype of Mediterranean Society. In D. Gilmore, ed., *Honor and Shame and the Unity of the Mediterranean*, pp. 75–89. Washington: American Anthropological Association.

Hourani, A. 1991. *A History of the Arab Peoples*. Cambridge, Mass.: Harvard University Press.

Ibn Battuta. 1983 [1929]. *Travels in Asia and Africa, 1325–1354*. London: Routledge & Kegan Paul.

Ibrahim, H. 1988. Leisure, Idleness and Ibn Khaldun. *Leisure Studies* 7:51–8.

Irvine, J.T. 1990. Registering affect: Heteroglossia in the Linguistic Expression of Emotion. In C. Lutz and L. Abu-Lughod, eds., *Language and the Politics of Emotion*, pp. 126–61. Cambridge: Cambridge University Press.

Jackson, M. 1983. Knowledge of the Body. *Man* 18:327–45.

Joseph, S. 1983. Working Class Women's Networks in a Sectarian State: A Political Paradox. *American Ethnologist* 10:1–22.

– 1986. Study of Middle Eastern Women: Investments, Passions, and Problems. *International Journal of Middle East Studies* 18:501–9.

– 1994. Brother/Sister Relationships: Connectivity, Love, and Power in the Reproduction of Patriarchy in Lebanon. *American Ethnologist* 21:50–73.

Kandiyoti, D. 1987. Emancipated but Unliberated: Reflections on the Turkish Case. *Feminist Studies* 13:317–38.

– 1991. End of the Empire: Islam, Nationalism, and Women in Turkey. In *Women, Islam, and the State*, pp. 22–47. Philadelphia: Temple University Press.

Kandiyoti, D., ed. 1991. *Women, Islam, and the State*. Philadelphia: Temple University Press.

Kanafani, A. 1983. *Aesthetics and Ritual in the United ArabEmirates*. Beirut: American University of Beirut.

Kapchan, D. 1992. Women in the Marketplace: Transitional Economies and Feminine Discursive Domains in Morocco. Ph.D. thesis, University of Pennsylvania.

Karp, I. 1980. Beer Drinking and Social Experience in an African Society: An Essay in Formal Sociology. In I. Karp and C.S. Bird, eds., *Explorations in African Systems of Thought*, pp. 83–119. Bloomington: Indiana University Press.

Kay, H.C. 1892. *Yaman, Its Early Medieval History*. London: E. Arnold.

Khazraji, A.H. al-. 1907. *The Pearl-Strings; A History of the Resuliyy Dynasty of Yemen*. Vol. II. Trans. J.W. Redhouse. Leiden: Brill.

Keall, E.J. 1982. *Zabid and Its Hinterland: 1982 Report*. Toronto: Royal Ontario Museum.

– 1983. The Dynamics of Zabid and Its Hinterland: The Survey of a Town on the Tihamah Plain of North Yemen. *World Archaeology* 14:378–92.

– 1989. A Few Facts About Zabid. Seminar for Arabian Studies, *Proceedings* 19:61–9.

– 1992. Mud, Sand and Sod's Law in Dusty Old Zabid. Toronto: Royal Ontario Museum *Newsletter*, Series II 48:1–4.

Knappert, J. 1990. Mawlid. *Encyclopedia of Islam*, pp. 895–7. Leiden: Brill.

– 1971. *Swahili Islamic Poetry*. Leiden: Brill.

Knauft, B. 1994. Foucault Meets South New Guinea: Knowledge, Power, Sexuality. *Ethos* 22:391–498.

Konig, R. 1973. *A La Mode*. New York: Seabury Press.

Lambek, M. 1990. Certain Knowledge, Contestable Authority: Power and Practice on the Islamic Periphery. *American Ethnologist* 17:23–40.

– 1992. Taboo as Cultural Practice among Malagasy Speakers. *Man* 27:245–66.

Lancaster, W. 1981. *The Rwala Bedouin Today*. Cambridge: Cambridge University Press.

Lapidus, I.M. 1984. Knowledge, Virtue, and Action: The Classical Muslim Conception of Adab and the Nature of Religious Fulfillment in Islam. In B.D. Metcalf, ed., *Moral Conduct and Authority*, pp. 38–61. Berkeley: University of California Press.

Lewis, B. 1970. *Race and Color in Islam*. New York: Octagon Books.

Lutz, C. and L. Abu-Lughod, eds. 1990. *Language and the Politics of Emotion*. Cambridge: Cambridge University Press.

Madelung, W. 1987. Islam in Yemen. In W. Daum, ed., *Yemen: 3000 Years of Art and Civilisation in Arabia Felix*, pp. 174–7. Frankfurt/Main: Umschau-Verlag.

Makhlouf, C. 1979. *Changing Veils: Women and Modernization in North Yemen*. Austin: University of Texas Press.

Marcus, G., ed. 1983. *Elites: Ethnographic Issues*. Albuquerque: University of New Mexico Press.

Marcus, J. 1984. Islam, Women and Pollution in Turkey. *Journal of the Anthropological Society of Oxford* 15:204–18.

– 1987. Equal Rites and Women in Turkey. *Mankind* 17:120–8.

Martin, R.C. 1985. *Approaches to Islam in Religious Studies*. Tucson: University of Arizona Press.

Mauss, M. 1970. *The Gift: Forms and Functions of Exchange in Archaic Societies*. Trans. Ian Cunnison. London: Routledge & Kegan Paul.

– 1973. Techniques of the Body. Trans. B. Brewster. *Economy and Society* 2:70–88.

– 1979. *Sociology and Psychology: Essays*. Trans. B. Brewster. London: Routledge & Kegan Paul.

McPherson, J.W. 1941. *The Moulids of Egypt: Egyptian Saints' Days*. Cairo: N.M. Press.

Meeker, M. 1976. Meaning and Society in the Near East: Examples from the Black Sea Turks and the Levantine Arabs. *International Journal of Middle East Studies* 7:243–70, 383–422.

Meisami, J.S. 1991. *The Sea of Precious Virtues: A Medieval Islamic Mirror for Princes*. Salt Lake City: University of Utah Press.

Messick, B. 1978. Transactions in Ibb: Economy and Society in a Yemeni Highland Town. Ph D Thesis, Princeton University.

– 1986. The Mufti, the Text and the World: Legal Interpretation in Yemen. *Man* 21:102–19.

– 1993. *The Calligraphic State: Textual Domination and History in a Muslim Society*. Berkeley: University of California Press.

Metcalf, B.D. 1984. Introduction. *Moral Conduct and Authority*, pp. 1–20. Berkeley: University of California Press.

– 1990. The Pilgrimage Remembered: South Asian Accounts of the Hajj. In D.F. Eickelman and J. Piscatori, eds., *Muslim Travellers: Pilgrimage, Migration, and the Religious Imagination*, pp. 85–107. Berkeley: University of California Press.

Miller, D. 1987. *Material Culture and Mass Consumption*. Oxford: Basil Blackwell.

– 1990. Fashion and Ontology in Trinidad. *Culture and History* 7:49–77.

Molyneux, M. 1991. The Law, the State, and Socialist Policies with Regard to Women: The Case of the People's Democratic Republic of Yemen 1967–1990. In D. Kandiyoti, ed., *Women, Islam, and the State*, pp. 237–71. Philadelphia: Temple University Press.

Moser, C. 1917. *The Flower of Paradise*. National Geographic Magazine 32:173–85.

Mundy, M. 1979. Women's Inheritance of Land in Highland Yemen. *Arabian Studies* 5:161–87.

– 1983. San'a Dress, 1920–75. In R.B. Serjeant and R. Lewcock, eds., *San'a': An Arabian Islamic City*, pp. 529–41. London: World of Islam Festival Trust.

– 1985. Agricultural Development in the Yemeni Tihama: The Past Ten Years. In B.R. Pridham, ed., *Economy, Society and Culture in Contemporary Yemen*, pp. 22–40. London: Croom Helm.

Myers, F.R. 1986. *Pintupi Country, Pintupi Self: Sentiment, Place, and Politics Among Western Desert Aborigines*. Washington/Canberra: Smithsonian Institute and Australian Institute of Aboriginal Studies.

– 1988. The Logic and Meaning of Anger Among Pintupi Aborigines. *Man* 23:589–610.

– 1993. Place, Identity, and Exchange in a Totemic System. In J. Fajans, ed., *Exchanging Products, Producing Exchange*, pp. 33–58. Oceania Monograph, 43. Sydney: Oceania Publications.

Myntti, C. 1979. *Women and Development in North Yemen*. Germany: German Agency for Technical Cooperation.

– 1984. Yemeni Workers Abroad: The Impact on Women. *Middle East Reports*, pp. 11–16.

– 1985. Changing Attitudes towards Health: Some Observations from the Hujariya. In B.R. Pridman, ed., *Economy, Society and Culture in Contemporary Yemen*, pp. 165–71. London: Croom Helm.

– 1988. Hegemony and Healing in Rural North Yemen. *Social Science Medicine* 27:515–20.

– 1990. Notes on Mystical Healers in the Hugariyyah. In R.B. Serjeant and R.L. Bidwell, eds., *Arabian Studies*, pp. 171–6. Cambridge: Cambridge University Press.

Nelson, C. 1974. Public and Private Politics: Women in the Middle Eastern World. *American Ethnologist* 1:551–63.

Olson, E.A. 1985. Muslim Identity and Secularism in Contemporary Turkey: The Headscarf Dispute. *Anthropological Quarterly* 58:161–89.

Papanek, H. and G. Minault, eds. 1982. *Separate Worlds: Studies of Purdah in South Asia*. Columbia, Mo.: South Asia Books.

Peristiany, J.G., ed. 1974 [1966]. *Honour and Shame: The Values of Mediterranean Society.* Chicago: University of Chicago Press. Midway Reprint.

Peterson, J.E. 1982. *Yemen: The Search for a Modern State.* Baltimore: Johns Hopkins University Press.

Rienhardt, A.K. 1990. Impurity/No Danger. History of Religions 30:1–24.

Riesman, P. 1983. On the Irrelevance of Child Rearing Practices for the Formation of Personality. *Culture, Medicine and Psychiatry* 7:103–29.

– 1992. *First Find Your Child a Good Mother: The Construction of Self in Two African Communities.* New Brunswick, NJ: Rutgers University Press.

Rogers, S. 1975. Female Forms of Power and the Myth of Male Dominance: A Model of Female\Male Interaction in Peasant Society. *American Ethnologist* 2:727–56.

Rosen, L. 1984. *Bargaining for Reality: The Construction of Social Relations in a Muslim Community.* Chicago: University of Chicago Press.

Rosenfeld, H. 1974. Non-Hierarchical, Hierarchical and Masked Reciprocity in an Arab Village. *Anthropological Quarterly* 47:139–66.

Sadek, N. 1989. Rasulid Women: Power and Patronage. Seminar for Arabian Studies, *Proceedings* 19:121–9.

– 1990. Patronage and Architecture in Rasulid Yemen, 626–858 A.H./1229–1454 A.D. Ph D thesis, University of Toronto.

Schimmel, A. 1985. *And Muhammad Is His Messenger: The Veneration of the Prophet in Islamic Piety.* Chapel Hill: University of North Carolina Press.

Seremetakis, N. 1990. The Ethics of Antiphony: The Social Construction of Pain, Gender, and Power in the Southern Peloponnese. *Ethos* 18:481–511.

– 1991. *The Last Word: Women, Death, and Divination in Inner Mani.* Chicago: University of Chicago Press.

Serjeant, R.B. 1962. Sex, Birth, Circumcision: Some Notes from South-West Arabia. In A. Leidlmaie, ed., *Herman von Wissman – Festschrift*, pp. 193–208. Tubingen.

– 1977. South Arabia. In C.A.O. Van Nieuvenhuize, ed., *Commoners, Climbers and Notables*, pp. 226–47. Leiden: Brill.

– 1987. Early Islamic and Mediaeval Trade and Commerce in the Yemen. In W. Daum, ed., *Yemen: 3000 Years of Art and Civilisation in Arabia Felix*, pp. 163–6. Frankfurt/Main: Umschau-Verlag.

– 1991. Tihamah Notes. Arabicus Felix: Luminosus Britannicus. In A. Jones, ed., *Essays in Honour of A.F.L. Beeston on His Eightieth Birthday*, pp. 45–60. Oxford: Ithaca Press Reading.

Sharafaddin, A.H. 1961. *Yemen: 'Arabia Felix.'* Rome: Daily American.

Simmel, G. 1950. *The Sociology of Georg Simmel.* Trans. K. Wolff, New York: The Free Press.

- 1957. Fashion. *The American Journal of Sociology* 112:541–58.
- 1971. *On Individuality and Social Form.* Chicago: University of Chicago Press.
- 1991. Style. *Theory, Culture and Society* 8:63–71.
Smith, G.R. 1987. The Political History of the Islamic Yemen Down to the First Turkish Invasion (1–945/622–1538). In W. Daum, ed., *Yemen: 3000 Years of Art and Civilisation in Arabia Felix*, pp. 129–39. Frankfurt/Main: Umschau-Verlag.
- 1989. Ibn al-Mujawir 7th/13th Century Arabia – the Wondrous and the Humorous. A.K. Irvine, R.B. Serjeant and G.R. Smith, eds., *A Miscellany of Middle Eastern Articles in Memoriam: Thomas Muir Johnstone 1924–83*, pp. 111–24. London: Longman.
- 1993. Some 'Anthropological' Passages from Ibn al-Mujawir's Guide to Arabia and Their Proposed Interpretations. In A. Gingrich, S. Haas, G. Paleczek, and T. Fillitz, eds., *Studies in Oriental Culture and History: Festschrift for Walter Dostal*, pp. 160–71. Frankfurt: Peter Lang.
Steedman, C. 1986. *Landscape for a Good Woman: A Story of Two Lives.* New Brunswick, NJ: Rutgers University Press.
Stirrat, R.L. 1984. Sacred Models. *Man* 19:199–215.
Stone, F., ed. 1985. *Studies on the Tihamah.* Salt Lake City: University of Utah Press.
Stookey, R.W. 1978. *The Politics of the Yemen Arab Republic.* Boulder, Colo.: Westview Press.
Tapper, N. 1983. Gender and Religion in a Turkish Town: A Comparison of Two Types of Formal Women's Gatherings. In P. Holden, ed., *Women's Religious Experiences: Cross Cultural Perspectives*, pp. 71–88. London: Croom Helm.
- 1990. Ziyaret: Gender, Movement, and Exchange in a Turkish community. In D.F. Eickelman and J. Piscatori, eds., *Muslim Travellers: Pilgramage, Migration, and the Religious Imagination*, pp. 236–54. Berkeley: University of California Press.
Tapper, N. and R. Tapper. 1987. The Birth of the Prophet: Ritual and Gender in Turkish Islam. *Man* 22:69–92.
Tuckerman, N. and N. Dunnan. 1995. *The Amy Vanderbilt Complete Book of Etiquette.* New York: Doubleday.
Turner, T. 1980. The Social Skin. In J. Cherfas and R. Lewin, eds., *Not Work Alone*, pp. 112–40. Beverly Hills: Sage Publications.
Veblen, T. 1979 [1899]. *The Theory of the Leisure Class.* New York: Viking Penguin.
Voll, J. 1987. Linking Groups in the Networks of Eighteenth-Century Revivalist Scholars: The Mizjaji Family in Yemen. In N. Levtzion and J. Voll, eds., *Eighteenth-Century Renewal and Reform in Islam*, pp. 69–92. Syracuse: Syracuse University Press.

von Arendonk, C. 1922. An Initiation Rite of the Sorcerer in Southern Arabia. In T.W. Arnold and R.A. Nicholson, eds., *A Volume of Oriental Studies Presented to Professor Edward G. Browne*, pp. 1–5. Cambridge: Cambridge University Press.

Walters, D. 1987. Perceptions of Social Inequality in the Yemen Arab Republic. Ph D thesis, New York University.

Weber, M. 1958 [1946]. *From Max Weber: Essays in Sociology*. Ed. H. Gerth and C. Mills. New York: Oxford University Press.

Weiner, A. 1976. *Women of Value, Men of Renown: New Perspectives in Trobriand Exchange*. Austin: University of Texas Press.

– 1985. Inalienable Wealth. *American Ethnologist* 12:210–27.

– 1992. *Inalienable Possessions: The Paradox of Keeping While Giving*. Berkeley: University of California Press.

Weiner, A., and J. Schneider, eds. 1989. *Cloth and Human Experience*. Washington: Smithsonian Institution Press.

Weir, S. 1985. *Qat in Yemen: Consumption and Social Change*. London: British Museum Publications.

Wikan, U. 1982. *Behind the Veil in Arabia: Women in Oman*. Chicago: University of Chicago Press.

– 1984. Shame and Honour: A Contestable Pair. *Man* 19: 635–52.

Williams, R. 1977. *Marxism and Literature*. Oxford: Oxford University Press.

Wilson, R.T.O. 1985. The Tihamah from the Beginning of the Islamic Period to 1800. In F. Stone, ed., *Studies on the Tihamah*, pp. 31–6. Salt Lake City: University of Utah Press.

Wolf, M. 1968. *The House of Lim: A Study of a Chinese Family*. Englewood Cliffs, NJ: Prentice-Hall.

– 1972. *Women and the Family in Rural Taiwan*. Stanford: Stanford University Press.

Wyman-Bury, G. 1915. *Arabia Infelix: or, the Turks in Yemen*. London: Macmillan.

Yamani, M.A.Z. 1987a. Birth and Behaviour in a Hospital in Saudi Arabia. *BRIMES* 13:169–76.

– 1987b. Fasting and Feasting: Some Social Aspects of the Observance of Ramadan in Saudi Arabia. In A. Al-Shahi, ed., *The Diversity of the Muslim Community: Anthropological Essays in Memory of Peter Lienhardt*, pp. 80–91. London: Ithaca Press.

Zein, M.A.H. el-. 1974. *The Sacred Meadows: A Structural Analysis of Religious Symbolism in an East African Town*. Evanston, Ind.: Northwestern University Press.

Index

'abid, 12, 15, 139

Abu-Lughod, L., 39, 46 n23, 73 n37, 81, 87, 88 n24, 89 n25, 93 n41, 149, 155 n21

Abu-Zahra, N., 38 n5, 49 n29, 96, 135 n61, 177 n37

Aden, 11, 17, 94, 156 n22, 185; cultural differences in, 84, 99; spatial organization of, 18, 99

Adornment, 91, 100, 108–16, 123, 192; cleanliness, 100–1, 115; dress, xiii, 34, 89–90, 109–10, 170; jasmine flowers, 26, 110–11, 125, 130, 170; for mourning, 131, 134–5, 138; perfume, 32, 91–2, 102–3. *See also* Gold jewelry

Akhdam (khadim), 5, 6, 12, 17, 30, 51, 97, 142, 189; emotion, 136 n65; greeting, 106; and Islam, 96, 165 n9; khadim, 23, 39, 87 n20, 106 n20, 137–40; modesty, 89 n27, 91 n36, 93–6, 150–2, 158; mourning for, 137–40; residence, 17, 61, 71; stigma, 13, 14–15, 16, 62, 83, 190–1; visiting, 55 n42; weddings, 121 n7, 122, 123, 126 n27, 127, 130; work, 14, 69, n28, 107 n24, 127; *zar* ceremony, 15, 151–2

Altorki, S., 20 n40, 38, 43, 46, 47 n24, 48, 49 n29, 77 n53, 105 n15, 121 n10, 133 n55, 143 n1

Anger, 141–58, 191; and *akhdam*, 150–2; and gossip, 143; and love, 146–7; and *nas*, 142–6, 154–8; and politeness, 147–8; and *qaba'il*, 152–4, 159

Appadurai, A., 5

Architecture, 17–19, 21, 88; inside houses, 61, 69–71

Asad, T., 83, 161, 162, 175

Aswad, B., 40 n6, 48 n28, 38 n4, 154 n15

Bayt kabir (al-kibar), 13, 17, 19, 112; family and household, 60–80, 154 n16, 194; mourning, 134, 136; neighbourhoods, 54–8, 190; visiting, 45, 47 n25, 49–51, 100, 102, 108, 168, 174, 190; weddings, 119–31, 192, 193; women, 29, 51, 93

Beidelman, T.O., 4, 56 n43, 104 n13, 107, 127 n30, 163 n5, 174

Betteridge, A., 104 n12, 172 n27

Boddy, J., 70 n31, 84, 85 n11, 98, 106 n21, 112 n39, 152 n13

Bourdieu, P., 5, 38, 41, 47, 57, 60, 70, 77, 101, 106, 112, 163

ANTHROPOLOGICAL HORIZONS

Editor: Michael Lambek, University of Toronto

Published to date: